CONVECTION CUISINE

CONVECTION CUISINE

RENÉ VERDON and
JACQUELINE MALLORCA

HEARST BOOKS
New York

Library of Congress Cataloging-in-Publication Data

Verdon, René, 1924–
  Convection cuisine.

  Includes index.
  1. Convection oven cookery.   I. Mallorca, Jacqueline.
II. Title.
TX840.C65V46 1989   641.5′8   88-16359
ISBN 0-688-08100-2

Printed in the United States of America

First Edition

1 2 3 4 5 6 7 8 9 10

BOOK DESIGN BY RICHARD ORIOLO

ILLUSTRATIONS BY JACQUELINE MALLORCA

ACKNOWLEDGMENTS

We would like to express our gratitude to all the friends and associates who helped to make this book possible. Cookbooks are not written in a vacuum, and we could not have accomplished this task without their invaluable help. In particular, we would like to thank:

Udo Nechutnys, chef of great talent, who lent his fine cooking skills and offered so many ideas.

Caryl Saunders, Inge Roberts, and Danielle Walker, who independently acted as catalysts for the whole project. Tom Wallerich, who so kindly shared his knowledge of personal computers. Fred Hill, our literary agent, and Ann Bramson, our editor, who showed such faith in us. Gerry Sweeney, who gave us the use of his test kitchen facilities, and Carl Sontheimer, for his invaluable advice on the technicalities of convection, microwave, and radiant heat.

And last but not least, we would like to thank our respective spouses, Yvette Verdon and Juan Mallorca, for their patience, understanding, and support.

RV AND JM

CONTENTS

INTRODUCTION

This book was written for people who want to get the most out of their convection ovens—and who appreciate really good food. If you don't own one yet, we hope the book will help you understand why a convection oven works as well as it does, and why switching to this kind of oven is such a good idea.

Like the food processor, the convection oven was first developed for professional use and is now standard equipment in all fine restaurants and bakeries. Of course, professional-size convection ovens are designed for volume cooking and require special ventilation and far more power than is available in the average home kitchen. However, convection ovens made for home use work on exactly the same principle: constantly circulating hot air.

Moving air heats or cools much more quickly than still air, as anyone who has ever stood in a cold wind on a winter's day will confirm. That's why weathermen speak of the "wind chill factor." Similarly, convection ovens cook by the "wind heat factor."

A standard conventional electric oven has "hot spots," and internal temperatures can vary by as much as 50 degrees Fahrenheit. Furthermore, the thermostat cycles on and off, which means that the oven temperature continually rises and drops. Solid foods such as roast meats and poultry respond badly to uneven heat—the internal juices escape from the underbrowned areas, and they have to be turned or basted continuously or they dry out. Repeatedly opening the oven door in order to do so doesn't help matters, and means that the cook has to hover about in the kitchen. Porous foods that are supposed to puff up as they cook—cakes, breads, cookies, soufflés, flaky pastry—are even more sensitive to uneven heat and abrupt changes in temperature, and will react accordingly. Soufflés sag, cookies brown too fast on the bottom, cakes droop in the middle, and flaky pastry sometimes refuses to rise or rises unevenly.

By contrast, the internal temperature in a convection oven is easier to regulate. The fan keeps hot air circulating, so foods cook uniformly and—most important—look and *taste* better. Heat is utilized more efficiently, so solid foods cook up to 30 percent faster, and often at a lower temperature than usual. This not only saves energy but is much better for the food being cooked—it loses less moisture and fewer nutrients. Roasts brown evenly on all sides and look more as though they had been cooked on a rotisserie than baked in an oven. Because forced air seals the outside surface, meats and poultry don't have to be basted, though we sometimes recommend that you turn foods over in a pan to absorb flavorings. Fish—always a delicate item to cook—remains juicy and flavorful.

Cakes, soufflés, breads, muffins, and other porous foods respond extremely well to the gentle, even heat of a convection oven. Cakes rise evenly, soufflés reach gratifying new heights, and breads develop an appetizingly crisp crust with a good airy crumb inside. Most of these foods, which cook fast anyway, bake in approximately the same length of time as in a conventional oven, but at a lower temperature than usual—on average, around 25 degrees lower—and have a markedly superior texture and appearance.

Another advantage of the convection oven is that a whole menu can be baked at the same time with no crossover of flavors. You can put a lot into a convection oven at once; everything will cook evenly. Just be sure to allow at least 1 inch of space around the edges of baking sheets, and stagger pans at different levels for maximum air circulation.

There are four different types of convection or semiconvection ovens available to the home cook: portable tabletop convection ovens (Farberware, Maxim); microwave/convection oven combinations such as those made by Sharp Electronics and Panasonic; built-in models (Gaggenau, JennAir), which are of course considerably more expensive than a standard electric oven; and a newly introduced portable converter, the Zephyr, which can turn almost any standard electric oven into a full-size semiconvection oven. Gas convection ovens are not yet available for home use, for complex technical reasons.

In a true convection oven, all the cooking (heating) takes place because of the forced flow of hot air. No heating element is visible; it is concealed within the wall of the oven. When a calrod or other heating element is visible in the oven, some of the cooking (heating) is due to radiation from the hot element. These are semiconvection ovens, but nonetheless give much better results than a conventional electric oven.

Due to the fact that a tabletop convection oven looks a lot like a microwave oven, some confusion exists. However, a microwave oven works on an entirely different principle: The source of heat is a magnetron tube that converts electrical energy into high-frequency microwaves. These reflect off the oven walls and are absorbed by the moisture in food. The resultant vibration of the food's molecules cause it to cook very rapidly, albeit without browning the exterior. By contrast, a convection oven utilizes a conventional heat source and cooks food from the outside in.

It is now possible to buy microwave/convection combination units. Convection heat seals and browns the outsides of foods, then microwave energy completes the interior cooking in a very short time. The best units can be operated independently: Briefly put, the microwave cycle alone is recommended for defrosting, reheating, and preparing recipes written for the microwave only; the convection cycle is recommended for baking small items; and the combination cycle for breads, cakes, casseroles, roast meats, and poultry.

Built-in convection ovens tend to be somewhat smaller than the average standard oven, but compensate by coming equipped with their own special racks, drip pans, baking sheets, and so on. When roasting in these ovens (or in the small tabletop convection ovens), it is recommended that you place the meat or poultry directly on one of the oven racks and slot a drip pan below it at the next level, or place it on the oven floor.

If you have a gas stove, a tabletop convection oven makes an invaluable second oven. It is also an excellent choice for a small kitchen or a holiday cottage. However, being small, you will find that roasts and some baked items have to be turned around from front to back in order to brown evenly, and many of your favorite baking dishes simply won't fit inside. A good microwave/convection combination fitted with a turntable and a sensor for automatically computing times for combination cooking, though considerably more expensive, does offer dual advantages.

If you have a standard electric stove, the relatively low-cost convection converter is easy to install, gives good results, and you can continue using all your existing roasting pans, baking sheets, and casseroles. Basically a fan with GE motor inside a housing, it looks somewhat like a flying saucer and plugs into the element. It rests on the floor of the oven below the bottom rack, out of the way. One caveat here: Test your oven thermostat with a portable oven thermometer from time to time, as they are notoriously inaccurate. You may have to either call in a repairman or simply compensate for the difference when you set the oven dial. (The same can apply to built-in convection ovens. A friend complained sadly that his new convection oven did a terrible job, until it was discovered that the thermostat had not been adjusted properly and was off by 40 degrees!)

A B O U T   T H E   R E C I P E S

All oven temperatures are given for a convection oven, and it is recommended that the oven be preheated despite some manufacturers' recommendations to the contrary. Naturally all the recipes may be cooked in a conventional oven; see page 13 for conversions.

The stated preparation times are approximate and presuppose that you have set out the ingredients and found all the necessary implements. (All cooks have a different pace at which they like to work in the kitchen.)

We hope you will be continually surprised and pleased with the results you get using these recipes. They were created for use in a home kitchen, using ingredients that are readily available and, where possible, inexpensive. You don't have to spend a lot of money to put good food on the table! We have included contemporary recipes that have their roots in countries as far removed as Italy and North Africa, which seems only right in a book written for American cooks, who are the most eclectic and open-minded in the world. Many of them are quick to prepare, a few are for special occasions and take a bit more time and attention, but all are "do-able" by the home cook. We wish you joy and satisfaction.

RV AND JM

CAN YOU USE THESE RECIPES WITH A REGULAR OVEN? YES, DEFINITELY.

All the recipes in this book may be cooked in a conventional gas or electric oven.

When cooking solid foods, leave oven temperatures the same or increase by up to 25 degrees for foods that cook in a very short time, such as fish. Basting and turning will be necessary for roast meats and poultry. Check for doneness at the stated time with an instant-reading meat thermometer, and continue cooking for as long as necessary, remembering that the internal temperature will rise by another 5 to 10 degrees while the roast stands after removal from the oven. (It is important to let roasts stand for 10 to 15 minutes before carving so that the internal juices, which get forced to the surface, can redistribute themselves.)

INTERNAL TEMPERATURES

Chicken, turkey, duck	170° breast meat; 185° thigh meat
Veal roasts	well done: 165°
Lamb roasts	medium rare: 125° to 130° well done: 145° to 150°
Fresh pork roasts	well done: 155°
Beef roasts	rare: 125° to 130° medium rare:135° to 140° medium: 145° to 150°

Cakes, soufflés, breads, muffins and other porous foods should be baked at 25° higher than the temperatures states in the recipes, for approximately the same length of time. However, check 10 minutes before the end of baking time to be on the safe side.

Some recipes are cooked covered, in which case cooking and temperature times remain the same.

CONVECTION CUISINE

FINGER FOODS AND FIRST 6 COURSES

CHICKEN LIVER, PRUNE AND COPPA APPETIZERS

SERVES 6

An easy but sophisticated appetizer that takes only 5 minutes to prepare and 6 minutes to bake. As they are served on toothpicks, these are a good choice for cocktail party hors d'oeuvres.

6 *chicken livers*

12 *thin slices of mild coppa (Italian cured ham)*

6 *soft pitted prunes, cut in half*

Black pepper

Preheat convection oven to 400 degrees. Trim chicken livers of connective tissue and any greenish parts (gall), and cut in half. Lay slices of coppa out on a work surface. Place half a chicken liver and half a prune on each slice, and season with pepper to taste. (Do not use salt, as coppa is salty.) Roll up and secure with a toothpick. Place on a baking sheet, and bake for 6 minutes. Serve hot.

PREPARATION TIME: 5 MINUTES / OVEN TIME: 6 MINUTES / EASY

CHICKEN LIVER
MOUSSE WITH TOMATO SAUCE

This delicious appetizer can be made for practically nothing, especially if you use chicken livers you've saved from whole birds. Duck fat is the first choice here for flavor and texture—always save the fat when you cook duck and store it in the freezer.

9 *ounces chicken livers*

1½ *cups bread crumbs made from day-old white bread*

7 *tablespoons duck fat (page 105) or butter*

½ *cup heavy cream*

1 *onion, finely chopped*

4 *cloves garlic, mashed and chopped*

1 *teaspoon chopped fresh parsley*

3 *teaspoons chopped fresh oregano, or 1½ teaspoons dried*

2 *large eggs*

Salt and pepper

2 *tablespoons olive oil*

2 *tablespoons all-purpose flour*

1 *can Italian plum tomatoes, 14½ ounces, chopped, with juice*

Preheat convection oven to 350 degrees. Grease a 1-quart soufflé dish generously with butter. Trim livers, removing any filaments or greenish (gall) areas. Place chicken livers, bread crumbs, duck fat, cream, half the onion and half the garlic, parsley, 1 teaspoon of the oregano, and the eggs in a food processor. Season with salt and pepper to taste. Process until smooth, and then strain through a fine sieve, pushing down on the mixture with a rubber spatula. Transfer purée to the prepared soufflé dish, and place in a baking pan. Add enough hot water to reach halfway up the sides of the dish. Bake for 30 to 35 minutes, until just set.

While the mousse is baking, prepare the sauce: Heat oil and sauté remaining onion and garlic until softened, about 5 minutes. Add remaining oregano, flour, and chopped tomatoes with their juice. Bring to a boil, stirring, and simmer for 2 minutes. Purée in a food processor, then strain and season to taste with salt and pepper. Reheat before serving.

Unmold the mousse or serve it from the baking dish, with tomato sauce.

PREPARATION TIME: 25 MINUTES / OVEN TIME: 30 TO 35 MINUTES

CHICKEN WINGS WITH SESAME OIL AND HONEY

These Chinese-style chicken wings take a little advance preparation, but they are delicious, inexpensive, and can be made in large quantities for a party. If you are serving them as hot cocktail appetizers, put paper frills on the bones to protect guests' fingers.

2 *pounds chicken wings, about 10*	1 *tablespoon Dry Sack sherry*
3 *tablespoons soy sauce*	1 *clove garlic*
1 *tablespoon Chinese sesame oil*	*Pinch Chinese five-spice powder*
½ *tablespoon honey*	*Salt and pepper*

Chop tips off wings and discard, or reserve for stock. Cut wings in half. Cut through skin just below the knob of one wing half, and scrape meat away from bone. Push bone toward the opposite end, turning meat inside out as you go, making a shape like a lollipop. (The lower part of the chicken wing will have two bones inside. Remove and discard the thinner one.) Chop the knob off the joint. Repeat with remaining wing halves.

In a shallow dish, combine the soy sauce, sesame oil, honey, sherry, garlic, five-spice powder, and salt and pepper to taste. Roll the prepared chicken wings in this mixture. Marinate, covered, in refrigerator for 2 hours, or longer if more convenient.

Preheat convection oven to 400 degrees, and heat a shallow roasting pan in the oven. Transfer the wings and marinade to the pan, and roast for 15 minutes. Serve hot.

PREPARATION TIME: 20 MINUTES; 2 HOURS MARINATING /
OVEN TIME: 15 MINUTES / EASY

GOAT CHEESE AND PEAR CANAPES

Cheese and pears are a classic combination; in this case they are layered on rounds of bread, covered with beaten egg white, and baked to make hot appetizers that can be served with wine or champagne before dinner.

9 *slices home-style white bread, ⅜ inch thick*

4 *tablespoons unsalted butter, softened*

8 *ounces fresh white goat cheese*

8 *ounces cream cheese*

4 *large egg yolks*
  Salt and pepper

4 *firm, ripe pears, 5 ounces each*

3 *large egg whites*

2 *ounces prosciutto, cut into narrow strips*

Preheat convection oven to 325 degrees. Using a 1½-inch cookie cutter, cut four rounds from each slice of bread. Spread one side lightly with butter, and place butter side down on a baking sheet. Combine goat cheese, cream cheese, and egg yolks in a bowl. Season to taste with salt and pepper, and mix with a fork until well combined. Slice pears ⅛ inch thick. Using the same cookie cutter, trim pear slices into 1½-inch rounds. Spread each round of bread with a layer of cheese mixture, a slice of pear, and a second layer of cheese.

Beat egg whites until very stiff, seasoning with a little salt. Top each canapé with a mound of beaten egg white, spreading a little on the sides as well. Bake for 10 minutes, until egg white is lightly browned and bread is crisp and brown on the bottom. Top each little "soufflé" with crossed strips of prosciutto, and serve warm.

PREPARATION TIME: 20 MINUTES / OVEN TIME: 10 MINUTES

LITTLE TURNOVERS WITH GROUND BEEF AND RED WINE

These excellent but inexpensive hot appetizers are made by forming a hamburger mixture into tiny balls, browning them lightly in butter, and then rolling them in a wine glaze. The meatballs are enclosed in puff pastry (which can be the frozen ready-to-use variety) and baked until golden.

8 ounces ground beef

6 ounces ground pork

3 tablespoons finely chopped onion

1 clove garlic, finely chopped

2 tablespoons chopped fresh parsley

1 teaspoon salt

½ teaspoon black pepper

1 large egg

1 tablespoon Cognac

2 cups dry red wine, such as Cabernet Sauvignon

2 tablespoons butter

½ teaspoon sugar

1½ pounds Quick Puff Pastry dough (page 244), or 1½ packages frozen puff pastry sheets, thawed

1 egg, beaten

In a bowl, combine beef, pork, onion, garlic, parsley, salt, pepper, egg, and Cognac, and mix well. Pour 1 cup of the wine into a separate bowl. Wet your fingers with the wine and form the meat mixture into 1-inch balls.

Heat butter in a nonstick skillet and sauté meatballs for 2 minutes, rolling them around so that they keep their shape. Remove to a large platter. (They will firm up, but will still be raw inside.) Add remaining 1 cup of wine and the sugar to the skillet. Bring to a boil and reduce liquid by three quarters, to form a syrupy glaze, about 7 minutes. Roll and toss the meatballs in this glaze, then remove and chill in the refrigerator for at least 10 minutes.

Preheat convection oven to 375 degrees. On a lightly floured surface, roll puff pastry out very thin. (If you are using 10 by 10-inch sheets of frozen puff pastry, roll them out to measure 20 by 20 inches.) Using a 3½-inch fluted-edge pastry cutter, cut out forty circles. Elongate the circles of dough slightly by pressing in the center with a rolling pin, and place a meatball to one side. Brush edges with water, fold pastry over, and press together to make a semicircular turnover. Repeat with remaining meatballs and place on baking sheets. Brush pastries with beaten egg, and bake for 15 to 18 minutes, until golden. Serve warm.

PREPARATION TIME: 30 MINUTES / OVEN TIME: 15 TO 18 MINUTES

ASPARAGUS AND PROSCIUTTO IN PUFF PASTRY CASES

SERVES 8

An impressive first course that is much easier to accomplish than it looks: poached asparagus tips rolled in thin slices of prosciutto and baked in puff pastry cases. This is all prepared ahead, along with a simple sauce made from puréed asparagus stalks, lemon juice, and lightly whipped cream. The filled pastries are warmed briefly in the oven before serving with the room-temperature sauce.

16 to 24 stalks asparagus, about 1 pound
½ tablespoon olive oil
Salt
8 ounces Quick Puff Pastry dough (page 244), or ½ package frozen puff pastry sheets, thawed

1 egg, beaten
8 thin slices prosciutto, 4 ounces total
Juice of 1 small lemon
½ cup heavy cream
White pepper

Peel asparagus and trim off woody ends. Bring a pot of water to a boil, add olive oil (this helps to hold the green color) and a pinch of salt, and poach asparagus until just tender, about 7 minutes. (Time depends on size of stalks.)

Preheat convection oven to 375 degrees. On a lightly floured surface, roll puff pastry dough out to form a 14 by 12-inch rectangle. Cut in half lengthways and stack the two strips. Trim strips to 11 by

5¼ inches; then cut in four equal pieces. This will give you eight 2¾ by 5¼-inch rectangles. Place on a baking sheet, well separated from each other. Chill for 10 minutes (to relax the dough so that it bakes evenly).

Brush dough with beaten egg. Make a cut ⅓ inch from the edge around each rectangle without going all the way through. (This will create sides to the pastry cases.) Make four light slanting cuts across the center of each one. Bake for 15 minutes, until well puffed. With the tip of a knife, cut around the lid of each pastry case and carefully remove. Discard any excess soft dough inside.

Cut off the top 3 inches of each asparagus stalk. Cut off the next 3 inches of stalk and reserve for sauce. (Discard any remaining, or use in soup.) Take two or three asparagus tips, roll up in prosciutto, place inside a pastry case with the tips sticking out a little, and top with pastry lid. Repeat with remaining cases.

Combine reserved stalks and lemon juice in the bowl of a food processor and purée. Whip cream lightly and fold into the asparagus purée. Season with salt and white pepper to taste.

When ready to serve, heat filled pastry cases at 350 degrees for 5 minutes. Make sure the dinner plates are very hot. Pour a little of the room-temperature sauce on each plate, and place pastry alongside.

PREPARATION TIME: 30 MINUTES / OVEN TIME: 15 MINUTES; 5 MINUTES

SPAGHETTI SQUASH WITH
GARLIC AND RED BELL PEPPER

This extraordinary vegetable makes an attractive and unusual substitute for pasta. Low in calories and cholesterol-free, it looks and tastes delicious. Serve this dish as a first course or as a vegetable with chicken, veal, or fish.

1 *spaghetti squash, 3 pounds*
Salt and pepper
3 *tablespoons olive oil*
1 *clove garlic, chopped*

½ *red bell pepper, seeded, peeled, and shredded (page 39)*
1 *tablespoon chopped fresh basil leaves*
Basil sprigs, for garnish

Preheat convection oven to 350 degrees. Cut squash in half lengthways, and wrap each half in foil. Bake for 40 minutes, or until squash gives to light pressure. Discard seeds and shred the squash into a bowl, unraveling the strands with a fork. Season with salt and pepper to taste. (Squash can be prepared ahead, or even the day before.) Cover and refrigerate.

Heat olive oil in a skillet, and sauté garlic and shredded bell pepper for 1 minute. Do not allow garlic to burn, as it will turn bitter. Add spaghetti squash and toss until heated through. Stir in chopped basil, and transfer to heated plates. Garnish with whole basil leaves.

PREPARATION TIME: 10 MINUTES / OVEN TIME: 40 MINUTES / EASY

CRAB CAKES WITH GREEN PEA SAUCE

SERVES 8

One Dungeness crab will serve eight as a very elegant appetizer when prepared this way: The flaked meat is mixed with shallot and bell pepper, ground sole, eggs, and cream. The mixture is then spread inside egg poaching rings (or clean tuna cans with both sides removed) and baked, and served on top of the green puréed pea sauce. If you plan to shell your own crab, allow extra preparation time. A 16-ounce Dungeness crab will yield about 6 ounces of meat.

It is important to peel bell peppers, as the skin is hard to digest. To do this quickly, cut the pepper into quarters, lay each section flat, and remove the skin with a vegetable peeler.

6 ounces cooked
  Dungeness crab meat
½ tablespoon unsalted
  butter
1 shallot, chopped
½ red bell pepper, seeded,
  peeled, and finely
  chopped (page 39)
¼ cup Dry Sack sherry
  Salt and pepper
4 ounces filet of sole
2 large egg yolks
¼ cup heavy cream
4 large egg whites

SAUCE

4 ounces (1 cup) peas,
  fresh or frozen
6 fresh mint leaves,
  chopped
2 tablespoons white wine
1 tablespoon heavy cream
  Salt and pepper
  Pinch sugar
1 small tomato, peeled,
  seeded, cut into
  julienne, and seasoned
  with salt and pepper

Pick over crabmeat for any bits of cartilage. Heat butter in a small skillet and simmer shallot in it for 1 minute. Stir in bell pepper, and cook for 1 minute. Add sherry and cook over medium-high heat until liquid has almost evaporated. Remove from heat, let cool a little, and combine with crab in a mixing bowl. Season with salt and pepper to taste. Blend sole and egg yolks in a food processor, and add cream. (Do not overmix or cream will turn to butter.) Season with salt and pepper to taste, and stir into crab mixture. Whip egg whites until stiff, and fold into crab and fish mixture. Cover and chill for 30 minutes, or longer if more convenient.

Preheat convection oven to 375 degrees. Line a baking sheet with baking parchment and butter it. Butter eight 3-inch pastry or poaching rings (½ inch high) and set on the baking sheet. Fill each one with crab mixture, and bake for 10 minutes.

To make Green Pea Sauce, blanch peas for 1 minute in boiling salted water. Plunge into cold water to set the color, and drain. Combine with mint in the bowl of a food processor and purée. Place in a saucepan with wine and cream, heat gently, and season to taste with salt, pepper, and sugar.

Divide sauce among eight heated dinner plates. Run a sharp knife around each baking ring and unmold the crab cakes upside down. Top each circle of pea sauce with a crab cake, browned side up, and garnish with julienne of tomato.

PREPARATION TIME: 20 MINUTES / OVEN TIME: 10 MINUTES

SHRIMP AND
BACON ON SKEWERS

If you are serving this dish as a hot cocktail appetizer, use medium-size shrimp and serve singly on toothpicks. If it is to be an entrée, add fluffy white rice.

12 *large shrimp, 1 pound total*

12 *strips lean bacon*

1 *cup bread crumbs made from day-old white bread*

Salt and pepper

SAUCE

½ *teaspoon chopped fresh tarragon, or ¼ teaspoon dried*

½ *teaspoon fresh lemon juice*

½ *cup heavy cream*

Preheat convection oven to 400 degrees. Shell and devein shrimp, and wrap each one in a strip of bacon. Thread onto bamboo skewers, leaving a little space between, three per skewer. Roll in the bread crumbs. (Shrimp can be prepared several hours ahead to this point, and refrigerated until required.) Place the skewers in a shallow baking dish and bake for 8 minutes, turning once.

Combine tarragon, lemon juice, and cream in a small saucepan. When shrimp are almost ready, bring this mixture to a boil. Divide sauce among heated dinner plates and top with the skewers.

PREPARATION TIME: 6 MINUTES / OVEN TIME: 8 MINUTES / EASY

SHRIMP IN CABBAGE LEAVES WITH RED CAVIAR

This is a striking appetizer for a formal dinner: The color and flavor contrasts are excellent. To remove large perfect leaves from a cabbage, cut through the white ribs at the base and then carefully pull away the leaves. Reserve the rest of the cabbage for Trout with Buttered Cabbage (page 34), or Gratin of Savoy Cabbage (page 205).

4 *large Savoy cabbage leaves*

16 *to 20 shrimp, 1 pound total*

2 *scallions, chopped*

1 *medium tomato, peeled, seeded, and coarsely chopped*

4 *small fresh basil leaves, chopped*

Pinch cayenne pepper

1 *tablespoon olive oil*

Salt and pepper

½ *cup fish stock or bottled clam juice*

2 *tablespoons butter, softened*

1 *ounce salmon roe (red caviar)*

Preheat convection oven to 350 degrees. Blanch cabbage leaves in boiling salted water for 1 minute, until just tender. Drain well. Peel and devein shrimp. Lay cabbage leaves on a work surface, and cut out white rib. Combine shrimp with scallions, tomato, basil, cayenne, and olive oil.

In the center of each leaf lay one quarter of the shrimp mixture. Season lightly with salt and pepper, and fold up sides of leaves to make a package. Lay cabbage packages seam side down in a shallow baking dish, and add fish stock. Top each package with a teaspoon of butter, cover surface with buttered baking parchment (or use butter wrappers), and bake for 6 minutes.

Remove cabbage packages to heated dinner plates. Transfer cooking juices to a saucepan, heat to boiling, and reduce by half about 2 minutes. Whisk in remaining butter, taste for seasoning, and pour sauce around cabbage packages. Top each one with a spoonful of salmon roe, and scatter a little more in the sauce.

PREPARATION TIME: 15 MINUTES / OVEN TIME: 6 MINUTES

SCALLOPS
WITH SCALLIONS

At their best when they are simply prepared, scallops require very brief cooking or they become rubbery. To serve this dish as a first course, you can divide it among four shirred egg dishes or natural scallop shells.

2 *tablespoons bread crumbs made from day-old white bread*

1 *tablespoon butter, chilled, cut into small dice*

16 *fresh sea scallops (or use small bay scallops), 12 ounces total*

2 *mushrooms, diced*

2 *scallions, white bulb and part of green stem, finely chopped*

Salt and pepper

2 *tablespoons dry white wine*

1 *tablespoon butter, melted*

Put bread crumbs in a small ovenproof dish and dot with the butter. Place in convection oven and heat to 375 degrees. By the time the oven is hot enough, in about 10 minutes, the crumbs will be golden and crispy. Remove dish of crumbs and set aside.

Butter a 9-inch shallow ovenproof baking dish. If scallops are large, cut into ½-inch-thick slices. In a bowl, combine mushrooms, scallions, salt and pepper to taste, wine, and melted butter. Add scallops and mix lightly together. Pour into baking dish and sprinkle with prepared crumbs. Bake for 6 minutes.

PREPARATION TIME: 10 MINUTES / OVEN TIME: 6 MINUTES / EASY

MARINATED
SHRIMP WITH HERBS

Easy and delicious, these herb-scented shrimp take only 5 minutes to bake and can be offered as an appetizer or as a main course. If possible, serve with freshly baked Baguettes (page 210) to mop up the good juices. Hold the shrimp by the tail to eat—this is an informal dish!

2 *pounds very fresh, medium-size unshelled shrimp*

3 *cloves garlic, finely chopped*

½ *cup chopped fresh parsley*

1 *teaspoon chopped fresh oregano*

1 *teaspoon chopped fresh tarragon*

1 *teaspoon chopped fresh basil*

1 *tablespoon Dijon mustard*

1 *teaspoon salt*

  Black pepper

½ *cup olive oil*

  Juice of 1 lemon

Shell and devein shrimp, leaving tails on. Rinse shrimp, pat dry, and place in a shallow baking dish. Combine remaining ingredients, pour over shrimp, and mix thoroughly. Cover and marinate for 2 hours at room temperature.

Preheat convection oven to 400 degrees. Bake shrimp for 4 minutes, then stir and return to oven for 1 minute. Shrimp should be pink and just cooked through. Serve at once.

PREPARATION TIME: 2 HOURS MARINATING; 15 MINUTES /
OVEN TIME: 5 MINUTES / EASY

CREAMY SALT COD IN BAKED POTATOES

Salt cod, a Mediterranean favorite, is combined with garlicky mashed baked potatoes and piled back into the shells. This makes an unusual and very easy first course, or it can be served as a light meal. If you have to buy salt cod in a 1-pound box, save the other half for The Original Eggs Benedict on page 48.

3 *baking potatoes, 8 ounces each*

8 *ounces dried salt cod, soaked overnight in two or three changes of cold water*

2 *cloves garlic, mashed and minced*

½ *cup heavy cream*

½ *cup olive oil*

¼ *teaspoon white pepper*

1 *tablespoon chopped fresh parsley*

Salt (optional)

2 *tablespoons dry white bread crumbs*

Preheat convection oven to 375 degrees. Bake potatoes for 45 minutes, until soft.

While potatoes are baking, place cod in a saucepan, cover with cold water, and bring to a boil. Simmer for a minute or two, until tender. Drain, and flake into a bowl.

Cut baked potatoes in half lengthways and scoop out pulp, leaving a thin shell. Place shells on a greased baking sheet. Mash potato pulp with flaked salt cod and garlic until very smooth. (Mash by hand; a food processor will turn mixture into glue.) Heat cream and olive oil, without boiling, and beat into mixture with a wooden spoon. Add white pepper and parsley. Taste for seasoning, and add salt only if necessary. Fill potato shells, and sprinkle with bread crumbs. (Potatoes can be prepared to this point several hours in advance. Cover and refrigerate.) Bake filled potatoes at 375 degrees for 15 minutes.

PREPARATION TIME: OVERNIGHT SOAKING; 20 MINUTES /
OVEN TIME: 45 MINUTES; 15 MINUTES / EASY

RED SNAPPER
WRAPPED IN ZUCCHINI

This dish looks elegant but is actually easy to prepare and very inexpensive. It serves four as an appetizer or two as a main course, and can be prepared well ahead of time.

1 *clove garlic, chopped*

1 *filet of red snapper, 8 ounces*

Salt and pepper

Paprika

2 *small zucchini, 4 ounces each*

1 *tablespoon olive oil*

¼ *cup dry white wine*

1 *teaspoon chopped fresh thyme leaves, or ½ teaspoon dried plus ½ teaspoon parsley*

¼ *cup heavy cream*

Preheat convection oven to 375 degrees. Grease a shallow baking dish and sprinkle with garlic. Remove any stray bones from snapper, sprinkle with salt, pepper, and paprika to taste, and cut into eight equal pieces. Cut zucchini lengthways into paper-thin slices. (An easy way to do this is to lay the zucchini flat, trim one end, and shave off slices with a wide-bladed vegetable peeler.) If the slices are not almost transparent, blanch in boiling water for a few seconds to make them pliable.

Place two zucchini slices, overlapping, on a work surface. Put a piece of fish on one end, and roll up the fish in the zucchini. Repeat with remaining fish and zucchini. Lay rolls in prepared baking dish and sprinkle with olive oil, wine, thyme, and salt, pepper, and paprika to taste. (Dish can be prepared ahead to this point, covered, and refrigerated.) Bake for 7 minutes.

Transfer rolls to heated plates and keep warm. Pour accumulated cooking juices into a skillet, bring to a boil, and reduce by half, about 3 minutes. Stir in cream, boil for 1 minute, and taste for seasoning. Pour sauce around fish.

PREPARATION TIME: 10 MINUTES / OVEN TIME: 8 MINUTES / EASY

SALMON QUENELLES
WITH LOBSTER SAUCE

If you have a food processor, this sophisticated first course is not at all hard to make. After chilling, the quenelle mixture is formed into ovals, poached, and later baked in the sauce. Using a top-quality canned lobster bisque as a base for the sauce is an acceptable shortcut; making a classic lobster sauce with pounded lobster shells takes a great deal of time and effort—and you just don't find piles of fresh lobster shells lying about in the average home kitchen!

10 *ounces fresh salmon, skinned and boned, well chilled*

2 *large eggs*

4 *tablespoons unsalted butter, softened*

½ *cup heavy cream, well chilled*

¾ *teaspoon salt*

¼ *teaspoon white pepper*

Dash nutmeg

SAUCE

1 *can lobster bisque, 15 ounces*

1 *tablespoon Cognac*

3 *tablespoons heavy cream*

All the ingredients should be very cold, except the room-temperature butter. Place the salmon in the bowl of a food processor, and grind it. Then, with the motor still running, add the eggs through the feed tube, one at a time, and blend. Add the butter and cream through the feed tube, blending only long enough to mix. Do not overbeat or allow the mixture to become warm. Season with salt, white pepper, and nutmeg. Transfer to a bowl, cover, and chill for 1 hour.

Grease a skillet with butter. Using two teaspoons dipped in cold water, form the salmon mixture into 2-inch-long oval quenelles. (Pack the mixture well by bringing the spoon up against the side of the bowl; to round the top of the quenelle, remove with the other spoon.) Place in the greased skillet. Add cold water to cover, and poach over medium-low heat for about 10 minutes. Do not allow water to boil. Let cool in the poaching liquid. (Quenelles will keep in cold poaching liquid for three to four days in the refrigerator.)

Preheat convection oven to 375 degrees. Drain quenelles and place in buttered 8 by 12-inch shallow ovenproof dish. Heat lobster bisque, and whisk in Cognac and cream. Cover quenelles with lobster sauce and bake for 10 minutes, until quenelles puff up and sauce is bubbly. Place two quenelles on each heated serving plate and surround with sauce.

PREPARATION TIME: 1 HOUR CHILLING; 30 MINUTES / OVEN TIME: 10 MINUTES

TROUT WITH BUTTERED CABBAGE

SERVES 8, OR 4 AS A MAIN COURSE

Boning a trout is much easier than you might think: Chop off the fins, make two parallel cuts through the back just above the backbone on each side, cut off the head—and that's it. Ready-boned trout are available in many supermarkets, but they cost more and it hardly seems worth it. You can substitute olive oil or avocado oil for the butter in this recipe if you prefer; the cabbage will still have a delicious flavor.

1 *medium Savoy or Nappa cabbage*
3 *tablespoons butter*
Salt and pepper

2 *teaspoons coriander seeds*
4 *trout, 8 ounces each, fileted and skinned*

Preheat convection oven to 350 degrees. Shred the cabbage, discarding the heavy white ribs. Heat butter in a wide, heavy pan and cook cabbage slowly until tender without letting it brown, about 10 minutes. Season to taste with salt and pepper.

Crack the coriander seeds in a mortar with a pestle, or crush them under a heavy saucepan. Toast in a dry skillet for a few seconds, until they become very aromatic.

Transfer cabbage to a large shallow baking dish. Lay trout filets on top, season lightly with salt and pepper, and scatter with toasted coriander seeds. Bake for 6 minutes. The trout filets will steam gently over the vegetable.

PREPARATION TIME: 15 MINUTES / OVEN TIME: 6 MINUTES / EASY

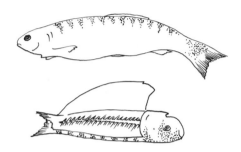

To bone and skin a trout, or any round fish, first cut off the sharp fins on the backbone and belly. Lay fish on its side and make a cut behind the gills, but do not cut the head off. Make a horizontal cut starting at the backbone, with the knife blade flat over the ribs. Make a shallow cut just above the tail and lift off the filet. Turn trout over and repeat on the other side, leaving the head and tail attached to the backbone. (These trimmings can be used for fish stock, if desired.)

To skin a filet, lay it skin side down and grasp the skin securely at the tail end. Insert the knife blade between flesh and skin and push the knife with the blade scraping against the skin—the flesh will peel away in one piece. Using your finger, feel filets for tiny bones; run the knife blade underneath the bones and remove them along with a sliver of flesh.

Warm Smoked Salmon
Mousse with Rich Tomato Sauce Serves 8

The recipe for this elegant first course can be halved if you like; or you can make the entire amount and serve half of it cold the following day, with Fresh Tomato, Olive Oil, and Coriander Sauce (page 305). Use tall bucket-shaped timbale molds if possible. The mousses unmold easily and look very attractive.

5 *ounces smoked salmon*
5 *large eggs*
1½ *cups heavy cream*
  Pinch cayenne pepper

Pinch nutmeg
Salt (optional)
1 *cup Rich Tomato Sauce (page 307)*

Preheat convection oven to 325 degrees. Line the bottom of a roasting pan with paper towels (which help to insulate the delicate mousse). Butter eight 3- to 4-ounce tin timbale molds or 4-ounce white porcelain ramekins.

Place salmon in the bowl of a food processor and grind it. With the motor running, add eggs one by one through the feed tube, scraping the bowl down as necessary. Add cream through the feed tube, but do not overprocess or it will turn to butter. Strain this mixture through a sieve into a bowl, pressing down with a wooden spoon. Add cayenne pepper and nutmeg. Taste, add salt only if necessary.

Place molds in prepared roasting pan, and fill with mousse. Add enough hot water to reach halfway up the sides of the molds, and cover pan with aluminum foil. Punch a few holes in the foil for steam to escape. Bake for 40 minutes, until mousse is just set. Run a knife around inside of molds, and turn mousse out onto warm plates while hot. Surround each serving with warm Tomato Sauce.

PREPARATION TIME: 10 MINUTES / OVEN TIME: 40 MINUTES / EASY

_L_IGHT MEALS

QUICHE WITH
SORREL AND SPINACH

Guests will wonder why your spinach quiche is so much better than anyone else's; the secret is the sorrel. Unlike basil, which has become very fashionable, you won't find sorrel everywhere, but it is a vegetable that is worth seeking out for its sharp piquancy. You will usually find it displayed with the fresh herbs. Always let a quiche cool before cutting it. If you wish to serve it warm, gently reheat it.

1 _Plain Pastry Shell (page 239), unbaked_

4 _ounces fresh sorrel leaves_

12 _ounces fresh spinach leaves_

4 _tablespoons unsalted butter_

3 _red or brown-skinned Spanish onions, thinly sliced_

4 _large eggs_

1½ _cups heavy cream_

Salt

White pepper

Pinch nutmeg

Preheat convection oven to 350 degrees. Bake pastry shell for 15 minutes, then set it aside to cool in the pan while you prepare the filling.

Rinse, drain, and devein sorrel. Rinse, drain, and de-stem spinach. Heat 2 tablespoons of the butter in a heavy pan and sauté sorrel and spinach until liquid evaporates and vegetables form a purée-like mass, about 2 minutes. In a separate sauté pan, heat remaining 2 tablespoons butter and cook onions over low heat, covered, until soft and transparent, 10 to 15 minutes, stirring occasionally. Combine sorrel, spinach, and onions and let cool to lukewarm.

In a large bowl, beat eggs and whisk in cream. Season to taste with salt, white pepper, and nutmeg, and add sorrel mixture. Pour into baked pastry shell and bake at 350 degrees for 30 minutes, or until custard is set. Serve lukewarm or cold—not hot, or the custard will be too soft.

PREPARATION TIME: 30 MINUTES / OVEN TIME: 30 MINUTES

MUSSEL QUICHE   SERVES 6 TO 8

This creamy seafood quiche, lightly perfumed with saffron, makes a good first course, or a light meal with a salad, and it's one of those dishes that you can put together "off the shelf" if you use bottled mussels. Be sparing with the saffron; too much can taste medicinal.

1 *Plain Pastry Shell (page 239), unbaked*
1 *tablespoon butter*
½ *leek, chopped, white part only*
1 *shallot, chopped*
2 *tomatoes, peeled, seeded, and chopped*
1 *clove garlic, chopped*

Small pinch saffron
½ *cup mussel juice or bottled clam juice*
Black pepper
2 *large eggs*
½ *cup heavy cream*
1 *cup shelled mussels (freshly steamed open, or bottled in brine and rinsed in water)*

Preheat convection oven to 350 degrees. Bake pastry shell for 15 minutes. Remove it from the oven, and set aside to cool in the pan.

Heat butter in a skillet and add the leek and shallot. Simmer slowly, covered, for 8 minutes. Add the tomatoes, garlic, saffron, and mussel juice, and season with pepper to taste. (The mussels and juice are salty; taste before adding any salt.) Cook for 2 minutes and allow to cool slightly.

Whisk eggs and cream together, and add vegetable mixture. Stir in mussels, and pour into baked pastry shell. Bake for 20 minutes at 350 degrees, until pastry is browned and filling is cooked. Serve lukewarm (not hot).

PREPARATION TIME: 30 MINUTES / OVEN TIME: 15 MINUTES; 20 MINUTES

SERVES 4, OR 8
AS AN APPETIZER

CRUSTLESS ARTICHOKE TART WITH BELL PEPPERS

In San Francisco delicatessens this kind of tart is known as a frittata, though it's hard to know why, since in Italy a frittata is a variety of omelet. Whatever you choose to call it, it's very good: a medley of lightly cooked vegetables bound together in a savory egg custard and baked in the oven. It's rather like a quiche without a pastry crust, and is delicious with salad and French bread for a light meal, or it can be served as an appetizer.

1 *package frozen artichoke hearts, 9 ounces, thawed*

1 *yellow bell pepper*

1 *red bell pepper*

1 *tablespoon olive oil*

2 *zucchini, 4 ounces each, sliced*

4 *scallions, white bulbs and half the green stems, chopped*

1 *clove garlic, chopped*

1 *teaspoon chopped fresh oregano, or ½ teaspoon dried*

½ *teaspoon salt*

¼ *teaspoon white pepper*

¼ *teaspoon nutmeg*

1 *tablespoon butter, softened*

2 *tablespoons dry white bread crumbs*

4 *large eggs*

1 *cup milk*

¼ *cup grated Parmesan cheese*

Preheat convection oven to 325 degrees. Blanch artichoke hearts in boiling salted water to cover for 1 minute. Drain and squeeze dry.

Peel peppers with a vegetable peeler; or cut into quarters, lay skin side down, and shave the meat off the skin with a sharp knife. Cut into strips. Heat oil in a large skillet. Sauté artichokes, zucchini, and bell pepper strips for 3 minutes. Add scallions and garlic, and sauté for 1 minute. Sprinkle with oregano, salt, white pepper, and nutmeg.

Grease an 8-inch glass or eathenware baking dish with the butter, and dust with bread crumbs.

Break eggs into a bowl, and whisk in milk. Stir in vegetables and Parmesan cheese, and spoon the mixture into the prepared dish. Bake for 25 minutes, and let cool in the dish. Unmold and serve at room temperature (not hot).

PREPARATION TIME: 20 MINUTES / OVEN TIME: 25 MINUTES / EASY

*V*EAL AND PORK TOURTE   *S E R V E S   8*

Like the double-crust Salmon Tourte on page 46, this is a good choice for lunch, accompanied by a green salad, or it can be served as an hors d'oeuvre. The flaky pastry contrasts nicely with the tender meat filling, and the tart is quick to assemble.

8 *ounces boneless veal*
8 *ounces boneless pork*
1 *shallot, chopped*
   Pinch thyme
1 *bay leaf*
½ *cup white wine*

1 *pound Quick Puff Pastry (page 244), or 1 package frozen puff pastry sheets, thawed*
1 *egg, beaten*
   Salt and pepper
2 *large eggs*
¾ *cup heavy cream*
   Dash nutmeg

Trim veal and pork of fat and skin, and cut into finger-length strips. (For this small amount of meat, it is probably easiest to buy chops.)

Combine in a bowl with shallot, thyme, bay leaf, and wine. Cover, and marinate for several hours or overnight in refrigerator.

On a lightly floured surface, roll pastry out about ⅛ inch thick. Using half the dough, line a 9-inch tart pan with removable base, being careful not to stretch the dough. Leave excess dough hanging over the edge. Brush edges with beaten egg. Drain meat and remove bay leaf. Fill shell with meat, and sprinkle with salt and pepper to taste. Cover with remaining dough, pushing the edges down over the filling at the sides to form a double edge. Trim edges flush with sides of pan. Brush dough with beaten egg, and cut a ½-inch round hole in the center. Line this hole with a funnel made of baking parchment. Cut dough trimmings into decorative shapes with a scalloped cutter, and place on top of the tourte. Brush these with beaten egg, and chill tourte uncovered for 20 minutes to relax the dough. (It will then rise more evenly.)

Preheat convection oven to 375 degrees. Bake tourte for 30 minutes. Beat eggs lightly with cream, and season with salt and pepper to taste, and nutmeg. Pour into tourte through funnel, and continue baking for a further 20 minutes. Remove tourte from pan and place on a rack. Serve lukewarm or cold.

PREPARATION TIME: SEVERAL HOURS OR OVERNIGHT MARINATING;
20 MINUTES CHILLING / OVEN TIME: 50 MINUTES

CORN CUSTARD WITH
HAM AND SWISS CHARD

Easy to make, inexpensive, and contemporary, this combination of young corn kernels, diced ham, Swiss chard, eggs, and cream makes a delectable lunch or supper dish. If fresh corn is not in season, frozen corn kernels can be substituted; they are not as sweet and tender, but cooking them in milk with a dash of sugar does help.

3 *ears young corn, about 7 inches long*

¼ *cup milk*

Pinch sugar

Salt

1 *bunch Swiss chard, 6 or 7 ounces, preferably with small leaves*

2 *tablespoons unsalted butter*

1 *small onion, chopped*

Black pepper

Pinch nutmeg

6 *ounces ham, diced*

2 *large eggs*

2 *tablespoons all-purpose flour*

1 *cup heavy cream*

Preheat convection oven to 375 degrees. Husk corn, remove silk, and place corn in a saucepan with enough water to cover. Add milk, sugar, and salt to taste, and bring to a boil. Simmer for 6 minutes, or until tender. Drain corncobs.

Remove stems from chard and reserve for another purpose. Shred leaves coarsely. Heat butter in a skillet and simmer onion for 5 minutes. Add chard, season to taste with salt, pepper, and nutmeg, and sauté for 5 minutes.

Butter an 8 by 10-inch baking dish. Lay chard on the bottom and cover with diced ham. Cut kernels from corncobs (there should be about 2 cups) and spread over ham. Beat eggs, whisk in flour and cream, and season to taste with salt and pepper. Pour over corn, and bake for 25 minutes. Serve hot.

PREPARATION TIME: 20 MINUTES / OVEN TIME: 25 MINUTES / EASY

ACORN SQUASH WITH HAM, BREAD CRUMBS, AND SHERRY

Even people who don't care for squash will enjoy it prepared this way. The sherry heightens the flavor combination, and the fluted squash cups look very attractive.

2 *fluted acorn squash, 18 ounces each, orange or green*

1½ *tablespoons butter*

1 *small onion, chopped*

1 *clove garlic, chopped*

8 *ounces ham, chopped*

2 *tablespoons chopped fresh parsley*

1 *teaspoon chopped fresh sage, or ½ teaspoon dried*

⅓ *cup Dry Sack sherry*

¾ *cup dry white bread crumbs*

Salt and pepper

3 *tablespoons heavy cream*

4 *teaspoons grated Parmesan cheese*

Preheat convection oven to 375 degrees. Cut squash in half and remove seeds. Place cut side down on a foil-lined baking sheet and bake for 25 minutes, or until tender.

While squash are baking, heat butter and sauté onion for 5 minutes, until soft. Add garlic, ham, parsley, and sage and cook for 3 minutes. Add sherry, remove from the heat, and stir in bread crumbs. Season to taste with salt and pepper.

Holding the squash halves with an oven mitt, scoop out and reserve the flesh, leaving a thick shell. If necessary, cut a little slice off the base of each so they will stand. Chop squash flesh, and combine with ham mixture. Stir in cream. Fill squash shells with this mixture and return them to the baking sheet. Sprinkle with cheese. (Squash may be prepared ahead to this point, covered, and refrigerated until required.) Bake at 375 degrees for 20 minutes, until lightly browned.

PREPARATION TIME: 20 MINUTES / OVEN TIME: 25 MINUTES; 20 MINUTES / EASY

GRATIN OF CARAMELIZED
ENDIVE WITH HAM

Most people are familiar with the crisp, creamy white leaves of Belgian endive in a salad, but the tightly closed heads are also delicious when left whole and cooked. In this recipe, which makes an outstanding lunch or supper dish, the precooked endive are caramelized in a skillet, wrapped in slices of ham, covered with cream and cheese, and baked.

4 *Belgian endive spears, 4 ounces each*

2 *tablespoons unsalted butter*

½ *teaspoon sugar*

¼ *teaspoon salt*

Juice of ½ lemon

4 *round slices ham, 1 ounce each, about ⅛ inch thick*

2 *ounces grated white New York cheddar cheese*

½ *cup heavy cream*

Preheat convection oven to 350 degrees. Rinse endive in water, then slice off root ends and just the tip of the pointed ends. Shake well to release water from inside. In a small ovenproof skillet just large enough to hold the endive, heat 1 tablespoon of the butter with the sugar and salt. Add endive with the small amount of water still clinging to the leaves, and the lemon juice (which will help to prevent discoloration). Bring to a boil and remove from the heat. Cover the endive with a circle of buttered parchment paper, and weight it down with an oven-proof pot lid that will fit inside the skillet. Bake for 30 minutes. Allow to cool. (This can be done a day ahead, covered, and refrigerated.)

To caramelize the baked endive, first squeeze them well to remove any liquid. Heat the remaining 1 tablespoon of butter in a small heavy skillet. Add the endive and sauté on both sides—they will turn a beautiful golden brown in about 2 minutes.

Butter a 9-inch baking dish. Roll each endive in a slice of ham and place seam side down in the prepared dish. Sprinkle with cheese and add cream. Bake for 10 minutes, until warmed through and bubbling.

PREPARATION TIME: 45 MINUTES / OVEN TIME: 30 MINUTES; 10 MINUTES

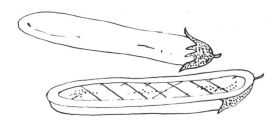

JAPANESE EGGPLANT WITH LAMB, FETA, AND MINT STUFFING

In this Middle Eastern–style recipe, the meat from a lamb chop is mixed with eggplant, sautéed onion, bread crumbs, feta cheese, mint, and cinnamon, and stuffed into the long, slender eggplant shells. It makes a good light meal for two, or an appetizer for six. (Don't try to eat the eggplant shells as you would potato skins; they get very tough when baked and are not meant to be eaten.)

3 *Japanese eggplants, 6 ounces each*
Olive oil
Salt
1 *tablespoon olive oil*
1 *small onion, chopped*
3 *ounces ground lamb (1 shoulder lamb chop, boned and ground in food processor)*
1 *tablespoon tomato paste*
Dash cinnamon

½ *cup Chicken Stock (page 300) or canned chicken broth*
5 *large fresh mint leaves, chopped*
1 *tablespoon chopped fresh parsley*
Black pepper
1 *cup dry white bread crumbs*
2 *ounces feta cheese, crumbled*
¼ *cup water*

Preheat convection oven to 350 degrees. Grease a shallow baking dish with olive oil. Cut eggplants in half lengthways. Make a shallow cut in the flesh all the way round the edge, and then make crisscross cuts without going through the skin. Sprinkle with olive oil and a little salt. Place in the prepared baking dish in one layer, and bake for 15 minutes.

While eggplants are baking, heat 1 tablespoon olive oil and sauté onion for 3 minutes, until soft. Add ground lamb and let brown a little.

Stir in tomato paste, cinnamon, chicken stock, mint, parsley, and salt and pepper to taste, and simmer for 10 minutes. Remove from the heat.

When eggplants are tender, remove from the oven and increase temperature to 375 degrees. Scoop out flesh with a spoon and chop fine. (Leave eggplant shells in the baking dish.) Combine eggplant flesh with meat mixture, and stir in bread crumbs. Let mixture cool. Fill eggplant shells, using a pastry bag or a spoon, and top with crumbled cheese. (Eggplant can be prepared to this point several hours ahead of time, covered, and refrigerated.) Pour water into the baking dish and bake for 10 minutes.

PREPARATION TIME: 25 MINUTES / OVEN TIME: 15 MINUTES; 10 MINUTES / EASY

SALMON TOURTE WITH MUSHROOMS AND PEAS

SERVES 8

Serve this savory double-crust tart for lunch with a green salad, or as an appetizer. The top layer of puff pastry is pressed around the edges inside a fluted quiche pan—it looks like a hat. When it is baked, the pastry rises dramatically to show the many layers around the sides.

14 *ounces filet of salmon, skinned*

1 *tablespoon Cognac*

2 *tablespoons olive oil*

5 *leaves fresh mint, chopped*

Salt and pepper

5 *ounces white mushrooms, sliced*

1 *shallot, chopped*

1 *tablespoon fresh parsley*

Juice of ½ lemon

⅓ *cup peas, fresh or frozen*

1 *pound Quick Puff Pastry (page 244), or 1 package frozen puff pastry sheets, thawed*

1 *egg, beaten*

1 *large egg*

⅓ *cup heavy cream*

Dash nutmeg

Cut salmon into 1 by 2-inch strips and place in a bowl with Cognac, 1 tablespoon of the olive oil, mint, and salt and pepper to taste. Marinate for 30 minutes.

Heat the remaining olive oil in a skillet, and sauté mushrooms with shallot and parsley for 5 minutes. Add lemon juice (to retain color), and let cool. Season with salt and pepper, and stir in peas. (They must be added last, or they lose their bright green color.)

On a lightly floured surface, roll pastry out about ⅛ inch thick. Using half the pastry, line a 9-inch tart pan with removable base, being careful not to stretch the dough. Leave excess dough hanging over the edge. Combine salmon with mushroom mixture and fill shell. Cover with remaining dough, pushing the edges down over the filling at the sides to form a double edge. Trim edges flush with side of pan. Brush with beaten egg, and a cut a ½-inch round hole in the center. Line this hole with a funnel made of doubled baking parchment. Cut dough trimmings into four fish shapes and four leaves, and place on top of the crust, alternating the two. Brush these with beaten egg, and chill tourte, uncovered, for 20 minutes to relax the dough. (It will then rise more evenly.)

Preheat convection oven to 400 degrees. Bake the tourte for 15 minutes. Beat egg lightly with cream, and season with salt, pepper, and nutmeg. Remove the tourte from the oven, and remove and reserve the leaves. Pour the cream mixture through the funnel in the center and through the holes left by the leaves. Return the tourte to the oven and bake for a further 15 minutes. Remove tourte from pan, and replace the reserved pastry leaves. Let rest for 10 minutes before cutting. Serve warm.

PREPARATION TIME: 30 MINUTES MARINATING; 20 MINUTES CHILLING   /
OVEN TIME: 30 MINUTES

THE ORIGINAL EGGS BENEDICT

The Benedictine monks of Fécamp, who in the 16th century perfected the famous liqueur known as Benedictine, are also credited with inventing a dish of poached eggs served over salt cod, which came to be known as Eggs Benedict. It seems quite logical: the good monks had to eat a great deal of fish, Fécamp has a harbor, and the only way to preserve the local catch—mainly cod—would have been to salt it. I like to believe that this legend is true, and I certainly prefer the happy combination of eggs with salt cod and creamy potatoes to the modern version of Eggs Benedict with ham and an English muffin.

3 baking potatoes, 8 ounces each

8 ounces dried salt cod, soaked overnight in two or three changes of cold water

2 cloves garlic, smashed and minced

½ cup heavy cream

½ cup olive oil

¼ teaspoon white pepper

Salt (optional)

1 tablespoon chopped fresh parsley

1 cup Hollandaise Sauce (page 303)

4 or 8 large eggs

1 tablespoon white wine vinegar

Preheat convection oven to 375 degrees. Bake potatoes for 45 minutes, until soft.

While the potatoes are baking, place cod in a saucepan, cover with cold water, and bring to a boil. Simmer for a minute or two, until tender. Drain, and flake into a bowl.

Cut baked potatoes in half lengthways, and scoop out flesh. Mash potato with flaked salt cod and garlic until very smooth. (Do this by hand; the mixture will turn to glue in a food processor.) Heat cream and olive oil, without boiling, and beat into potato mixture with a wooden spoon. Add white pepper and parsley. Taste for seasoning, and add salt only if necessary. Butter four 3 by 6-inch porcelain shirred egg dishes, and divide the mixture among them. (Potatoes can be prepared to this point several hours in advance, covered with plastic wrap and refrigerated.) Bake for 15 minutes.

While potato mixture is baking, prepare Hollandaise Sauce. Poach the eggs briefly in simmering water to which the vinegar has been added, removing them as soon as the whites have set. The yolks should be soft. Trim off any ragged bits of egg white. To serve, top each dish with one or two poached eggs, and mask with Hollandaise Sauce.

PREPARATION TIME: OVERNIGHT SOAKING 25 MINUTES /
OVEN TIME: 45 MINUTES; 15 MINUTES

BAKED EGGS WITH BACON AND MUSHROOMS

SERVES 4

A good choice for brunch guests, as it looks attractive, tastes delicious, and can be prepared an hour or two ahead of time. Small white oval ovenproof baking dishes are worth buying; they are useful in the kitchen as well as being excellent individual serving dishes.

4 *strips bacon*
6 *mushrooms, medium, sliced*
Black pepper
¼ *cup fine dry white bread crumbs*

4 *eggs*
Salt
1 *tablespoon butter, cut into small dice*
Chopped fresh parsley

Preheat convection oven to 275 degrees. Chop bacon and fry until soft. Add mushrooms, season with black pepper to taste, and cook for 2 minutes. Butter four shallow ovenproof porcelain shirred egg dishes, and sprinkle each one with a teaspoon of bread crumbs. Break an egg into each dish, and season lightly with salt. Top with bacon and overlapping mushroom slices. Sprinkle with remaining crumbs, and dot with butter. (Dish can be prepared ahead to this point and left to stand at room temperature for an hour or two, covered with plastic wrap.) Bake for 10 to 12 minutes, and garnish with parsley before serving.

PREPARATION TIME: 10 MINUTES / OVEN TIME: 10 TO 12 MINUTES / EASY

ASPARAGUS SOUFFLÉ

SERVES 4

On special occasions, gild the lily and serve this impressive soufflé with Hollandaise Sauce on the side.

To make a cheese soufflé, omit the asparagus and stir in 1 cup of grated Swiss cheese, ¼ cup grated Parmesan cheese, and a dash of cayenne pepper after adding the egg yolks.

2 tablespoons butter
2 tablespoons grated
  Parmesan cheese
1 cup 3-inch tips of tender
  green asparagus, 6
  ounces
2 tablespoons all-purpose
  flour

1 cup milk, heated
4 large egg yolks, well
  beaten
4 large egg whites, beaten
  until stiff
Salt and pepper
Pinch nutmeg

Preheat convection oven to 350 degrees. Grease a 1-quart soufflé dish with a little of the butter, and dust with Parmesan cheese. Cut asparagus tips diagonally into 1-inch lengths, and poach for 3 minutes in simmering water. (Asparagus will finish cooking in the oven.) Plunge into cold water to stop the cooking and preserve the color, and drain. Reserve three asparagus points, and place the remainder in the bottom of the soufflé dish.

In a saucepan, melt remaining butter over low heat and blend in the flour, stirring constantly. When the mixture is smooth, remove from the heat and whisk in the hot milk. Gradually whisk in the beaten egg yolks. Add salt, pepper, and nutmeg and stir well. Stir one quarter of the stiffly beaten egg whites into the mixture, then gently fold in the remainder. Pour over asparagus tips. Cut reserved asparagus tips in half lengthways, and arrange in a star pattern, flat sides down, on the top of the soufflé. Bake for 25 minutes, until well puffed and golden brown. Serve immediately.

PREPARATION TIME: 20 MINUTES / OVEN TIME: 25 MINUTES

PIZZA AND PASTA

BASIC PIZZA DOUGH

It is difficult to make yeast dough in very small quantities; this recipe is sufficient for two 12-inch pizzas. However, the dough freezes well, so you can freeze the extra if you're making only one. Let the dough come to room temperature before rolling it out.

1½ teaspoons dry yeast
2½ cups unbleached bread
    flour, sifted

1 cup warm water (110
    degrees)
½ teaspoon salt

Preheat convection oven to 85 degrees, or barely warm. In a small bowl, combine yeast with 1 tablespoon of the flour, and add half the water. Set aside to proof until bubbly, about 10 minutes.

Measure remaining flour and salt into bowl of an electric mixer. Using a wooden spoon, stir in remaining water and the yeast mixture. Set bowl on mixer stand and knead with the dough hook for 10 to 15 minutes, adding more flour if necessary to make a supple and elastic dough. Place dough in a greased bowl, turning to grease all sides, and cover with a hot damp terry-cloth towel. Place bowl in the oven and let dough rise until doubled in bulk, about 45 minutes to 1 hour. (The moist warmth will encourage rising; dampen the towel with more hot water occasionally.)

Remove dough from bowl and punch down. Form into two balls and let rest for 5 minutes. Then roll each ball into a 12-inch circle (on a baking sheet is easiest) and let rise in the barely warm oven for 20 minutes.

Add pizza ingredients of choice.

PREPARATION TIME: 2 HOURS / OVEN TIME: NONE / EASY

ONION PIZZA WITH BLACK OLIVE PASTE

SERVES 2, OR 6 TO 8 AS AN APPETIZER

Black olive paste, made from oil-cured Mediterranean olives, herbs, and garlic, takes only seconds to blend in a food processor. It seems to affect people the way catnip affects cats, and makes this crispy pizza irresistible.

½ *recipe Basic Pizza Dough (page 51), or 10-ounce roll of ready-prepared pizza dough*

2 *tablespoons olive oil*

1 *onion, 6 ounces, sliced*

2 *cloves garlic, minced*

1 *leek, white part only, rinsed well and shredded*

½ *red bell pepper, seeded, peeled, and shredded (page 39)*

6 *tablespoons Black Olive Paste (page 308)*

Black pepper

Preheat convection oven to 400 degrees. Roll pizza dough into a 10 to 12-inch circle (on a baking sheet is easiest), making the edge a little thicker than the rest. Heat olive oil in a skillet and sauté onion for 5 minutes, until softened but not colored. Add garlic, leek, and bell pepper and sauté for 3 minutes.

Spread pizza dough with olive paste, and top with sautéed vegetables. Season with coarsely ground black pepper (but no salt as the olive paste is salty). Bake for 20 minutes, until crust is crispy around the edge. Serve warm.

PREPARATION TIME: 15 MINUTES / OVEN TIME: 20 MINUTES / EASY

EGGPLANT, MUSHROOM, AND GOAT CHEESE PIZZA

The combination of the crisp crust with the juicy eggplant, sliced mushrooms, slightly oily sun-dried tomatoes, and goat cheese is delightful. Long slender Japanese eggplants have very tender skins and do not require peeling for this dish. They can be any shade from pale mauve to deep purple, and cook very quickly.

½ recipe Basic Pizza Dough (page 51), or 10-ounce roll of ready-prepared pizza dough

4 Japanese eggplants, 7 to 8 ounces each, unpeeled

2 tablespoons olive oil

1 small leek, shredded

1 clove garlic, minced

6 mushrooms, sliced

Pinch oregano

Salt and pepper

¼ cup Chicken Stock (page 300), canned chicken broth, or water

½ cup sun-dried tomatoes in oil, drained if necessary and cut in strips

5 ounces goat cheese or feta cheese, crumbled

2 ripe tomatoes, 5 to 6 ounces each, sliced

Preheat convection oven to 400 degrees. Roll pizza dough into a 10 to 12-inch circle (on a baking sheet is easiest), making the edges a little thicker than the rest.

Trim eggplants and cut in half lengthways. Slice into 1-inch pieces. Heat 1 tablespoon of the oil in a nonstick skillet and sauté eggplant for 1 minute, then add leek, garlic, mushrooms, oregano, and salt and pepper to taste. Add chicken stock or water, cover pan, and steam for 1 minute. Uncover pan and boil off any excess liquid. Spread the sautéed vegetables over the pizza dough, and top with strips of sun-dried tomato. Cover with crumbled cheese and a layer of sliced fresh tomatoes. Season with black pepper, and salt if necessary (the sun-dried tomatoes may be salty), and sprinkle with the remaining tablespoon of olive oil. Bake for 20 minutes, until crust is crispy around the edge. Serve warm.

PREPARATION TIME: 15 MINUTES / OVEN TIME: 20 MINUTES / EASY

ALSATIAN PIZZA WITH
CREAM CHEESE AND BACON

This is an ancient recipe from Alsace, where it is generally known as *Tarte Flambé* because it was cooked over burning wood and flames licked the top of the tart.

½ recipe Basic Pizza Dough (page 51) or 10-ounce roll of ready-prepared pizza dough

10 strips lean bacon, chopped in ½-inch pieces

1 large onion, thinly sliced

8 ounces cream cheese (preferably fresh), softened

2 large egg yolks

½ cup heavy cream

Salt and pepper

Pinch nutmeg

Preheat convection oven to 400 degrees. Roll pizza dough into a 12-inch circle (on a baking sheet is easiest), making the edge a little thicker than the rest. Sauté bacon in a skillet until fat starts to run, about 3 minutes, then remove and drain on paper towels. Discard half the remaining fat, add onion to the skillet, and cook, covered, until very soft but not browned, about 10 minutes.

Combine cream cheese, egg yolks, cream, a little salt (the bacon is salty), pepper, and nutmeg. Sprinkle the onion over the crust, and then top with dollops of the cream cheese mixture, leaving an edge of dough showing. Scatter bacon over the surface, and bake for 15 minutes, until crust is browned at the edges. Let cool on a rack for 15 minutes before serving.

PREPARATION TIME: 20 MINUTES / OVEN TIME: 15 MINUTES / EASY

TOMATO AND ANCHOVY PIZZA

If it is available, use buffalo mozzarella cheese on this pizza: it melts better and has a good flavor. On the other hand, you can use Monterey Jack or Swiss cheese if that's what you happen to have in the refrigerator. The wonderful thing about making your own pizza is that you can improvise as you go along, and no one will report you to the Un-Italian Culinary Activities Committee! If you find that most anchovies are too salty for your taste, rinse them off in water and pat dry before using, and sprinkle a little extra olive oil on top of the pizza.

½ recipe Basic Pizza
   Dough (page 51), or
   10-ounce roll of ready-
   prepared pizza dough

2 tomatoes, sliced

1 teaspoon oregano

6 to 8 ounces mozzarella
   cheese, thinly sliced

1 can anchovies, 2
   ounces, drained and
   split lengthways

12 dry oil-cured black
   olives, pitted and cut in
   half

1 teaspoon olive oil

Preheat convection oven to 400 degrees. Roll pizza dough into a 10 to 12-inch circle (on a baking sheet is easiest), making the edge a little thicker than the rest. Cover dough with a layer of sliced tomatoes, and sprinkle with oregano. Top tomatoes with thinly sliced mozzarella. Form a lattice on top with strips of anchovy filets. Place half an olive within each square, and sprinkle the pizza with olive oil. Bake for 20 minutes, until crust is browned and crispy around the edge. Serve warm.

PREPARATION TIME: 10 MINUTES / OVEN TIME: 20 MINUTES / EASY

FETTUCINE BAKED
WITH BLUE CHEESE

An outstanding—and very easy—pasta dish to serve with salad for a light meal. It can also be offered as a first course, or as a side dish with roast pork or pork chops.

6 *ounces fettucine or egg noodles*

1 *teaspoon vegetable oil*

Salt

1 *cup cream-style cottage cheese*

2 *ounces blue cheese, crumbled (½ cup)*

½ *cup chopped fresh parsley*

¼ *cup chopped scallions, white bulbs and half of green tops*

1 *large egg, well beaten*

1 *small clove garlic, chopped (optional)*

Black pepper

1½ *cups half-and-half or light cream*

Preheat convection oven to 325 degrees. Bring a large pot of water to a boil and add oil (to prevent pasta from sticking together). Add salt to taste, and cook pasta until just tender (approximately 2 minutes for fresh pasta or according to package directions if dried). Rinse under cold water to remove any loose starch, and drain. Combine remaining ingredients in a large bowl, add pasta, and toss well. Butter a 1-quart ovenproof casserole or soufflé dish, add mixture, and bake for 30 minutes. Push the brown crispy bits down into the sauce before serving.

PREPARATION TIME: 20 MINUTES / OVEN TIME: 30 MINUTES / EASY

GNOCCHI PARISIAN STYLE, WITH MUSHROOM SAUCE

The lightest of all gnocchi, these are really feather-light dumplings made from a *pâte à choux* mixture. A convenient and elegant first course for guests, Parisian gnocchi can be prepared well ahead of time and then combined with the sauce and baked until lightly browned and bubbly.

1 *cup water*
6 *tablespoons butter*
¼ *teaspoon salt*
⅛ *teaspoon white pepper*
⅛ *teaspoon nutmeg*
   Scant ¾ cup (4 ounces) all-purpose flour, sifted
3 *large eggs*
1 *tablespoon vegetable oil*

MUSHROOM SAUCE

2 *tablespoons butter*
2 *tablespoons all-purpose flour*
1 *cup Chicken Stock (page 300) or canned chicken broth*
½ *cup milk*
   Salt
   White pepper
   Nutmeg
4 *mushrooms, sliced*
1 *tablespoon grated Parmesan cheese*

In a heavy saucepan, combine water, butter, salt, white pepper, and nutmeg. Bring to a boil. Add flour and stir vigorously until mixture thickens, about 30 seconds. Remove from the heat and whisk in eggs one at a time, beating well after each addition.

Bring a large pot of salted water to a boil and add oil (to prevent gnocchi from sticking). Transfer flour mixture to a pastry bag fitted with a plain ½-inch tube. Pipe out 1-inch lengths into the boiling water, cutting them off with a knife. (Or form into small ovals with two teaspoons.) Simmer for about 3 minutes, until gnocchi swell and rise to the surface. Cool off in cold water, then drain. Gnocchi will keep for 2 days in the refrigerator if placed in cold salted water.

To make the sauce, heat butter and stir in flour. Add chicken stock and milk, whisking continuously, and season to taste with salt, pepper, and nutmeg. Add sliced mushrooms and simmer for 5 minutes. The sauce should be quite thin. Remove from the heat.

Preheat convection oven to 375 degrees. Combine gnocchi and sauce in a shallow baking dish and sprinkle with Parmesan. Bake for 15 minutes, until bubbly.

PREPARATION TIME: 25 MINUTES / OVEN TIME: 15 MINUTES / EASY

GNOCCHI PIEDMONT STYLE, WITH POTATO AND FONTINA

SERVES 4

Gnocchi vary from district to district in Italy, but most are made of some kind of paste of flour and eggs, formed into corklike shapes and poached in water before being combined with a sauce and baked in the oven. It's actually a variation on fresh pasta that can be made very quickly, without kneading or rolling the dough. In Piedmont it is common to include mashed potatoes with the basic gnocchi mixture.

The amount of dough in this recipe will make about 80 gnocchi. Serve half with the cream and Fontina; at another meal serve the other half in Rich Tomato Sauce (page 307), sprinkled with grated Parmesan cheese. The gnocchi dough can be kept for up to three days in the refrigerator, covered with plastic wrap.

1 *pound russet or all-purpose potatoes*
1 *cup (5 ounces) all-purpose flour*
2 *large eggs*
½ *teaspoon salt*

¼ *teaspoon white pepper*
½ *teaspoon nutmeg*
  Dash olive oil
1 *cup heavy cream*
3 *ounces Fontina cheese, very thinly sliced*

Peel potatoes, cut into evenly sized chunks, and boil in salted water until tender, about 25 minutes. Drain immediately (or they will absorb water). While potatoes are still warm, push them through a sieve into a bowl and incorporate flour, eggs, salt, white pepper, and nutmeg. Chill for 20 minutes.

Remove half the dough, reserving the balance for another use. (Cover and store in refrigerator for up to three days.) With lightly floured hands, form dough into little cigar shapes, ½ inch in diameter and 1 inch long. Press each one with the tines of a fork, to make crossways ridges. Arrange, without touching, on a lightly floured surface.

Bring a large pot of salted water to a boil and add a dash of oil (to prevent the gnocchi from sticking together). Add the gnocchi a few at a time, removing them with a perforated spoon as they rise to the surface, about 3 minutes. Plunge into cold water.

Preheat convection oven to 375 degrees. Butter a shallow ovenproof dish. Fill the dish with gnocchi, cover with cream, then cover with slices of Fontina. Bake for 10 minutes, until bubbling and starting to brown.

PREPARATION TIME: 40 MINUTES; 20 MINUTES CHILLING TIME   /
OVEN TIME: 10 MINUTES   /   EASY

GNOCCHI ROMAN
STYLE, WITH TOMATO SAUCE

SERVES 6
AS AN APPETIZER

The Roman-style gnocchi mixture includes semolina and is chilled in the form of a flat cake before being cut into diamonds or triangles. In Italy, these gnocchi are usually dipped in melted butter before being baked with lots of Parmesan cheese and yet more butter. In this extra-light version, the gnocchi are dipped in beaten egg before baking. The light tomato sauce makes a delicious contrast.

These gnocchi can be served for lunch, as a first course, or as a starch with meat or poultry. Two per person is usually enough as an appetizer. The dough will keep in the refrigerator for three or four days.

Incidentally, Asiago cheese, made in the United States, makes a good and less costly substitute for imported Parmesan. If you *are* buying Parmesan, don't bother with copies. Get the best: Parmigiano Reggiano.

2 *cups milk*

2 *tablespoons butter*

Heaping ½ cup (3¼ ounces) imported Italian semolina

½ *teaspoon salt*

¼ *teaspoon white pepper*

¼ *teaspoon nutmeg*

2 *large eggs*

1 *large egg yolk*

Grated Parmesan or Asiago cheese for dredging, 1½ to 2 cups

SAUCE

½ *tablespoon olive oil*

1 *clove garlic, smashed and chopped*

½ *onion, chopped*

1 *can peeled tomatoes, 14½ ounces, drained and chopped, juice reserved*

½ *bay leaf*

1 *sprig fresh thyme, or pinch dried*

Salt and pepper

Combine milk and butter in a saucepan and bring to a boil. Slowly sprinkle in semolina, stirring constantly with a whisk so that it does not form lumps. Cook for 2 minutes, until thick, and season with salt, white pepper, and nutmeg. Remove from the heat and whisk in 1 whole egg and the egg yolk.

Moisten the bottom of an 8 by 10-inch baking dish with water and spread the dough in it, using a wet spatula to make it smooth and even. Refrigerate until set, about 30 minutes, or until required. Turn the dough out onto a flat surface and cut into 2-inch-wide bands. Cut the bands diagonally into diamond shapes.

To make the sauce, heat olive oil in a skillet and sauté onion for 3 minutes, until softened. Add garlic, chopped tomatoes, bay leaf, thyme, and salt and pepper to taste. Cook for 2 minutes, then add reserved tomato juice. Simmer for 10 minutes. Remove from the heat and discard bay leaf.

Preheat convection oven to 375 degrees. Spoon tomato sauce into a shallow baking dish. Beat remaining egg lightly. Dip gnocchi into egg, and then into grated cheese. Lay on top of sauce. Bake for 20 minutes, until sauce is bubbling and gnocchi are starting to turn golden brown.

PREPARATION TIME: 25 MINUTES; 30 MINUTES CHILLING   /
OVEN TIME: 20 MINUTES   /   EASY

MACARONI, LAMB, AND FETA CASSEROLE

This savory Greek layered casserole, called *pastitsio*, is a distant cousin of baked lasagne, and is a good choice for a casual buffet-style meal.

8 *ounces elbow macaroni*

8 *tablespoons butter, melted*

1 *tablespoon olive oil*

1 *onion, chopped*

2 *cloves garlic, minced*

12 *ounces ground lean lamb (preferably from shoulder chops, freshly ground in food processor)*

Salt and pepper

1 *teaspoon chopped fresh oregano, or ½ teaspoon dried*

Pinch cinnamon

1 *cup Chicken Stock (page 300) or canned chicken broth*

1 *tablespoon tomato paste*

1 *tablespoon chopped fresh parsley*

10 *sheets phyllo dough, thawed if frozen*

8 *ounces feta cheese, crumbled*

¼ *grated Parmesan cheese*

6 *large eggs*

2 *cups milk*

Cook macaroni in a large pot of boiling salted water until *al dente,* or just done. Drain, plunge into cold water, drain again, and mix with ¼ cup of the melted butter. Set aside.

Heat oil in a skillet and simmer onion for 5 minutes, until softened. Add garlic and lamb and sauté for 5 minutes, until meat loses its pink color. Add salt and pepper to taste, oregano, cinnamon, chicken stock, and tomato paste. Cook until liquid has evaporated, about 20 minutes. Stir in parsley.

Preheat convection oven to 375 degrees. Lay five phyllo sheets in a 14 by 11-inch baking dish, brushing each sheet with some of the remaining melted butter. Top with half the macaroni. Sprinkle with half the feta and half the Parmesan. Spread meat mixture on top, and cover with remaining macaroni and cheeses.

Beat eggs and combine with milk. Season lightly with salt and pepper, and pour over mixture in baking dish. Cover with remaining five sheets of phyllo, brushing each with remaining melted butter. Bake for 35 minutes, until golden. Let stand for 10 to 15 minutes before cutting into squares.

PREPARATION TIME: 40 MINUTES / OVEN TIME: 35 MINUTES / EASY

𝓕ISH AND SEAFOOD

HALIBUT WITH GREEN HERB SAUCE

An elegant main course for guests—the contrast between the white fish steaks and the brilliant green sauce is spectacular. The fish bakes in 10 minutes and the sauce is easy to make. A complementary first course would be the Gnocchi Roman Style (page 60), which can be made ahead of time, and the Lemon Soufflé Tart (page 260) is a good choice for dessert. There's a nice balance of colors, textures, and flavors in this menu, and you won't have to spend much time in the kitchen between courses.

2 tablespoons minced shallots

4 halibut steaks, 6 ounces each

2 tablespoons butter, cut into small dice

Salt and pepper

8 ounces mushrooms, sliced

⅔ cup dry white wine

SAUCE

1 sprig fresh tarragon, 4 to 5 inches long

3 sprigs fresh dill, 4 to 5 inches long

1 bunch fresh young spinach leaves, 6 ounces, blanched, squeezed dry, and cooled

2 tablespoons crushed ice

1 tablespoon butter

Salt and pepper

Dill sprigs for garnish

Preheat convection oven to 350 degrees. Sprinkle shallots in a shallow baking dish, and top with fish steaks. Dot with butter, and season with salt and pepper to taste. Top with mushrooms, and pour wine over all. Bake for 10 minutes.

To make the sauce, strain the cooking juices into a saucepan; there will be about 1 cup. Heat to boiling and reduce by half, about 5 minutes. Keep fish and mushrooms warm in the meantime.

In the bowl of a food processor, combine tarragon and dill leaves (discard stems) and spinach. Process to a purée, adding crushed ice after the first few seconds to set the brilliant green color. Whisk the butter into the purée, then whisk purée into the reduced fish juices. Taste for seasoning and add salt and pepper as required. Heat through but do not allow to boil.

To serve, pour a little sauce on each plate and spread it out to form a circle. Remove skin from halibut and lift out the central bone. Reassemble each steak on top of the sauce, and garnish with a sprig of dill. Lay mushroom slices around the fish, in the sauce.

PREPARATION TIME: 25 MINUTES   /   OVEN TIME: 10 MINUTES

ORANGE ROUGHY WITH BASIL

SERVES 4

Orange roughy is a mild, sweet-flavored white fish from Australia with
a nice texture somewhere between that of sole and snapper. This is a
good dish to prepare when fresh basil is available, and when you are
in a hurry: it takes very little time to prepare and bakes in just 6
minutes.

1 *shallot, chopped*
4 *filets of orange
  roughy, 6 ounces each*
  Salt and pepper
¼ *cup dry vermouth*
½ *cup fish stock or
  bottled clam juice*
2 *tablespoons olive oil*
1½ *tablespoons shredded
  fresh basil leaves*

2 *tablespoons butter*
1 *tablespoon fresh lemon
  juice*
1 *tomato, peeled, seeded,
  and chopped*
1 *tablespoon torn flat-
  leaf parsley or chopped
  curly parsley*

Preheat convection oven to 375 degrees. Butter a shallow ovenproof
dish, and add the shallots. Place the orange roughy filets on top, and
season with salt and pepper to taste. Sprinkle with vermouth, fish
stock, olive oil, and basil leaves. Bake for 6 minutes.

Remove the dish from the oven and pour the accumulated juices
into a saucepan. Keep fish warm. Bring juices to a simmer. Over low
heat, whisk in butter bit by bit. Add lemon juice and taste for seasoning. Pour the sauce over the filets, then sprinkle with the tomato
and parsley.

PREPARATION TIME: 12 MINUTES / OVEN TIME: 6 MINUTES / EASY

RED SNAPPER WITH HERB CRUMB STUFFING

Two snapper filets are sandwiched together with a simple herb and bread crumb mixture. More of this green stuffing goes on top, which in turn is covered with a layer of thinly sliced bright red tomatoes. The fish is baked, and the juices are made into a simple sauce. Plain boiled new potatoes make a good accompaniment.

1 to 2 tablespoons olive oil

2 filets of red snapper or rockfish, 6 ounces each

¾ cup bread crumbs made from day-old white bread

6 tablespoons milk

1 small onion, chopped

2 tablespoons chopped fresh parsley

2 teaspoons chopped fresh basil

1 teaspoon chopped fresh thyme

Salt and pepper

2 ripe tomatoes, very thinly sliced

½ cup white wine

SAUCE

½ cup bottled clam juice

6 scallions, chopped, white bulbs and half of green tops

2 tablespoons chopped fresh parsley

½ tablespoon butter

Preheat convection oven to 375 degrees. Grease a shallow baking dish with the olive oil and lay one of the snapper filets in it, skin side down. In the bowl of a food processor, combine bread crumbs, milk, onion, parsley, basil, thyme, and salt and pepper to taste. Process briefly to form a light stuffing. Spread half of this mixture on the filet in the dish, and top with the other filet, skin side up. Spread remaining mixture over the second filet. Top with sliced tomatoes, overlapping the slices like scales. Season lightly with salt and pepper, and sprinkle with a little olive oil. Pour wine into the baking dish, and bake for 25 minutes.

Pour cooking juices from the baking dish into a saucepan. (Keep fish warm in the dish.) Add clam juice, scallions, and parsley and bring to a boil. Whisk in butter, taste for seasoning, and pour around fish. Serve from the baking dish.

PREPARATION TIME: 15 MINUTES / OVEN TIME: 25 MINUTES / EASY

RED SNAPPER WITH
MUSHROOMS AND WHITE WINE   SERVES 3 TO 4

A fast and easy entrée that can be prepared and baked in 20 minutes or less. Fairly thick filets of other firm-fleshed white fish such as cod, perch, or orange roughy are also excellent cooked this way. Serve with boiled new potatoes; or offer fresh pasta with Genoese Pesto Sauce (page 304) as a first course.

1 *large shallot, finely chopped*

4 *ounces mushrooms, sliced*

½ *cup Chardonnay, or other dry white wine*

1 *pound filets of red snapper, 1½ inches thick*

Salt and pepper

¼ *cup bread crumbs made from day-old white bread*

2 *tablespoons butter, chilled, cut into small dice*

Preheat convection oven to 375 degrees. Butter a shallow ovenproof dish large enough to hold the fish in one layer. In a small saucepan, combine the chopped shallot, mushrooms, and wine. Boil for 1 minute. Lay the fish filets in the baking dish. Pour the mushroom and wine mixture over them, and season with salt and pepper to taste. Sprinkle with bread crumbs and dot with butter. Bake for 8 to 10 minutes, until fish is just cooked and no longer translucent in the center.

PREPARATION TIME: 10 MINUTES / OVEN TIME: 8 TO 10 MINUTES / EASY

SALMON FILETS
WITH BLACK OLIVE PASTE

A good choice for a main course if you're running late—or even if you're not. It takes about 15 minutes to prepare and bake. Have quick-cooking fresh pasta to start with (or Gnocchi Roman Style, page 60, if you have any already made), and serve with a green salad.

2 *salmon filets, 4 ounces each*

1 *tablespoon olive oil*

1 *teaspoon chopped shallots*

Salt and pepper

½ *cup dry white wine*

1 *scallion, chopped, white bulbs and half of green top*

1 *teaspoon Black Olive Paste (page 308) or store-bought Italian*

1 *tomato, 4 ounces, peeled, seeded, and coarsely chopped*

1 *tablespoon butter*

1 *tablespoon flat-leaf parsley, torn up, or 1 teaspoon chopped curly parsley*

Preheat convection oven to 375 degrees. If salmon still has its skin, remove by placing the filet skin side down on a cutting board and cutting the flesh away from the skin. (See illustration for skinning trout filets on page 35.) Cut off any dark areas of salmon flesh—it is bitter. Pour olive oil into a small ovenproof skillet and add shallots, salt and pepper to taste, salmon filets, and wine. Bake for 5 minutes.

Remove salmon to heated plates and keep warm. Place skillet over high heat and add scallions, olive paste, tomato, and pepper to taste. (Be cautious with salt, as the olive paste is salty.) Bring to a boil and whisk in butter. Taste for seasoning, and pour around salmon. Sprinkle sauce with parsley.

PREPARATION TIME: 10 MINUTES / OVEN TIME: 5 MINUTES / EASY

SALMON WITH MINT
AND CUCUMBER EN PAPILLOTE

Here's a wonderful way to cook salmon: Slices of filet are combined with fresh mint, lemon, and shredded cucumber and baked in parchment paper packages. It could hardly be easier, and can be served as an appetizer or as an entrée. I like to slide the packages onto warmed dinner plates and let each diner make a semicircular slit in the paper at the table, which releases the fine aromas, and eat from the package. (Some people open the packages in the kitchen and put the contents onto plates there, but you lose the concentrated aromas that way.) The dish can be prepared several hours ahead of time and refrigerated. Naturally, if you are serving this as an appetizer, divide the ingredients among four packages instead of two.

1 *cucumber, about 8 inches long*

2 *sheets of baking parchment, each 15 by 18 inches*

2 *tablespoons butter*

4 *slices of salmon filet, 2 ounces each*

Salt and pepper

3 *leaves fresh mint, chopped*

4 *segments lemon, all peel and pith and membrane removed*

1 *egg white, beaten*

Preheat convection oven to 375 degrees, and place a baking sheet in the oven to preheat. Peel cucumber, then cut in half. Run each half lengthways across a mandoline (or use wide-bladed vegetable peeler) to create very thin 4-inch-long slices. Discard the seedy center-portion slices. Stack and cut into long thin strips.

Fold sheets of baking parchment in half. Cut each into a half heart shape, as large as the paper allows, and butter lightly. Open the folded paper and lay flat.

Heat butter in a skillet and turn salmon slices in it for a few seconds. Lay 2 slices on one half of a paper heart. Sprinkle with salt and pepper to taste, and half the chopped mint. Cover with half the cucumber strips. Season lightly with salt and pepper, and top with 2 segments of lemon. Brush edges of paper with egg white. Fold other half of paper heart over contents. Repeat with the other paper and ingredients. Seal the packages by folding and crimping the two edges together all the way round, starting at the top of the heart. Secure the point with an upward twist of the paper. Place on the heated baking sheet and bake for 5 or 6 minutes. Transfer the packages to plates, and serve.

PREPARATION TIME: 15 MINUTES / OVEN TIME: 5 TO 6 MINUTES / EASY

SERVES 4

SOLE STUFFED WITH ARTICHOKES AND MUSHROOMS

A flavorful and appetizing dish that can be prepared well ahead, this takes a little time but is not difficult. Be sure to use very fresh fish; old or defrosted sole has a flabby texture. Offer crisp French bread with the fish for mopping up the delicious sauce. Asparagus and Prosciutto in Puff Pastry Cases (page 22) would make a suitable first course; and a flourless Chocolate Soufflé Cake (page 271) would round out the menu.

8 *sole filets, 6 to 7 inches long, 1½ pounds total*
  Salt and pepper
2 *tablespoons butter*
1 *shallot, chopped*
2 *freshly cooked or canned artichoke bottoms (well rinsed and drained if canned), diced*
4 *ounces mushrooms, diced*
1 *tablespoon chopped fresh parsley*

1 *tomato, peeled, seeded, and coarsely chopped*
1 *cup dry white wine*
1 *cup heavy cream*
2 *egg yolks*
1 *tablespoon diced artichoke bottom, for garnish*
1 *tablespoon chopped tomato, for garnish*
1 *teaspoon chopped chives, for garnish*

Preheat convection oven to 375 degrees. Flatten sole lightly with the flat of a large knife, and cut out the slender cartilage in the center.

Butter an ovenproof dish large enough to hold four filets in one layer, and sprinkle it lightly with salt and pepper. Lay four of the filets in the dish, reassembling the split halves.

Heat 1 tablespoon of the butter in a skillet and sauté the shallot for 1 minute. Add diced artichoke, mushrooms, parsley, and tomato and sauté for 2 minutes. Season lightly with salt and pepper. Spoon one quarter of the vegetable mixture over each sole filet, heaping it in the center. Cover with remaining sole filets, letting the filling show through the split in the middle. Dot with the remaining tablespoon of butter, and pour wine into the dish. Top fish with buttered paper—baking parchment or butter wrappers. (Can be prepared ahead to this point, covered, and refrigerated.) Bake for 7 minutes.

Pour cooking juices into a skillet, and keep fish warm. Bring juices to a boil and reduce by half, about 5 minutes. Then stir in cream and bring to a boil. Taste, and season with salt and pepper if necessary. Over low heat, whisk in the egg yolks and let thicken slightly without boiling, about 1 minute. When mixture will coat a spoon, it is ready. Divide sauce among four heated dinner plates and top with stuffed sole filets. Scatter sauce with artichoke, tomato, and chives.

PREPARATION: 20 MINUTES / OVEN TIME: 7 MINUTES

SOLE WITH KALAMATA OLIVES

Richly flavored Kalamata olives from Greece add wonderful flavor to this quickly prepared main course, which is just as good made with snapper or other white fish. If you are using thicker filets, bake for 7 rather than 5 minutes. Serve with rice cooked in fish stock or bottled clam juice, and steamed green beans sprinkled with lemon juice.

1 *pound very fresh filets of sole, flounder, or snapper*
White pepper
2 *tablespoons butter*
½ *stalk celery, destringed and cut into julienne*
2 *mushrooms, cut into julienne*

½ *cup dry white wine*
½ *cup bottled clam juice*
6 *Kalamata olives, pitted and cut into slivers*
¼ *cup heavy cream*
1 *tablespoon chopped fresh parsley*

Preheat convection oven to 375 degrees. Butter a shallow baking dish large enough to hold the fish in one layer, and lay the filets in it. Season lightly with white pepper (but no salt as both olives and clam juice are salty).

In a skillet, melt butter and simmer celery and mushrooms for 5 minutes. Stir in wine, clam juice, and olives, and cook for 2 minutes. Pour over fish, and bake for 5 to 7 minutes.

Remove fish and vegetables to a warm plate and keep warm. Pour cooking liquid into same skillet, bring to a boil, and reduce by half, about 5 minutes. Add cream, let bubble for a minute or two, and taste for seasoning. Strain over the fish, and sprinkle with parlsey.

PREPARATION TIME: 10 MINUTES / OVEN TIME: 5 TO 7 MINUTES / EASY

TROUT WITH
MINT EN PAPILLOTE

Whole trout are cooked inside foil packages with onion, tomato, Canadian bacon, mint, and wine. The packages can be prepared ahead and refrigerated; they bake in just 10 minutes.

4 *tablespoons butter*

1 *onion, chopped*

4 *whole trout, 8 ounces
  each*

2 *tomatoes, peeled,
  seeded, and coarsely
  chopped*

4 *slices Canadian bacon,
  3 ounces total, julienned*

6 *to 8 leaves fresh mint,
  chopped*

Salt and pepper

⅓ *cup dry vermouth*

⅓ *cup dry white wine*

Preheat convection oven to 350 degrees. Grease the center area of four 12 by 16-inch sheets of aluminum foil with ½ tablespoon of the butter. In a skillet, heat remaining butter and simmer chopped onion until lightly colored, about 5 minutes.

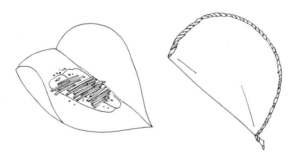

Lay one trout across each sheet of foil (with or without head, as you please). Top each fish with one quarter of the cooked onions, tomato, Canadian bacon, mint, and salt and pepper to taste. Turn up the edges of the foil by 1 inch so the liquid won't run out, and sprinkle trout with vermouth and white wine. Gather up the edges of the foil and crimp together on top, leaving as much air inside as possible, to form four long packages. (Can be prepared ahead to this stage and refrigerated for several hours.) Place packages on a baking sheet and bake for 10 minutes.

To serve, place package on a heated dinner plate and cut open with scissors. Carefully pull away the foil, leaving the trout on the plate with the vegetables and sauce.

PREPARATION TIME: 15 MINUTES / OVEN TIME: 10 MINUTES / EASY

ROAST TUNA WITH BELL PEPPER AND TOMATO

SERVES 2

Tuna steaks are delicious when they're served lightly cooked, but they taste like pieces of two-by-four if overdone, so treat them with care!

2 tablespoons olive oil

2 tuna steaks, 6 ounces each

Salt and pepper

½ onion, sliced

1 green bell pepper, seeded, peeled, and shredded (page 39)

2 cloves garlic, chopped

2 tomatoes, peeled, seeded, and quartered

1 bay leaf

½ teaspoon chopped fresh thyme, or ¼ teaspoon dried

2 tablespoons chopped fresh parsley

1 tablespoon red wine vinegar

½ teaspoon chopped fresh dill, or ¼ teaspoon dried mixed with ½ teaspoon chopped fresh parsley

Preheat convection oven to 350 degrees. Heat olive oil in an ovenproof skillet. Season tuna with salt and pepper to taste, and quickly sauté on both sides, about 1 minute altogether. Remove fish and set aside. In the same pan sauté onion for 2 minutes. Add bell pepper, garlic, tomatoes, bay leaf, thyme, and salt and pepper to taste. Cook over medium heat for 6 minutes. Stir in parsley, and lay tuna on top of vegetables. Sprinkle with wine vinegar. Transfer skillet to the oven and bake for 8 minutes. Garnish with dill before serving.

PREPARATION TIME: 15 MINUTES / OVEN TIME: 8 MINUTES / EASY

CHICKEN AND OTHER BIRDS

BUTTERFLIED CHICKEN WITH HONEY-MUSTARD GLAZE

SERVES 2

A simple and inexpensive entrée for two, with a good sauce. Plain rice and steamed zucchini and carrot matchsticks would round this dish off nicely.

1 *chicken, 2 to 2½ pounds*
Salt and pepper
1 *tablespoon butter, chilled, cut into small dice*

¼ *cup honey*
¼ *cup Dijon mustard*
1 *tablespoon fresh lemon juice*
½ *cup water*

Preheat convection oven to 350 degrees. Grease a shallow baking pan lightly with butter. Insert a sharp chef's knife inside the cavity of the chicken and cut through the ribs on either side of the backbone (see illustration). Lay chicken out flat and pull out the keelbone (white cartilage) between the two breast halves. Turn chicken skin side up and chop off the wing tips. Fold the wings under bird. To keep the legs in place while cooking, make two little slits in the skin on either side near the tail and insert the leg ends in them. Place chicken in baking pan, skin side up, and surround with backbone, wing tips, and

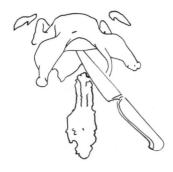 

giblets. (Reserve liver for another use.) Sprinkle with salt and pepper to taste, and dot with butter. Roast for 15 minutes, then turn chicken over and roast skin side down for 10 minutes.

In the meantime, combine honey, mustard, lemon juice, and a pinch of salt. Brush surface of chicken with some of this glaze, and roast for a further 15 minutes. Remove pan from the oven and set chicken aside to keep warm. Place roasting pan over medium-high heat, add water, and bring to a boil, loosening any browned bits with a wooden spoon. Strain into a saucepan and skim off fat. Stir in remaining honey-mustard mixture, and boil for 2 minutes. Taste for seasoning, and serve with chicken. Cut bird in half to serve.

PREPARATION TIME: 15 MINUTES / OVEN TIME: 40 MINUTES / EASY

Butterflied chicken with lemon and sherry

Cooking a "flat" chicken is faster than leaving it whole, and inserting the notched slices of lemon into the skin adds both flavor and visual interest. A Gratin of Potatoes with Cream (page 195) and steamed asparagus would complement the flavors and textures.

1 *frying chicken, 2 to 2½ pounds*

1 *lemon*
  Salt and pepper

1 *tablespoon butter, chilled, cut into small dice*

2 *tablespoons Dry Sack sherry*

½ *cup heavy cream*

Preheat convection oven to 375 degrees. Grease a shallow baking pan lightly with butter. Insert a sharp chef's knife inside the cavity of the chicken, and cut through the ribs on either side of the backbone. Lay chicken out flat and pull out the keelbone (white cartilage) between the two breast halves. Turn chicken skin side up and chop off wing tips. Fold the wings under bird. To keep the legs in place while cooking, make two little slits in the skin on either side near the tail, and insert the leg ends in them (see illustration).

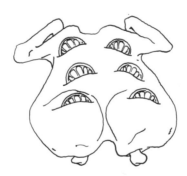

Score the lemon lengthways six times, then cut into thin slices. Make six incisions in the top surface of the chicken, three on each side, and insert the notched lemon slices. Sprinkle with salt and pepper to taste, and dot with butter. Place in baking pan and surround with backbone, wing tips, and giblets. (Reserve liver for another use.) Bake for 15 minutes, then reduce heat to 350 degrees and bake for a further 20 to 25 minutes.

Remove chicken and set it aside to keep warm. Pour off fat from roasting pan, and place pan over medium-high heat. Add the sherry and bring to a boil, scraping up the browned bits in the pan. Reduce liquid by one third, about 2 minutes, then add cream. Bring to a boil and simmer for 2 to 3 minutes. Cut chicken in half, and strain this sauce over it.

PREPARATION TIME: 15 MINUTES / OVEN TIME: 35 TO 40 MINUTES / EASY

CHICKEN ROLLS WITH SPINACH AND SHIITAKE MUSHROOMS

SERVES 4

This is a very attractive way to serve breast of chicken: It is pounded flat and rolled up with a layer of spinach leaves and sliced mushrooms. After the chicken rolls are wrapped in parchment paper and baked, they are cut into oval slices, which show off the filling, and fanned out on top of a light sauce. Regular mushrooms can be substituted for the shiitake, but they are not as flavorful, so in that case it's a good idea to add a big pinch of fresh or dried tarragon to the chicken stock.

4 *chicken breast halves, 6 ounces each*
Salt and pepper
4 *ounces large spinach leaves, rinsed and patted dry*
4 *ounces fresh shiitake mushrooms, caps sliced and stems reserved*

Pinch thyme
½ *bay leaf*
1 *cup Chicken Stock (page 300) or canned chicken broth*
½ *carrot, cut in julienne*
½ *stalk celery, destringed and cut in julienne*
1 *cup heavy cream*

Preheat convection oven to 375 degrees. Cut breast meat off the bone and pull off the small filet. Make a horizontal cut into the breast meat without going all the way through, and open out flat, like a book. Place between sheets of plastic wrap and pound flat. Remove tendon from filet and pound meat flat. Sprinkle the four portions of breast meat with salt and pepper to taste, and cover with a layer of spinach leaves. Top each with sliced mushroom caps and the small filet. Roll each into a sausage shape, and then roll up in a small rectangle of baking parchment. Pinch ends shut—the packages will be about 5 inches long. Place in a shallow baking dish with the chicken bones, mushroom stems, thyme, bay leaf, and stock. Cover, and bake for 10 minutes.

While chicken is baking, cook carrot and celery julienne in boiling salted water for 3 minutes, then drain and keep warm.

Remove chicken rolls from broth, and keep warm. Transfer broth to a skillet, bring to a boil, and reduce to 2 tablespoons, about 5 minutes. Add cream and boil for 2 minutes. Strain, and spoon onto hot dinner plates. Remove paper from chicken rolls and slice rolls ½ inch thick at a 45-degree angle, to form ovals. Fan out on top of sauce and garnish with the vegetable julienne.

PREPARATION TIME: 20 MINUTES / OVEN TIME: 10 MINUTES

CHICKEN AND THREE CHEESES IN PHYLLO, WITH PEAR SAUCE

SERVES 4

An elegant, very contemporary entrée for a special dinner. The combination of cheese with pears is a classic one, but is presented here in an interesting new way: Chicken breasts are stuffed with cheese, wrapped in flaky phyllo dough, and then baked. Pears are cooked in chicken broth to make the sauce, and the plates are garnished with slices of the poached fruit.

4 chicken breast halves, 5 ounces each, boned and skinned

Salt and pepper

2 ounces Stilton cheese, crumbled

3 tablespoons grated Parmesan cheese, about 1 ounce

½ cup grated imported Gruyère cheese, about 2 ounces

2 tablespoons unsalted butter

Flour for dredging

8 sheets phyllo dough, thawed if frozen

2 tablespoons butter, melted

SAUCE

2 ripe but firm pears, 6 ounces each

½ lemon

1 cup Chicken Stock (page 300) or canned chicken broth

¼ cup demi-sec white wine, Sauvignon Blanc type

¼ teaspoon green peppercorns in brine, drained

1 tablespoon heavy cream

Detach small filets from chicken breast halves and remove tendon. Place filets between sheets of plastic wrap and pound to flatten. Make a horizontal cut in each chicken breast and open it out flat, like a book. Sprinkle with a very little salt (the cheeses are salty) and pepper to taste. Blend the cheeses to form a paste, and divide into four portions. Form each portion of cheese into a roll and place on each chicken portion, slightly to one side. Top with a filet and fold the breast back together.

Heat butter in a heavy skillet. Dredge chicken breasts lightly with flour, and immediately sauté quickly on both sides, about 30 seconds in all. Remove and let cool.

CHICKEN AND OTHER BIRDS   *81*

Preheat convection oven to 375 degrees. Cut sheets of phyllo in half. Stack sheets in sets of four, brushing each sheet with melted butter. Lay a sautéed chicken breast in the center of each stack and enclose it in the phyllo, bringing up the sides to make multiple layers on top. Lay packages on a baking sheet, multiple layered side uppermost. (The dish can be prepared ahead to this point, covered, and refrigerated.) Bake for 15 minutes.

While phyllo packages are baking, make Pear Sauce: Peel, halve, and core pears, reserving skin and cores. Rub fruit with lemon to prevent discoloration. Place pears in a saucepan along with skin and cores. Add chicken stock, wine, and green peppercorns. Bring to a boil and simmer for 6 or 7 minutes. Remove pear halves and keep warm. Bring juices back to a boil, and reduce to 1 cup, about 5 minutes. Strain, pressing down on the pear skins to extract all the flavor, but not so hard as to push them through the sieve. Add cream and heat through. Pour a portion of the sauce onto each heated dinner plate. Place a phyllo package on top, with a thinly sliced and fanned-out pear half to one side.

PREPARATION TIME: 30 MINUTES / OVEN TIME: 15 MINUTES

CHICKEN BREASTS WITH PROSCIUTTO EN PAPILLOTE
SERVES 2

An easy, fast entrée for two. The chicken breast is combined with an aromatic stuffing, enclosed in foil, and baked for 12 minutes. Serve it with rice cooked in chicken stock or Bulgur Pilaf (page 205) to take up the good juices, and a salad.

1½ tablespoons butter,
   softened
½ onion, finely chopped
1 small carrot, julienned
3 mushrooms, sliced
1 large tomato, peeled,
   seeded, and coarsely
   chopped
¼ cup prosciutto or
   Canadian bacon,
   julienned, about 1
   ounce

Salt and pepper
Pinch thyme
2 chicken breast halves,
   5 to 6 ounces each,
   skinned and boned
2 tablespoons dry white
   wine
2 teaspoons Cognac

Preheat convection oven to 350 degrees. Grease center area of two 12 by 16-inch sheets of aluminum foil with ½ tablespoon of the butter. In a skillet, heat remaining butter and sauté onion and carrot for 2 minutes. Add mushrooms and tomato, and cook for 1 minute. Stir in prosciutto and season with salt and pepper to taste, and thyme. Be careful with salt as prosciutto is salty. Let cool slightly.

Cut a horizontal pocket into each piece of chicken and stuff with one fourth of the sautéed mixture. Lay each chicken breast on a sheet of foil, placing it slightly right of center. Cover with the remaining vegetables. Turn the edges of the foil up slightly so the liquid won't run out, and sprinkle each chicken breast with 1 tablespoon wine and 1 teaspoon of Cognac. Fold the foil over the chicken (like closing a book), and crimp the edges firmly together, leaving as much air space inside the foil as possible. The two packages should be somewhat D-shaped. (They can be prepared ahead to this point several hours ahead of time and refrigerated.) Transfer to a baking sheet and bake for 12 minutes.

To serve, place package on a heated dinner plate and cut open with scissors along the non-crimped edge. Gently pull the foil away, leaving the chicken on the plate with the vegetables and sauce.

PREPARATION TIME: 15 MINUTES / OVEN TIME: 12 MINUTES / EASY

CRISP CHICKEN CUTLETS
WITH BELL PEPPER VINAIGRETTE

Because these cutlets are made with dark meat, they are exceptionally juicy. The contrast between the hot crisp chicken and the cold piquant sauce is fantastic. The dish can be served as a light summer entrée, or cut into small pieces and presented as a hot cocktail appetizer.

4 *whole chicken legs, 6 to 8 ounces each*

Salt and pepper

¼ *red bell pepper, seeded, peeled, and shredded (page 39)*

¼ *green bell pepper, seeded, peeled, and shredded (page 39)*

1 *tomato*

2 *tablespoons wine vinegar*

½ *cup plus 2 tablespoons olive oil*

1 *clove garlic, smashed and minced*

2 *scallions, slivered, white bulb and half of green stem*

½ *small onion, very thinly sliced*

Flour for dredging

1 *egg, beaten*

1½ *cups bread crumbs made from day-old white bread*

Skin chicken legs and chop off the knobs at the ends of the drumsticks. Make a cut along the drumstick and thigh and remove leg bones, scraping around them with the knife to leave the meat in one piece. Lay meat out flat between sheets of plastic wrap, and flatten slightly with the flat of a cleaver to make cutlets of even thickness. Season with salt and pepper to taste.

Cut red and green bell peppers into extra-fine slivers. Cut the tomato into quarters. Lay the tomato quarters skin side down on a cutting board, and shave the flesh off the skin. Cut flesh into fine slivers.

Prepare vinaigrette by dissolving a pinch of salt in the vinegar, then beating in ½ cup of the olive oil and the garlic. Add pepper to taste. Add shredded bell peppers, tomato, scallions, and sliced onion.

Preheat convection oven to 400 degrees. Grease a rimmed baking sheet with 1 tablespoon olive oil, and heat in the oven until very hot.

Heat remaining tablespoon of oil in a nonstick skillet. Dredge chicken in flour, then dip in beaten egg, and then in crumbs. Sauté very quickly on both sides, about 1 minute. (Do this in two batches if necessary.) Transfer chicken to the heated baking sheet and bake for 15 minutes, turning once. Serve very hot, on warmed plates, with the room-temperature vinaigrette poured on top.

PREPARATION TIME: 20 MINUTES / OVEN TIME: 15 MINUTES / EASY

CHICKEN IN
WHISKEY AND CREAM SAUCE

SERVES 4

Since this dish has a Scottish flavor, it's a nice idea to start the menu with smoked salmon and thin slices of buttered brown bread, such as the Rye Bread with Walnuts (page 218). Garnish the main course with broccoli florets and steamed new potatoes. For dessert, have something with a touch of bitter orange—Pépé's Citrus Meringue Tart (page 262), for instance.

1 *chicken, 3½ pounds*
All-purpose flour for dredging
1 *tablespoon olive oil*
1 *tablespoon butter*
2 *shallots, chopped*
1 *onion, chopped*
Salt and pepper
1 *bay leaf*

½ *teaspoon chopped fresh thyme, or ¼ teaspoon dried*
½ *cup Chicken Stock (page 300) or canned chicken broth*
¼ *cup Scotch whiskey*
1 *cup heavy cream*

Preheat convection oven to 350 degrees. Cut the chicken into fourteen pieces (see illustration on page 86), and discard the backbone. Dredge chicken lightly in flour. In an ovenproof skillet, heat oil and butter.

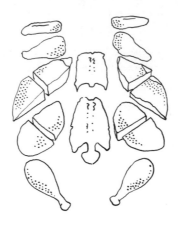

Brown chicken, about 10 minutes. Add shallots and chopped onion, and season to taste with salt and pepper. Cook for 2 minutes, then add bay leaf, thyme, and chicken stock. Transfer to the oven and bake, uncovered, for 20 minutes.

Place the skillet over medium heat (watch the handle as it will be very hot), and spoon off any fat. Pour Scotch over chicken, and carefully flame with a match. Shake the pan until the flame dies down. Stir in cream, and cook for 2 minutes.

PREPARATION TIME: 20 MINUTES / OVEN TIME: 20 MINUTES

CHICKEN LEGS
STUFFED WITH GOAT CHEESE

Chicken legs prepared this way are really succulent, and the skin gets nice and crispy in a convection oven. It's cheaper to buy two whole chickens than to pay a premium for the legs alone; you can reserve the breasts for any of the chicken breast recipes in this book. (Fresh raw chicken breast can be kept in the refrigerator for two days.) Freeze the carcasses and giblets for Chicken Stock (page 300), the livers for Chicken Liver Mousse (page 18), and the wings for Chicken Wings with Sesame Oil and Honey (page 19). Be sure to label your packages unless you want to follow the example of a restaurateur we know of in California's Gold Rush country. She invites all her friends for a surprise Christmas dinner every year, at which they use up all the UFOs— unidentified frozen objects—in her big freezer!

6 *ounces goat cheese*

¼ *cup bread crumbs made from day-old white bread*

¼ *cup heavy cream*

¼ *cup chopped fresh parsley*

1 *teaspoon chopped fresh thyme*

1 *teaspoon chopped fresh oregano*

Salt and pepper

4 *chicken legs with thighs attached, 8 ounces each*

2 *tablespoons butter, softened*

½ *cup unflavored yogurt, preferably creamy type*

1 *teaspoon mixed chopped fresh herbs: parsley, thyme, and oregano*

2 *tablespoons diced, peeled, seeded tomato*

Preheat convection oven to 350 degrees. Crumble goat cheese into a bowl and blend with bread crumbs, cream, parsley, thyme, oregano, and salt and pepper to taste. With your finger, carefully separate chicken skin from the meat on the thigh and drumstick, being careful to leave the skin attached at the sides. Stuff the cheese mixture under the skin of each chicken leg, making the layer as even as possible. Place on flat rack in a shallow baking pan. Rub the chicken skin with the butter, and season lightly with salt and pepper. Bake for 30 minutes, until the skin is brown and crisp.

Heat the yogurt, but do not allow to boil. Pour a portion of yogurt on each heated dinner plate, scatter with mixed chopped herbs and diced tomato, and top with a chicken leg.

PREPARATION TIME: 10 MINUTES / OVEN TIME: 30 MINUTES / EASY

CHICKEN,
BACON, AND EGG PIE

SERVES 4

This is good family fare: unpretentious and tasty. Add a salad, and try Yellow Summer Squash Pudding with Raspberry Sauce (page 290) for dessert.

4 *chicken legs with thighs attached, 6 ounces each*

4 *strips bacon, cut in quarters*

All-purpose flour for dredging

½ *onion, finely chopped*

Pinch thyme

Salt and pepper

1 *tablespoon Worcestershire sauce*

½ *cup Chicken Stock (page 300) or canned chicken broth*

2 *hard-boiled eggs, cut in half*

8 *ounces Quick Puff Pastry (page 244), or ½ package frozen puff pastry sheets, thawed*

1 *egg, beaten*

Preheat convection oven to 350 degrees. Cut chicken legs in half, through the joint. Chop the knobs off the ends of the drumsticks, and then cut out leg bones, leaving the meat in large pieces. Remove skin or not, as preferred.

Cook the bacon in a heavy skillet until the fat starts to run. Dredge the chicken meat lightly in flour and add to the pan. Brown slowly on all sides, then stir in chopped onion. Add thyme, salt and pepper to taste (be careful with amount of salt as both bacon and Worcestershire sauce are salty), Worcestershire sauce, and chicken stock. Continue cooking for 5 minutes. Transfer mixture to a 9-inch ovenproof glass pie pan. Push egg halves under the meat.

On a lightly floured surface, roll pastry out ⅛ inch thick. Cut out a 10-inch circle for the top of the pie, and a 1½-inch-wide strip (or strips) long enough to cover the rim of the pie pan. Cut several leaf shapes from trimmings. Brush rim of pie pan with water, cover with pastry strip, and then brush with some of the beaten egg. Cover pie with pastry circle, and press around rim to seal. Make a hole in the center for steam to escape. Decorate top with pastry leaves, and brush with remaining egg glaze. Bake for 35 minutes, until pastry is golden brown. Serve at once, while pastry is still very puffy.

PREPARATION TIME: 25 MINUTES / OVEN TIME: 35 MINUTES / EASY

CHICKEN LEGS WITH MUSHROOMS, ARTICHOKES, AND SCALLIONS

SERVES 4

A wonderful dish for a weeknight dinner: doesn't take much preparation, is quite low in calories, cooks in about 30 minutes, and is extremely tasty. Serve it with rice cooked in chicken stock to soak up the good sauce.

4 *chicken legs with thighs attached, 8 to 10 ounces each*

1 *package frozen artichoke hearts, 9 ounces, thawed*

2 *tablespoons butter*

Flour for dredging

12 *mushrooms, quartered*

3 *scallions, sliced, including most of green tops*

Salt and pepper

½ *cup Chicken Stock (page 300) or canned chicken broth*

¼ *cup dry white wine*

Preheat convection oven to 350 degrees. Chop knob off the end of each drumstick, and pull out the white tendons. Cut out the thigh bones, leaving whole chicken legs with only one short bone in the lower portion. Blanch artichoke hearts in boiling salted water for 1 minute, and drain.

Melt butter in a sauté pan. Dredge chicken legs in flour, shaking to remove excess, and brown well, about 7 minutes. Add mushrooms, artichoke hearts, and scallions. Sprinkle with salt and pepper to taste. Add chicken stock and wine, and simmer for 5 minutes. Transfer the mixture to a large shallow baking dish attractive enough to bring to the table, and bake for 20 minutes, until tender.

PREPARATION TIME: 25 MINUTES / OVEN TIME: 20 MINUTES / EASY

SPICED ROAST CHICKEN WITH SAFFRON RICE   *SERVES 4*

Exotically spiced roast chicken is cut into serving portions and served on a bed of saffron rice with toasted almonds. A suitable first course would be Japanese Eggplant with Lamb, Feta, and Mint Stuffing (page 45), and as an accompaniment you can serve a simple salad of sliced cucumber with plain yogurt. As it's a North African–style meal, you might want to finish with baklava, the layered honey and nut pastry made with phyllo dough, and mint tea. (To make mint tea, combine 3 teaspoons green Chinese tea leaves, 1 tablespoon sugar, and 3 tablespoons chopped fresh mint in a warmed teapot. Cover with 4 cups boiling water and let steep for 5 minutes. Stir, allow to settle, and strain into cups or small glasses.)

1 *chicken, 3½ pounds*
1 *lemon, cut in half*
2 *tablespoons butter,*
  melted
1 *teaspoon Ras el Hanout*
  (Moroccan spice
  mixture, page 310)
  Salt and pepper
½ *onion, chopped*

1 *cup long-grain rice,*
  well rinsed and drained
½ *cup raisins*
  Pinch saffron
3 *cups Chicken Stock*
  (page 300) or canned
  chicken broth
¼ *cup sliced almonds,*
  with skins

Preheat convection oven to 350 degrees. Remove any excess fat from chicken and chop off wing tips. Rub chicken inside and out with lemon halves, and then place the lemon inside the cavity. Melt 1 tablespoon of the butter with ½ teaspoon of the Ras el Hanout and brush over the chicken. Tie legs and wings to body with string, and place breast side up on a roasting rack. Rest rack *across* the roasting pan for better air circulation. Sprinkle with salt and pepper to taste. Place wing tips and giblets in roasting pan (reserve liver for another use), and roast chicken for 55 minutes. There is no need to turn or baste chicken when roasted in a convection oven.

When the chicken has cooked for 30 minutes, prepare rice: Heat remaining butter in an ovenproof skillet, and simmer onion for 2 minutes, until soft but not browned. Add rice, and stir for 2 or 3 minutes to coat the grains with butter. Add raisins, remaining ½ teaspoon Ras el Hanout, saffron, 2 cups of the chicken stock, and bring to a boil. Add salt to taste (depending on seasoning of chicken stock). Cover, transfer to the oven, and bake for 18 minutes. Spread almonds on a baking sheet, and bake (also at 350) for 7 or 8 minutes, until lightly toasted.

Remove the roasting pan from the oven and let the chicken stand for 10 minutes. Discard the fat, and place the pan over high heat. Add the remaining 1 cup chicken stock and deglaze, scraping up any browned bits. Boil until reduced by one third, about 5 minutes. Taste for seasoning, and strain into a sauceboat. Spread cooked rice on a heated platter. Cut chicken into serving pieces and place over rice. Scatter toasted almonds on top, and present platter at the table. Serve the sauce separately.

PREPARATION TIME: 20 MINUTES / OVEN TIME: 55 MINUTES / EASY

WHOLE BONELESS CHICKEN STUFFED WITH RICE AND SHIITAKE MUSHROOMS

Boning the chicken and stuffing it with rice and mushrooms makes it very easy to carve later, and an average-size chicken will then serve six. Accompany it with an oriental green vegetable such as baby bok choy or snow peas, as this is really a Chinese-style ballotine. Any leftovers can be served cold, like pâté.

2 *tablespoons butter*

1 *onion, chopped*

1 *cup long-grain rice, rinsed and drained*

1 *ounce dried shiitake mushrooms, stems removed, coarsely chopped (do not soak)*
Black pepper

3½ *cups Chicken Stock (page 300) or canned chicken broth*

1 *chicken, 3½ pounds*
Salt

1 *large egg*

½ *teaspoon Chinese five-spice powder*

2 *tablespoons sliced almonds, lightly toasted*

1 *tablespoon Chinese sesame oil*

1 *onion, unpeeled, quartered*

1 *carrot, cut into chunks*

1 *cup white wine*

1 *teaspoon cornstarch, dissolved in a little cold water*

Preheat convection oven to 350 degrees. Heat butter in an enameled cast-iron casserole, and sauté onion for 5 minutes, until softened. Slowly add rice, then stir in pieces of dried mushroom and almonds. Season with pepper to taste (do not add salt unless chicken stock is salt-free). Stir in 2 cups of the chicken stock and bring to a boil. Cover, transfer to the oven, and bake for 15 minutes; rice should be slightly undercooked.

While the rice is cooking, bone the chicken, leaving wings and drumstick bones in place (see illustration). Reserve the bones.

Lay the boned chicken flat on a work surface, skin side down, and sprinkle with salt and pepper to taste. Place the trimmed liver

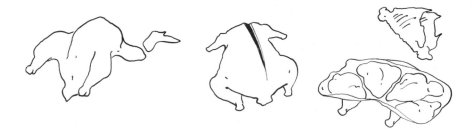

To bone a chicken, game hen, squab, or quail, place bird breast side up and cut off the wings at the second joint. Turn bird over and slit the skin down the backbone. Start scraping the meat away from the carcass along the backbone, on both sides. Find the ball joint of each thigh and cut through the tendon to disconnect. Repeat for shoulder. Scrape meat away from breastbone and disconnect the keelbone (soft cartilage) without cutting through the skin. Keep scraping with the knife blade against the boney carcass until it can be lifted away from the now-flat bird. Scrape meat away from thighbones and cut through joint. Leave drumstick bone in place or not, as desired, but chop off knobby joint at the end and expose the bone slightly by scraping with the knife.

and the two small filets from the breast in the bowl of a food processor. Add egg and five-spice powder, and process until ground. Combine with the cooked rice and stir in almonds. Mound rice mixture on top of chicken, then draw up sides and ends and turn bird over, keeping it as compact as possible. Place on a sheet of aluminum foil, folding the sides tightly against the bird to make a shallow case. There is no need to truss with string. Place in a shallow baking pan, and rub with sesame oil. Surround with onion, carrot, and chopped bones from bird. Roast at 350 degrees for 1 hour.

Remove chicken and set aside to keep warm. Pour off fat and place roasting pan over high heat. Add wine and deglaze pan, then stir in remaining chicken stock. Bring to a boil and reduce to 1¼ cups, about 5 minutes. Strain, taste for seasoning, and stir in dissolved cornstarch. Let cook for a few seconds until mixture thickens and clears. Cut chicken straight across in thick slices, and serve with sauce.

PREPARATION TIME: 35 MINUTES / OVEN TIME: 18 MINUTES; 1 HOUR

WHOLE CHICKEN BAKED IN SALT CLAY

This is a spectacular way to serve chicken: wrapped inside a paste made of flour, salt, and water, which hardens in the oven and forms an airtight, chicken-shaped clay casserole. You will find that the chicken is exceptionally tender, juicy, and somewhat salty, like a good brine-cured ham. The dish can be kept warm in the oven for an hour or two; it won't matter. A green salad and Baguettes (page 210) make ideal accompaniments.

3½ cups all-purpose flour

3 cups coarse (kosher) salt

1½ cups water

1 tablespoon fresh rosemary leaves, chopped, or ½ tablespoon dried

1 chicken, 3 to 3½ pounds
   Black pepper

½ leek, white part only, cut into julienne

½ stalk celery, destringed and cut into julienne

½ small carrot, cut into julienne

¼ turnip, cut into julienne

1 clove garlic, chopped

1 teaspoon chopped fresh thyme, or ½ teaspoon dried

1 teaspoon chopped fresh tarragon, or ½ teaspoon dried

2 tablespoons butter, melted

1 egg, beaten

In the bowl of an electric mixer, combine flour, salt, and water. Mix with the flat beater to form a smooth dough. Turn out onto a lightly floured surface, and knead in the rosemary.

Preheat convection oven to 375 degrees. Season chicken with pepper inside and out. Combine all the vegetables with the herbs and melted butter, and season to taste with pepper. Stuff the chicken with this mixture and tie legs together with string.

Roll the dough out to form an oval large enough to enclose the chicken. Place chicken in the center, breast side up. Draw up sides of dough and pinch together on top to seal. Gently elongate the ends of the dough with a rolling pin and cut off excess. Fold remainder

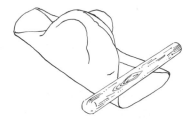

under package to seal completely; there must be no holes. (If necessary, patch with leftover dough, sticking it down with water.) Mold the dough with your hands to follow the contours of the chicken, and decorate top with shapes cut from leftover dough. Brush with beaten egg. Transfer to baking sheet and bake for 1 hour and 20 minutes.

To serve, carefully cut through the hard-baked dough about 3 inches up from the bottom to form a clay casserole with a lid. Be sure to use a knife with a short, rigid blade as the baked clay will be hard. If you are not yet ready to serve, replace the lid—the chicken will stay warm for at least half an hour, or can be returned to a low oven. Remove the chicken to a carving board and cut into serving portions, discarding the juices in the bottom of the container as they will be very salty. Serve some of the julienned vegetables from inside the bird with each portion. (If you like, you can pour the juices out of the container, put a piece of aluminum foil in the bottom, replace the carved chicken and vegetable garnish and cover with the lid. Serve from the container at the table.)

PREPARATION TIME: 20 MINUTES / OVEN TIME: 1 HOUR AND 20 MINUTES

WHOLE ROAST
CHICKEN IN A PIE

A casual family-style dish that you bring to the table in a casserole. The chicken can be roasted ahead of time—it will reheat as the pastry bakes. Serve with Gratin of Green Beans with Almonds (page 197), which is baked for 10 minutes at the same temperature as the pie. For dessert, offer chilled Orange and Raisin Custard with French Toast Topping (page 284).

5 *tablespoons butter*

1 *onion, chopped*

8 *ounces spinach leaves, shredded*

⅓ *cup long-grain rice*

⅔ *plus ¾ cup Chicken Stock (page 300) or canned chicken broth*

Salt and pepper

1 *chicken, 3½ pounds*

4 *strips lean bacon*

6 *mushrooms, sliced*

2 *tomatoes, peeled, seeded, and quartered*

2 *tablespoons Worcestershire sauce*

8 *ounces Quick Puff Pastry (page 244), or ½ package frozen puff pastry sheets, thawed*

1 *egg yolk, beaten*

Preheat convection oven to 350 degrees. Heat 2 tablespoons of the butter in a skillet, and sauté onion for 2 minutes. Stir in spinach and simmer for 1 minute.

Place rice in a small casserole and add ⅔ cup chicken broth and salt and pepper to taste. Cover, transfer to the oven, and bake for 18 minutes. Let cool, and then mix with spinach and onion.

Season chicken inside with salt and pepper to taste, and stuff with rice and spinach mixture, closing opening with skewers. Rub outside of bird with 1 tablespoon soft butter, and sprinkle with salt and pepper to taste. Place breast side up on a rack laid *across* a roasting pan, for maximum air circulation, and roast for 1 hour. Five minutes before the chicken is done, add bacon strips to the roasting pan. Heat remaining 2 tablespoons butter in a skillet, and sauté mushrooms and tomatoes for 3 minutes. Remove from the heat.

Remove chicken and bacon from roasting pan, and pour off fat. Place pan over medium-high heat, add ¾ cup chicken stock and Worcestershire sauce, and mix well. Let simmer for 1 minute.

Place chicken in a cast-iron casserole just large enough to hold it, and cover with the mushrooms, tomatoes, and strips of bacon. Pour the sauce on top. (Chicken can be prepared ahead to this point and held, covered, in refrigerator.)

Preheat convection oven to 375 degrees. Roll the puff pastry out to form a circle large enough to cover the casserole, allowing an extra inch all around. Brush it with some of the egg yolk and reverse it over the casserole, pressing the overhanging pastry against the sides. Brush the top with the remaining egg yolk, and decorate with leaves cut from pastry trimmings. Bake for 15 minutes, until pastry is brown and well risen. Serve from the casserole.

PREPARATION TIME: 35 MINUTES / OVEN TIME: 18 MINUTES; 1¼ HOURS

ROAST CHICKEN WITH BABY ARTICHOKES AND RED POTATOES

SERVES 4

Serve this one-dish meal when little red potatoes appear in the markets. If baby artichokes are unavailable, substitute frozen artichoke hearts.

1 *chicken, 3 pounds*

2 *teaspoons butter, softened*

Salt and pepper

8 *baby artichokes (12 ounces), or 1 package frozen artichoke hearts (9 ounces), thawed*

8 *small red potatoes, ½ pound total, unpeeled*

1 *tablespoon Chinese sesame oil*

2 *tablespoons butter*

2 *cloves garlic, unpeeled*

Pinch thyme

½ *cup water*

1 *tablespoon fresh lemon juice*

Preheat convection oven to 350 degrees. Remove any excess fat from chicken, and truss with string for more even cooking. (Tie legs and wings to body, crossing the string underneath and tying it on top.) Rub with softened butter and sprinkle lightly with salt and pepper. Place breast side up on a rack resting *across* a roasting pan, for maximum air circulation. Roast for about 55 minutes, until juices no longer run pink when thigh is pricked. (There is no need to turn or baste a chicken roasted in a covection oven.)

Wash and trim artichokes, pulling off the outer leaves until you reach the pale green under leaves. Trim ½ inch off the tip and cut each artichoke in half. (Cut slightly larger artichokes in quarters and remove tiny triangle of fuzzy choke with knife tip.) Cut potatoes in half. In a sauté pan, combine sesame oil, butter, garlic, thyme, water, and lemon juice. Add artichokes and potatoes and bring to a boil. Season lightly with salt and pepper, cover, and cook for 1 minute.

When the chicken has cooked for 20 minutes, add vegetables to the roasting pan. Continue roasting for a further 35 minutes or until bird tests done.

Transfer bird and vegetables to a heated platter, and keep warm. Reserve the garlic cloves. Pour cooking juices into a glass measuring cup and let stand for a few minutes so fat can rise to the top. Transfer juices to a saucepan and discard fat. (One way to do this is to draw the clear juices off from below the fat with a bulb baster.) "Pop" the garlic cloves out of the skins, mash if necessary, and add to the pan. Reheat sauce and serve with chicken and vegetables.

PREPARATION TIME: 30 MINUTES / OVEN TIME: 55 MINUTES / EASY

ROAST CHICKEN WITH RICOTTA CHEESE AND HERBS

Poultry is always at its best when roasted in a convection oven: It's juicy and succulent and doesn't need turning or basting. Here, the under-the-skin stuffing of cheese and herbs adds a wonderful flavor to the meat. Serve with a classic Gratin of Potatoes with Cream (page 195) and spinach.

1 *roasting chicken, 5 pounds*
Salt and pepper
1 *lemon*
1 *tablespoon butter, softened*

STUFFING

8 *ounces ricotta cheese*
2 *tablespoons finely chopped onion*
½ *teaspoon grated lemon peel*
1 *teaspoon chopped fresh mint*

1 *tablespoon chopped fresh parsley*
Salt and pepper

SAUCE

½ *onion, coarsely chopped*
1 *carrot, cut into chunks*
1 *stalk celery, cut into chunks*
1 *bay leaf*
Large pinch thyme
½ *cup white wine*
1 *cup Chicken Stock (page 300) or canned chicken broth*

Preheat convection oven to 350 degrees. Remove wing tips from chicken and reserve, along with giblets and neck. Loosen skin over body by inserting your fingers and gently pushing skin away from the meat. Season cavity with salt and pepper to taste. Prick lemon all over and place inside cavity.

Combine stuffing ingredients. Push stuffing under skin of chicken body, making as even a layer as possible. Truss bird with string, tying legs together first and looping string underneath before tying on top. Smear with butter and sprinkle with salt and pepper to taste. Place on rack resting *across* a roasting pan, and roast for 1¾ to 2 hours, or until juices no longer run pink when thigh is pricked. (There is no need to turn or baste a chicken roasted in a convection oven.)

About 30 minutes before bird is ready, add giblets, wing tips, vegetables, and herbs to roasting pan. When the chicken is done, remove and set aside to keep warm. Pour off any fat and place roasting pan over high heat. Add white wine and deglaze pan, then add chicken stock and reduce by one third, about 5 minutes. Taste for seasoning and strain. (Do not thicken this sauce.) Serve sauce separately.

PREPARATION TIME: 20 MINUTES / ROASTING TIME: 1¾ TO 2 HOURS / EASY

CORNISH GAME HENS WITH ALMONDS AND CINNAMON IN PHYLLO
SERVES 4

A classic Moroccan dish, *bisteeya* is phyllo dough filled with boned squab, exotic spices, ground almonds, and scrambled eggs. It is lightly sweetened, in authentic North African style, and is always decorated with cinnamon. Squab (farm-raised young pigeons) are very expensive here, but game hens or a cut-up chicken can be substituted.

To blanch almonds, drop them in boiling water for a few seconds and then drain. Rub in a dish towel to help loosen the skins and then pop the nuts free.

2 *Cornish game hens, 20 ounces each*

1 *onion, sliced*

2 *cloves garlic*

1 *teaspoon Ras el Hanout (Moroccan spice mixture, page 310)*

Salt and pepper

Pinch saffron

1½ *teaspoons cinnamon*

3 *sprigs parsley*

1 *sprig cilantro*

2 *cups water*

¾ *cup blanched almonds*

Generous ¼ cup confectioners' sugar

Juice of 1 lemon

6 *large eggs, lightly beaten*

4 *tablespoons butter, melted*

6 *sheets phyllo dough, thawed if frozen*

Confectioners' sugar, for garnish

Cinnamon, for garnish

Preheat convection oven to 325 degrees. Place hens in a flameproof casserole with their giblets, and add onion, garlic, Ras el Hanout, salt and pepper to taste, saffron, 1 teaspoon of the cinnamon, parsley, cilantro, and water. Bring to a boil over high heat, then cover, transfer to the oven, and bake for 1 hour.

While game hens are baking, grind almonds coarsely in a food processor and blend with confectioners' sugar and remaining cinnamon.

When hens are tender, remove from the casserole and set aside to cool. Strain cooking liquid—there should be about 2 cups. Add lemon juice, and pour half of the mixture, including the chicken fat, into a saucepan. Bring to a boil and whisk in the eggs. Keep stirring until they coagulate, like scrambled eggs. Transfer to a colander and let drain. Discard fat from remaining liquid. Bring liquid to a boil and reduce almost to a glaze in the bottom of the pan, about 10 minutes. When hens are cool enough to handle, take the meat off the bones. Shred meat and chop giblets. (The dish can be prepared in advance to this point, covered, and held in refrigerator.)

Preheat convection oven to 375 degrees. Grease a 9 by 2-inch round baking dish or cake pan with some of the melted butter. Line with five sheets of the phyllo dough, overlapping them and letting the excess hang over the sides, and brushing each with melted butter. Spread the nut mixture over the bottom, and layer with half of the shredded poultry, the scrambled eggs, the rest of the poultry, and the reduced glaze. Cover with the remaining sheet of phyllo dough, folded to fit and brushed with butter, and bring the overhanging leaves up over the top. Bake for 25 minutes, until golden brown. Turn out onto a platter, and sift confectioners' sugar over the top. Decorate in traditional style with crisscrossed lines of powdered cinnamon.

PREPARATION TIME: 30 MINUTES / OVEN TIME: 1 HOUR; 25 MINUTES

CORNISH GAME HENS WITH EGGPLANT AND MUSHROOM STUFFING

Inexpensive, readily available Cornish game hens are boned, stuffed with aromatic vegetables, and placed in little paper cases to roast. Depending on the rest of the menu, half a hen is sufficient for most appetites. Bulgur Pilaf (page 205) makes a good accompaniment.

2 Cornish game hens, 20 ounces each

5 strips lean bacon, chopped

2 tablespoons finely chopped onion

2 stalks celery, destringed and finely chopped

3 mushrooms, 2 ounces total, finely chopped

¾ cup diced unpeeled eggplant

Black pepper

3 fresh sage leaves, chopped

1 teaspoon chopped fresh thyme, or ½ teaspoon dried

1 tablespoon chopped fresh parsley

½ cup Chicken Stock (page 300) or canned chicken broth

½ cup bread crumbs made from day-old white bread

Salt

2 sheets baking parchment or aluminum foil, 8 by 10 inches each

1 tablespoon butter, softened

SAUCE

½ cup Dry Sack sherry

½ cup Chicken Stock (page 300) or canned chicken broth

Bone game hens (see illustration on page 93) and lay flat, skin side down. Reserve carcasses and giblets for sauce.

In a skillet, cook bacon for 2 minutes. Stir in onion and celery, and simmer for 5 minutes. Add mushrooms, eggplant, a sprinkling of black pepper, sage, thyme, and parsley. Cook for 3 minutes, then add chicken stock and simmer for 7 to 8 minutes. Remove from the heat, and stir in bread crumbs, which will absorb the liquid. Taste for seasoning, adding salt if necessary (the bacon is already salty), and

let cool. (This can be done quickly by spreading the mixture on a plate and placing it in the freezer for a few minutes.)

Preheat convection oven to 375 degrees. Heap half the chilled stuffing in the center of each game hen. Fold both sides over stuffing, then the ends, and turn bird over. Place breast up on one of the sheets of baking parchment. Double the paper at the edges and make a snug "boat" around the hen (see illustration), tucking the ends underneath. Place packages in a shallow roasting pan and surround with carcass and giblets. Smear tops of hens with butter, and roast for 40 minutes.

Remove hens from roasting pan and keep warm. Make the sauce: Pour off fat and place pan over medium-high heat. Add sherry and deglaze, loosening the browned bits with a wooden spoon, then stir in chicken stock. Boil for 3 minutes, taste for seasoning, and strain into a bowl. Remove hens from paper cases and cut in half, discarding backbone. Place on heated dinner plates and spoon sauce around them.

PREPARATION TIME: 30 MINUTES / OVEN TIME: 40 MINUTES

DUCK WITH
BRAISED RED CABBAGE

This is a succulent family-style dish: The duck is preroasted for a few minutes to brown and release excess fat, and then baked on a bed of cabbage. Serve it with boiled red potatoes with a strip of skin pared from the middle, like a wide belt.

1 *duckling, 4 to 5 pounds*
Salt
1 *red cabbage, cored and shredded*
2 *tablespoons sugar*
1 *clove garlic, chopped*
1 *tablespoon chopped fresh parsley*
1 *tart green apple, unpeeled, diced*

1 *teaspoon chopped fresh thyme, or ½ teaspoon dried*
1 *teaspoon chopped fresh marjoram, or ½ teaspoon dried*
¼ *cup cider vinegar*
1 *cup red wine*
Black pepper

Preheat convection oven to 400 degrees, and heat a shallow baking pan in it. Cut duck into twelve serving pieces, cutting each breast half crossways into three pieces and the legs through the joint (see illustration on page 105). (Reserve pieces of extra skin with fat.) Salt the duck pieces and place in the hot pan, skin side down. Roast for 5 to 6 minutes, turning once, to brown the outside. Remove the pan from the oven, and reduce heat to 350 degrees.

In a large enameled cast-iron casserole, sauté reserved duck skin for 3 minutes, long enough to render some fat. (Add more duck fat from roasting pan if required.) Add cabbage, and stir in all the remaining ingredients, seasoning with salt and pepper to taste. Stir over medium-high heat for 5 minutes. Top with pieces of duck, transfer to the oven, and bake, uncovered, for 1 hour.

PREPARATION TIME: 20 MINUTES / OVEN TIME: 5 TO 6 MINUTES; 1 HOUR

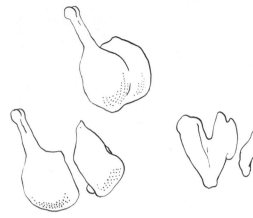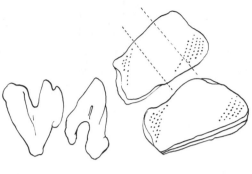

DUCK WITH WHITE BEANS AND CANADIAN BACON

This is a simple version of cassoulet, without the large quantity of fat that this old-fashioned French country dish often contains.

Duck fat is excellent in cooking when used in small amounts, as it is very flavorful. After it has been rendered off the carcass, strain well, put in a screw-top jar, and label. It will keep for weeks in the refrigerator, or it can be frozen.

1 *pound dried white beans*

½ *onion, peeled, in one piece*

3 *cloves garlic, unpeeled*

Pinch thyme

1 *bay leaf*

1 *duckling, 4 to 5 pounds*

1 *onion, chopped*

2 *cloves garlic, chopped*

1 *cup dry white wine*

1½ *cups Chicken Stock (page 300) or canned chicken broth*

4 *tomatoes, peeled, seeded, and quartered*

1 *tablespoon tomato paste*

Salt and pepper

6 *thick slices Canadian bacon*

2 *tablespoons bread crumbs made from day-old white bread*

1 *teaspoon butter, chilled*

The night before, cover beans with plenty of cold water and soak overnight. (If you are short of time, cover beans with 6 cups cold water and bring to a boil. Cook for 2 minutes, cover pan, and let stand for 1 hour.)

Drain beans and place in a large pot. Add onion half, garlic cloves, thyme, and bay leaf. (Do not add salt at this stage, as it would make the beans hard.) Cover with cold water and bring to a boil. Simmer, uncovered, for about 1 hour, until tender, adding more water if necessary to keep beans submerged. Discard onion and bay leaf. Squeeze garlic pulp out of husks and stir into beans. Drain, and transfer to a large casserole or baking dish.

Preheat convection oven to 400 degrees. Cut legs and breast meat off duck. Cut legs in two, through the joint, and chop off the knob at the end of each drumstick. Cut each breast half across into four pieces. Lay duck pieces in a roasting pan with the chopped-up carcass, wings, and giblets. (Reserve liver for another use.) Surround with chopped onion and garlic, and roast for 30 minutes, to render the fat. Remove from the oven, and reduce heat to 300 degrees.

Pour duck fat off pan and reserve for another use. Transfer serving pieces of duck to the casserole containing beans. Place roasting pan over high heat, add wine, and deglaze, scraping the bottom well to gather up the browned bits. Strain into a saucepan. Add chicken stock, tomatoes, and tomato paste to strained liquid, season to taste with salt (not much, as the bacon is salty) and pepper, and bring to a boil. Stir into casserole and add Canadian bacon, pushing it under the surface. Cover, and bake for 30 minutes.

Taste for seasoning. Sprinkle surface with bread crumbs and dot with butter. Increase oven heat to 375 degrees and bake for 10 minutes, until crumbs have browned.

PREPARATION TIME: OVERNIGHT OR 1 HOUR FOR SOAKING; 1¼ HOURS /
OVEN TIME: 1 HOUR AND 10 MINUTES

LEAN DUCKLING WITH GREEN OLIVES

Duck can be really delicious, but it must be cooked with care if it is not to be either fatty or dried out. The breast of a roast duck should always be served rare in order to be tender, but the legs require more cooking. In this recipe the fat drips off the bird during the initial roasting, and should be reserved as it is wonderful when used in small amounts. The breast is cooked for less time than the legs, and is then reheated with the legs in the wine sauce, with the olives making a nice counterpoint to the rich meat. If you are serving this to four persons—appetites do differ—cut the leg and breast meat in half so that everyone gets some of each. Serve with Wild Rice Pilaf (page 207) and Beet Mousse (page 191).

1 *duckling, 4 to 5 pounds*	2 *cloves garlic, unpeeled*
Salt and pepper	½ *cup pitted green cocktail olives*
1 *carrot, cut into chunks*	
1 *onion, quartered*	1 *tablespoon butter*
1 *stalk celery, cut into chunks*	4 *ounces mushrooms, quartered*
3 *parsley sprigs*	½ *bottle dry red wine*
1 *bay leaf*	½ *cup Chicken Stock (page 300) or canned chicken broth*
Pinch thyme	

Preheat convection oven to 350 degrees. Remove excess fat from duck, and reserve giblets. Chop off wings. Season inside of duck with salt and pepper to taste, and place breast side up in a shallow roasting pan with the carrot, onion, celery, parsley sprigs, bay leaf, thyme, and garlic. Add the wings and giblets to the pan, reserving liver for another use. Roast for 1 hour.

Remove the duck from the oven and cut breast meat away from either side of the breastbone, discarding the skin. (The meat should be rare.) Cut legs from carcass and chop knobs off drumsticks. Return duck legs to the roasting pan and roast for another 15 minutes.

Boil olives in water for 5 minutes (to reduce saltiness), and drain. Heat butter in a skillet and sauté mushrooms for 5 minutes.

Remove duck legs from roasting pan. Pour off all fat from pan, and place pan over high heat. Add the wine, bring to a boil, and deglaze, stirring to scrape up all the brown bits. Add chicken stock, and boil until sauce is reduced to 1 cup, about 5 minutes. Strain into skillet containing mushrooms, and add olives. Squeeze garlic pulp from the husks into the sauce, and stir. Taste for seasoning. Add duck breast and legs to sauce and heat through, but do not allow to boil.

PREPARATION TIME: 30 MINUTES / OVEN TIME: 1¼ HOURS

BONED TURKEY WINGS
STUFFED WITH PORK AND SPINACH

Here is an entrée with a lot to recommend it: It looks elegant, tastes wonderful, and costs practically nothing. The wings can be prepared ahead of time and reheated, so it's a good dish for guests—who will probably think they are eating sliced stuffed veal.

Buy fresh turkey wings, not frozen ones, for the best flavor. To remove the bones, which takes a little time but is worth the effort, cut through the skin at top and bottom and then scrape your knife blade along the bones until you can work them free, leaving a cavity for the stuffing. It is preferable to buy boneless pork chops and grind the meat yourself rather than to get ready-ground pork, which is often very fatty and might not be fresh. Duck fat is the most flavorful choice—save this useful fat whenever you cook any of the duck recipes in this book.

3 *large fresh turkey wings, about 3½ pounds total*

10 *ounces spinach, rinsed well and stems removed*

1 *tablespoon duck fat, lard, or butter*

1 *small onion, finely chopped*

1 *clove garlic, chopped*

7 *ounces boneless pork chops with some fat*

2 *tablespoons bread crumbs made from day-old white bread*

6 *Kalamata olives, pitted*

1 *large egg*

Pinch nutmeg

Black pepper

Salt

1 *carrot, sliced*

1 *onion, quartered*

Pinch thyme

2 *tablespoons vegetable oil*

½ *cup Dry Sack sherry*

1 *cup Chicken Stock (page 300) or canned chicken broth*

½ *cup heavy cream*

Pinch oregano

Preheat convection oven to 375 degrees. Cut tips off turkey wings. Separate wings through the joint and remove bones (see illustration on page 110). Place wing tips and bones in a shallow roasting pan.

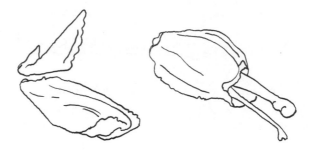

Blanch spinach in boiling salted water for 1 minute and drain. Plunge into cold water, drain, and squeeze dry. Chop coarsely.

Heat duck fat in a small skillet and sauté onion for 5 minutes, until softened. Add garlic and cook for 30 seconds.

Cut pork into large pieces, and grind coarsely in a food processor. (For best results, drop pieces through feed tube while motor is running.) Add spinach, onion and garlic, bread crumbs, olives, egg, nutmeg, and black pepper and process only long enough to blend. Fry a small ball of this mixture in a skillet and taste for seasoning. Add salt if required (the olives are salty). Stuff boned turkey wings with the mixture (no need to tie them), and place on top of the bones in the roasting pan. Surround with sliced carrot and onion, and add thyme. Sprinkle with vegetable oil, season lightly with salt and pepper, and roast for 1 hour.

Remove stuffed turkey wings from the roasting pan and transfer to an enameled cast-iron casserole. Pour fat off, then place pan over high heat. Add sherry, bring to a boil, and deglaze, scraping pan with a wooden spoon. Stir in chicken stock, and strain this sauce over the turkey wings. Cover casserole and bake for a further 30 minutes. Remove turkey wings to a cutting board. Place casserole over high heat, bring to a boil, and reduce sauce by one quarter, about 5 minutes. Stir cream and oregano into sauce and boil for 2 minutes. Taste for seasoning. While the sauce is cooking, cut each stuffed wing diagonally into ½-inch-thick slices. Serve fanned out on heated dinner plates, on a pool of sauce.

PREPARATION TIME: 35 MINUTES / OVEN TIME: 1½ HOURS

BREAST OF TURKEY,
OVEN-STEAMED OVER HERBS

A contemporary way to cook turkey breast—it is marinated in cider vinegar, vermouth, and honey for a couple of hours before being steamed with fresh herbs, which permeate the meat. Good accompaniments would be steamed potatoes—the little yellow Finnish ones if possible—and slender whole string beans. Any leftovers are infinitely better-tasting and juicier than the turkey breast you can buy in a delicatessen. And last but not least, this low-calorie dish looks very inviting.

1 *breast of fresh turkey, 2 to 2½ pounds, with bone*	2 *large sprigs oregano*
	2 *large sprigs thyme*
2 *tablespoons cider vinegar*	2 *large sprigs basil*
	2 *large sprigs sage*
2 *tablespoons dry vermouth*	½ *teaspoon black peppercorns*
2 *tablespoons honey*	½ *cup Chicken Stock (page 300) or canned chicken broth*
½ *teaspoon salt*	
Black pepper	*Additional fresh herbs, for garnish*
1 *cup water*	
2 *large sprigs marjoram*	

Rinse turkey breast and pat dry. Remove any excess fat. In a large bowl, combine cider vinegar, vermouth, honey, salt, and pepper to taste. Mix well and add turkey breast, turning to coat. Marinate skin side down for 2 hours, or overnight in the refrigerator if more convenient, covered with plastic wrap.

Preheat convection oven to 350 degrees. Place water, fresh herbs, and peppercorns in a deep ovenproof pot and bring to a boil. Insert a folding steamer or rack and place the turkey breast on it, skin side down. (Reserve the marinade.) Make sure that the turkey is above the liquid; rest the steamer on a custard cup or something similar if necessary. (A large two-part steamer with a lid is even better, if available.) Cover, transfer to the oven, and cook for 1 hour. The gentle heat will not cause the herb infusion to boil away, the meat will absorb the herb flavors, and turkey juices will drip into the liquid. Remove the turkey from the pan, and strain the herb infusion.

Pour reserved marinade into a sauté pan or wide skillet and boil until the honey caramelizes, about 5 minutes. Add turkey skin side down, and move it around until the meat is lightly browned, about 1 minute. Remove the turkey and keep warm. Stir herb infusion into the pan and add chicken stock. Boil until reduced by one quarter, about 5 minutes, and taste for seasoning, adding salt and pepper if necessary. Carve meat into thin slices and arrange on a deep platter. Top with sauce and garnish with fresh herbs.

PREPARATION TIME: 20 MINUTES; 2 HOURS MARINATING / OVEN TIME: 1 HOUR

BREAST OF TURKEY
STUFFED WITH PORK FILET

An exceptional main course for Thanksgiving or Christmas if you don't want to have a whole roast turkey. Few guests will be able to identify the juicy, succulent "eye" of the roast, surrounded with green herb stuffing and tender white meat of turkey. (Someone once described eternity as two people and a ham; the same could be said of two people with lots of leftover turkey.) Pumpkin Pancake with Scallions (page 203) and Wild Rice Pilaf (page 207) go well with this dish.

1 *half breast of turkey, 3 to 3¼ pounds*

1 *whole pork filet, 12 ounces to 1 pound*

1 *bunch watercress*

4 *ounces spinach*

2 *to 3 tablespoons butter*

1 *onion, chopped*

3 *cloves garlic, chopped*

3 *slices white bread, crusts removed*

½ *teaspoon chopped fresh sage, or ¼ teaspoon dried*

Pinch thyme

Salt and pepper

1 *large egg, lightly beaten*

SAUCE

1 *onion, quartered*

Pinch thyme

1½ *cups Chicken Stock (page 300) or canned chicken broth*

Cut turkey breast meat off the bone, leaving skin intact, and reserve bones. Remove the small filet and pull out the white tendon, scraping a knife blade against it as you go. Butterfly the filet by slicing it horizontally but not all the way through, and open it like a book. Lay the turkey breast skin side down on a work surface and butterfly it like the filet. Pound the meat a little to flatten it. Leave skin attached, including the neck skin.

Trim all the silver membrane off the pork filet. Cut pork to the same length as the turkey meat, reserving the thin tapered end.

Twist leaves off the bunch of watercress and rinse well, discarding lower portions of stems. De-stem spinach leaves and rinse well. Blanch the greens in boiling salted water for 1 minute, then drain and plunge into cold water to set the color. Drain, squeeze dry, and chop coarsely.

Heat 1 tablespoon of the butter in a skillet, and sauté pork filet until nicely browned, about 3 minutes. Remove and set aside. In the same skillet, adding another tablespoon of butter if necessary, cook the onion until soft, about 5 minutes, adding garlic toward the end.

Place bread and reserved end of pork filet (cut up) in a food processor, and grind. In a large bowl, combine bread crumb and pork mixture, sautéed onions and garlic, sage, and thyme. Add salt and pepper to taste. Stir in spinach and watercress, and add the egg.

Preheat convection over to 350 degrees. Place turkey skin side down on a work surface. Spread a layer of stuffing along the center. Top with pork filet, and spread with remaining stuffing, covering pork completely. Wrap the turkey breast around the filling and turn it over, covering exposed filling at one end with neck skin. Tie into a roll, starting with a length of string around the circumference, then looping it around the roast several times. Place in a shallow roasting pan and smear with remaining ½ tablespoon of butter. Surround with reserved turkey bones. Season to taste with salt and pepper, and roast for 1 hour. Fifteen minutes before the time is up, add the quartered onion to the pan—it will caramelize and add flavor to the sauce.

Remove the turkey from the oven and keep warm until ready to serve. Pour off any fat from the roasting pan and place pan over high heat. Add the chicken stock and boil for 2 minutes, scraping the pan with a wooden spoon. Add thyme. Taste for seasoning, and strain (do not thicken). Serve roast in ½-inch-thick slices, topped and surrounded with sauce.

PREPARATION TIME: 35 MINUTES / OVEN TIME: 1 HOUR

POT-AU-FEU
CALIFORNIA STYLE

The classic French pot-au-feu is made with beef. Here we use turkey drumsticks instead, and the results are truly spectacular. Nobody can believe that such an inexpensive part of the turkey can be made into so delicious and succulent a meal! It is an easy dish to prepare, and very low in calories into the bargain. Be sure to trim the vegetables into neat and even pieces; it adds to the look of the dish.

2 *fresh turkey drumsticks, 1¼ to 1½ pounds each*

2 *to 3 teaspoons coarse (kosher) salt*

2 *tablespoons butter*

1 *onion, cut in half*

2 *cloves garlic, minced*

¼ *teaspoon pepper*

2 *carrots, cut into 2-inch lengths*

2 *turnips, cut into eighths*

2 *small leeks, white and some green portion, well rinsed*

1 *small celery head, cut in half lengthways (use interior stalks only)*

1 *bay leaf*

¼ *teaspoon whole aniseeds*

1 *teaspoon chopped fresh thyme, or ½ teaspoon dried*

1 *cup Chicken Stock (page 300) or canned chicken broth*

HORSERADISH CREAM

1 *cup heavy cream*

2 *tablespoons grated fresh horseradish (or use bottled type and adjust amount to taste)*

¼ *cup chopped fresh parsley*

GARNISH

Dijon mustard

Cornichons (French pickled gherkins)

Coarse salt crystals

The day before, rub turkey drumsticks with the salt and place in a shallow dish. Cover and refrigerate overnight.

Preheat convection oven to 350 degrees. In a heavy enameled cast-iron casserole with a tight-fitting lid, melt the butter. Rinse turkey and pat dry. Add to pan and allow to brown slowly, covered, for 10 to 15 minutes, turning once. Add onion, cut side down in the butter, garlic, and pepper. Arrange remaining vegetables around and on top of the turkey, and add bay leaf, aniseeds, and thyme. Cover, and bake for 1 hour and 20 minutes.

When turkey is almost ready, prepare Horseradish Cream: Whip cream until it holds its shape gently, and fold in the grated horseradish and parsley. Transfer to a serving dish.

To serve, remove turkey drumsticks to a cutting board and cut the meat from the bones, discarding the tough tendons. (The meat will be very tender and succulent.) Cover four heated deep dinner plates with sauce from the pot, and top with turkey meat. Garnish with the vegetables, and serve with dishes of Horseradish Cream, Dijon mustard, cornichins, and coarse salt crystals. Offer crusty Baguettes (page 210) or other French bread for mopping up the juices.

PREPARATION TIME: OVERNIGHT MARINATING; 30 MINUTES / OVEN TIME: 1 HOUR AND 20 MINUTES / EASY

Spiced Turkey and Pork Meat Loaf

SERVES 6

Similar to a well-seasoned pork sausage but with the addition of lean ground turkey, this meat loaf is also outstanding served cold with salad, or in sandwiches. Be sure to buy freshly ground turkey, as the compacted frozen variety has too mushy a texture and very little flavor. The raw mixture can also be shaped into patties and fried, like hamburgers.

1 *tablespoon butter*

1 *small onion, chopped*

3 *slices home-style white bread, crusts removed*

2 *large eggs*

1 *pound freshly ground turkey*

1 *pound ground pork*

1 *tablespoon Spiced Salt (recipe follows) (page 118)*

1 *tablespoon Cognac*

Preheat convection oven to 325 degrees. Heat butter in a small skillet and sauté onion until soft but not browned, about 5 minutes. In the bowl of a food processor, process bread to crumbs. Add eggs and process until beaten. Add crumbled turkey and pork, onion, Spiced Salt, and Cognac. Process briefly to combine, but do not purée. Transfer mixture to a 2-quart ovenproof terrine, soufflé dish, or glass loaf pan and smooth the surface with a rubber spatula. Bake uncovered for 45 minutes.

PREPARATION TIME: 15 MINUTES / OVEN TIME: 45 MINUTES / EASY

TURKEY DRUMSTICKS WITH SAUERKRAUT

SERVES 4

A savory country dish that is both simple and inexpensive. The turkey drumsticks can be baked in sauerkraut a day ahead—the mixture is even better reheated. The dish is accompanied by freshly boiled potatoes, frankfurters, and German mustard. Serve with cold beer rather than wine, which would quarrel with the sauerkraut.

2 *turkey drumsticks, 1¼ to 1½ pounds each*
  Salt and pepper
1 *tablespoon juniper berries*
1 *teaspoon black peppercorns*
1 *bay leaf*
1 *sprig thyme*
2 *tablespoons butter*
1 *tablespoon vegetable oil*
1 *onion, chopped*
1 *clove garlic, chopped*

4 *cups fresh sauerkraut; or 3 pounds bottled sauerkraut, well rinsed and squeezed dry*
1 *cup white wine*
1 *cup Chicken Stock (page 300) or canned chicken broth*
8 *small boiling potatoes*
4 *best-quality veal frankfurters*
  Mild German mustard

Preheat convection oven to 350 degrees. Cut the knobby bone off the end of each drumstick. Sprinkle with salt and pepper to taste, remembering that sauerkraut is salty. Tie the juniper berries, peppercorns, bay leaf, and thyme in a cheesecloth bag.

Heat butter and oil in an enameled cast-iron casserole and brown drumsticks on all sides, about 7 minutes. Remove to a plate. Add the onion and garlic to the pot and sauté for 3 minutes, then stir in the sauerkraut. Add the wine and chicken stock. Bury the turkey in the mixture, add the cheesecloth bag of herbs, cover, and bake for 1 hour and 20 minutes.

Half an hour before the turkey is done, boil potatoes for approximately 20 minutes or until tender. Poach frankfurters in water for 5 minutes. To serve, cut the turkey meat off the bones and divide among four plates. Garnish with sauerkraut, potatoes, and frankfurters, and offer German mustard on the side.

PREPARATION TIME: 30 MINUTES / OVEN TIME: 1 HOUR AND 20 MINUTES / EASY

SPICED SALT

MAKES ¼ CUP

¼ teaspoon crumbled bay leaf

¼ teaspoon thyme

¼ teaspoon cloves

¼ teaspoon cinnamon

¼ teaspoon nutmeg

¼ teaspoon ginger

¼ teaspoon mace

¼ teaspoon coriander

¾ teaspoon black and white peppercorns, mixed

Pinch of cayenne pepper

3 tablespoons salt

For the best flavor, use whole spices wherever possible, and grind in a mortar with a pestle.

Combine all ingredients, mix well, and store in an airtight jar.

ROAST TURKEY
WITH PECAN CORNBREAD
AND CHESTNUT STUFFING

A convection oven is unbeatable for producing a succulent turkey, brown and crisp on the outside and tender and juicy within. Serve the Gratin of Corn and Spinach (page 193) as your vegetable dish; and as a new twist on an old theme, present the Pumpkin Soufflé Salzburg Style, with Cranberry Sauce (page 287), for dessert.

1 oven-ready fresh turkey, 10 to 12 pounds, with giblets

2 tablespoons butter, melted

STUFFING

3 onions, finely chopped

1½ cups finely diced de-stringed celery

4 tablespoons butter

1 tablespoon Cognac

1 recipe Pecan Cornbread (page 224), one day old, crumbled

3 cups shelled unsweetened chestnuts (buy ready-prepared, or roast and shell according to recipe on page 299)

½ cup finely chopped fresh parsley

½ teaspoon chopped fresh thyme, or ¼ teaspoon dried

2 large leaves chopped fresh sage, or ½ teaspoon dried

1½ teaspoons salt

Black pepper

2 large eggs, beaten

1¾ cups Chicken Stock (page 300) or canned chicken broth

GIBLET SAUCE

1 onion, chopped

1 carrot, chopped

1 stalk celery, chopped

2 cups Chicken Stock (page 300) or turkey stock

Salt and pepper

2 teaspoons cornstarch, dissolved in a little cold water

Rinse and dry turkey, inside and out. Trim turkey liver, dice, and set aside. Chop remaining giblets and set aside.

Prepare stuffing: Sauté onion and celery in butter for 5 minutes until softened, and add turkey liver. Cook for 1 minute and remove from heat. Sprinkle with Cognac. In a large bowl, combine the onion mixture, crumbled cornbread, chestnuts, parsley, thyme, and sage. Season with salt and a generous grinding of black pepper. Stir in the eggs and stock. The mixture should be moist but not sloppy.

Fill the turkey loosely with this mixture, stuffing from both ends. Close vent and cavity with poultry pins through the skin, and tuck wings underneath body. Spoon remaining stuffing into a buttered 1-quart baking dish. Place bird on a rack in a shallow roasting pan. (Use a rack that holds the turkey above the level of the pan, or rest rack across pan sides to get the best possible air circulation.) Brush the outside of the bird with melted butter, and season with salt and pepper to taste.

Preheat convection oven to 325 degrees. Roast turkey for 15 minutes per pound, or until internal temperature of thigh meat registers 180 degrees on a meat thermometer. (There is no need to turn the bird or baste in a convection oven.) After 1 hour, add the chopped giblets, onion, carrot, and celery to the roasting pan. Cover the dish of extra stuffing with aluminum foil and bake along with the turkey for 1 hour.

When the turkey is done, place on a heated platter and let rest in a warm place for at least 20 minutes so that the internal juices can settle.

To make the giblet sauce, transfer giblets and vegetables from the roasting pan to a heavy skillet and place over medium heat. Pour off fat from pan and add any remaining juices to skillet. Sauté for 5 minutes; then stir in the stock and deglaze the pan. Simmer until reduced by half, about 10 minutes. Stir in any juices that have accumulated on the roast platter, then taste for seasoning and add salt and pepper as needed. Strain into a saucepan and add dissolved cornstarch. Boil for a few seconds, until sauce thickens and clears, then pour into a warmed sauceboat.

PREPARATION TIME: 30 MINUTES / OVEN TIME: 2½ TO 3 HOURS / EASY

MEATS

BACON-WRAPPED CABBAGE ROLLS

This savory dish can be reheated successfully, so it's a good one to make a day ahead, or for dinner when you suspect everyone is going to be late. If you are grinding your own meat in a food processor, cut it up and drop it through the feed tube while the motor is running. This gives a more even consistency.

1 *green cabbage*
1 *tablespoon butter*
1 *onion, chopped*
1 *cup soft white bread crumbs*
½ *cup milk*
8 *ounces ground pork*
8 *ounces ground veal*
4 *leaves fresh sage, chopped, or ¼ teaspoon dried*
1 *teaspoon chopped fresh thyme, or ½ teaspoon dried*
2 *tablespoons chopped fresh parsley*

½ *teaspoon nutmeg*
1 *teaspoon salt*
½ *teaspoon pepper*
2 *large eggs, beaten*
12 *strips lean bacon*
1 *carrot, sliced*
  Pinch thyme
  Black pepper to taste
  Pinch nutmeg
1 *bay leaf*
1½ *cups Chicken Stock (page 300) or canned chicken broth*

Bring a large pot of salted water to a boil. Cut the cabbage through the core near the stalk, and carefully separate the leaves. Blanch for

1 minute in the boiling water, and drain. Heat butter in a small skillet and sauté half of the onion for 5 minutes, until softened. Set aside to cool slightly.

Preheat convection oven to 350 degrees. In a bowl, combine bread crumbs and milk. Add pork, veal, sage, 1 teaspoon thyme, parsley, ½ teaspoon nutmeg, salt, ½ teaspoon pepper, eggs, and sautéed onion. Blend well and form into six balls. Line six large cabbage leaves with one or two small tender ones, and top with a portion of meat. Form each into a tight package and turn over. Wrap each with two strips of bacon at right angles to each other, tucking the ends underneath. (If preferred, use only one strip of bacon per roll.) Place the cabbage rolls in a 10 by 16-inch ovenproof dish. Add remaining chopped onion, carrot, bay leaf, pinch of thyme, generous grinding of pepper, and pinch of nutmeg to the dish. Pour in chicken stock. Cover dish with aluminum foil and bake for 30 minutes. Remove foil and bake for a further 15 minutes, uncovered. Transfer cabbage rolls to heated dinner plates and surround with sauce.

PREPARATION TIME: 20 MINUTES / OVEN TIME: 45 MINUTES / EASY

FILET OF PORK WITH
CAPER AND CORNICHON SAUCE

Filet of pork makes a good small roast for two or four people, and when cooked this way—which takes less than 30 minutes from start to finish—it is nice and juicy, not dry. It should be very slightly pink in the center when done. (The USDA now says that pork is perfectly safe when cooked to an internal temperature of over 137 degrees, and it certainly tastes a lot better.) Good accompaniments include new potatoes boiled in their jackets and then sliced, or rounds of zucchini dusted with flour and quickly sautéed in olive oil.

1 *whole filet of pork, 12 to 16 ounces*
1 *tablespoon olive oil*
½ *stalk celery, slivered*
½ *leek, white part only, rinsed well and slivered*
2 *cloves garlic, chopped*
Pinch thyme
1 *bay leaf*
Black pepper to taste

SAUCE

1 *tablespoon all-purpose flour*
¾ *cup white wine*
¾ *cup water*
1 *tablespoon capers, drained*
1 *teaspoon chopped fresh parsley*
1 *tablespoon chopped cornichons (French pickled gherkins)*
1 *egg yolk*
Salt (optional)

Preheat convection oven to 350 degrees. Trim the pork filet, removing any fat or silver membrane. Cut off the thin tapered end and reserve it for another use, or discard. Heat olive oil in an ovenproof skillet, brown the meat over high heat very quickly, about 1 minute, and stir in celery, leek, garlic, thyme, bay leaf, and pepper to taste. Transfer skillet to oven and bake for 12 minutes. Remove meat and keep warm. Stir flour into skillet, then add wine and water. Bring to a boil and reduce to 1 cup, about 7 minutes. Stir in capers, parsley, and cornichons. Remove ¼ cup of the sauce and mix it with the egg yolk. Return this to the pan, but do not allow to boil. Taste for seasoning, and add salt if desired.

To serve, make a pool of sauce on each heated dinner plate. Carve pork filet diagonally into thin slices, and fan out on top of sauce. Spoon more sauce on top of meat.

PREPARATION TIME: 10 MINUTES / OVEN TIME: 12 TO 15 MINUTES / EASY

LOIN OF PORK
WITH MUSTARD AND SAGE
SERVES 6 TO 8

Pigs are now bred to be a lot leaner than they were ten or twenty years ago. Since there is now very little internal fat, the meat dries out quickly when cooked, so timing is important if you want to enjoy juicy, succulent pork. Both the USDA and the National Pork Producers Council advise that any trichinae pork might contain (and this is extremely rare today) are killed at 137 degrees, and they recommend roasting pork to an internal temperature of 155 degrees, which will rise a few more degrees as the meat rests before carving. Pork should look juicy when cooked, not white and dried out.

1 *loin of pork, 4 pounds (see below)*

1 *tablespoon Dijon mustard*

1 *teaspoon chopped fresh sage, or ½ teaspoon dried*

1 *tablespoon white wine*

1 *stalk celery, chopped*

1 *carrot, chopped*

1 *onion, chopped*

1 *cup Chicken Stock (page 300) or canned chicken broth*

½ *cup heavy cream*

Salt and pepper to taste

Have your butcher bone the roast and chop the bones for you, or buy a ready-tied roast that weighs about 3 pounds plus some extra pork bones, such as spareribs.

Preheat convection oven to 350 degrees. Blend the mustard, sage, and wine together. If meat is rolled up, untie and brush a little of this mixture inside. Retie and place on a rack resting across (not in) a shallow roasting pan. (This allows maximum air circulation.) Brush remaining mustard mixture over meat. Place bones under the rack. Roast for 30 minutes, then add celery, carrot, and onion to the pan. When meat has cooked for 1 hour, test internal temperature with a meat thermometer. When it reaches 155 degrees, remove meat (it will continue to cook internally when outside the oven, and the temperature will rise another 5 to 10 degrees). Transfer pork to a warm platter and let rest for 15 minutes so the juices can settle.

Pour fat off roasting pan, and place pan, with bones and vegetables, over medium-high heat. Add chicken stock, bring to a boil, and deglaze, scraping up any browned bits on the bottom of the pan. Simmer until reduced by half, about 7 minutes. Add any juices that have accumulated on the roast platter, and strain into a saucepan. Stir in cream and simmer for 2 minutes, until slightly thickened. Taste for seasoning, and add salt and pepper if necessary. To serve, pour a little sauce on each heated dinner plate and top with a ½-inch-thick slice of pork.

PREPARATION TIME: 20 MINUTES / OVEN TIME: 1¼ TO 1½ HOURS / EASY

MEDALLIONS OF PORK WITH GINGER AND CHINESE FIVE-SPICE POWDER

This is a wonderful way to prepare pork chops so that they are tender and succulent. It is of course a Chinese dish, though not cooked in a wok. Serve the sliced meat with boiled rice and snow peas. A complementary first course would be the Chicken Wings with Sesame Oil and Honey (page 19), and the crunchy Cornmeal Almond Cookies (page 230) make an appropriate dessert, along with some jasmine tea.

If your pork chops are closer to 1 inch thick, bake for only 10 minutes and then slice into one to see if it is cooked. The meat should look juicy and be a very pale pink inside. Return to the oven for a short time if the meat is still rosy.

4 *boneless loin pork chops, about 1½ inches thick, 4 to 6 ounces each*	5 *scallions finely chopped, white bulbs and half of green tops*
1 *tablespoon soy sauce*	1 *clove garlic, mashed and chopped*
3 *quarter-size slices peeled ginger root*	2 *tablespoons Dry Sack sherry*
Pinch Chinese five-spice powder	1 *cup Chicken Stock (page 300) or canned chicken broth*
2 *tablespoons vegetable oil*	
6 *mushrooms, sliced*	2 *teaspoons cornstarch*

Trim any excess fat from pork chops. Combine soy sauce, ginger, and five-spice powder in a shallow dish, and turn chops in this mixture. Marinate for 20 minutes (or overnight in refrigerator if more convenient).

Preheat convection oven to 375 degrees, heating a shallow oven-proof dish at the same time. In a heavy skillet, heat 1 tablespoon of the oil and brown pork chops and ginger slices very quickly, about 1 minute. Transfer pork to the preheated dish, discarding ginger, and bake for 15 minutes.

Meanwhile, add remaining tablespoon of oil to the skillet and sauté mushrooms for 3 minutes. Add scallions and garlic, and cook for 1 minute. Stir in sherry and chicken stock, and simmer for 5 minutes. Just before serving, dissolve the cornstarch in a little cold water and stir into sauce. Boil until it thickens and clears, about 30 seconds.

Remove pork from oven and carve diagonally into ¼-inch-thick slices. The meat should be slightly pink inside. Fan out onto heated dinner plates and cover with sauce.

PREPARATION TIME: 10 MINUTES; 20 MINUTES MARINATING /
OVEN TIME: 15 MINUTES / EASY

MEDALLIONS OF PORK WITH PRUNES AND RED CURRANT JELLY

SERVES 4

This is an elegant and delicious way to cook boneless pork chops— they are sautéed to brown the exterior and are then baked very briefly so that they do not dry out. A simple sauce is made from the wine in which the prunes were marinated, red currant jelly, and a little cream. If your pork chops are closer to 1 inch thick, bake for only 10 minutes and then slice into one to check for doneness. The interior should be very pale pink and look juicy. If it is still too rosy, return them to the oven for a short time.

12 *soft pitted prunes*
1 *cup demi-sec white wine, such as Sémillon or Sauvignon Blanc*
½ *tablespoon vegetable oil*
4 *boneless loin pork chops, about 1½ inches thick, 4 to 6 ounces each, well trimmed*

Salt and pepper to taste
1 *tablespoon red currant jelly*
½ *cup heavy cream*

Place prunes in a saucepan with the wine and soak for 4 hours, or overnight if more convenient.

Preheat convection oven to 375 degrees, and heat a small shallow baking dish at the same time. Heat oil in a heavy skillet and brown pork chops very quickly on both sides, about 1 minute. Transfer to the heated baking dish and bake for 15 minutes.

Meanwhile, bring prunes and wine to a boil and simmer for 5 minutes. Remove prunes and reserve. Reduce liquid almost to a glaze in the bottom of the pan, about 7 minutes, and then stir in jelly. Add cream, bring to a boil, and reduce by one third, about 4 minutes. Season with salt and pepper to taste. Return prunes to sauce and heat through, about 1 minute.

Place pork on a cutting board and pour any pan juices into the sauce. Carve pork into thin slices and fan out on heated dinner plates. Cover with sauce and garnish with prunes.

PREPARATION TIME: 4 HOURS OR OVERNIGHT SOAKING; 15 MINUTES   /
OVEN TIME: 15 MINUTES   /   EASY

BAKED VEAL CHOPS WITH HERB STUFFING

An easy and unexpected way to cook veal chops that requires very little attention. The meat absorbs the herb flavors and the stuffing gets nice and crispy on top. Serve with the Gratin of Eggplant, Mushrooms, and Tomatoes (page 194), which can bake in the oven at the same time.

½ tablespoon olive oil

2 tablespoons butter

2 veal chops, 6 ounces each

1 small onion, chopped

2 tablespoons ham, chopped

2 mushrooms, diced

½ cup bread crumbs made from day-old white bread

2 tablespoons grated Swiss Gruyère cheese

1 tablespoon fresh parsley

1 teaspoon chopped fresh thyme, or ½ teaspoon dried

Salt and pepper

2 tablespoons white wine

½ cup Brown Veal Stock (page 302) or canned beef broth

Preheat convection oven to 350 degrees. Heat oil in a skillet with 2 teaspoons of the butter. Brown veal chops very quickly, about 3 minutes. Remove and set aside. Add remaining butter to pan and sauté onion until soft, about 5 minutes. Stir in ham and mushrooms, and cook for 2 minutes. Transfer to a bowl and add bread crumbs, cheese, parsley, thyme, and salt and pepper to taste. Press stuffing on top of chops and place in a small shallow baking dish. Cover with aluminum foil and bake for 15 minutes. Then add wine and veal stock and bake uncovered for 1 hour, until veal is very tender and stuffing is brown and crispy on top.

PREPARATION TIME: 10 MINUTES / OVEN TIME: 1¼ HOURS / EASY

BREAST OF VEAL STUFFED WITH SPINACH

This is a sophisticated way to serve a cheap cut of meat, and any leftovers are excellent sliced thin and served cold, with salad. You may find that the butcher has already made a couple of individual odd-looking pockets in the meat. Ignore these and make one clean slice instead, holding the meat flat with the palm of one hand as you do so.

1 *boneless breast of veal,*
3¼ pounds
Salt and pepper
2 *tablespoons butter,*
softened

STUFFING

12 *ounces spinach, rinsed*
12 *ounces ground pork*
3 *tablespoons butter*
1 *onion, chopped*
¼ *teaspoon nutmeg*
1 *teaspoon chopped fresh*
thyme, or ½ teaspoon
dried

1 *teaspoon chopped fresh*
oregano, or ½ teaspoon
dried
1 *teaspoon salt*
½ *teaspoon pepper*
½ *cup white bread crumbs*
2 *large eggs, beaten*

VEGETABLE GARNISH

1 *onion, quartered*
2 *carrots, cut into chunks*
1 *stalk celery, de-stringed*
and cut into chunks
4 *potatoes, quartered*
1 *cup Chicken Stock*
(page 300) or canned
chicken broth

Preheat convection oven to 375 degrees. Make a pocket in the veal by cutting it horizontally but not all the way through, and open it out like a book. Sprinkle with salt and pepper to taste.

Make the stuffing: Blanch spinach in boiling salted water for 1 minute, and plunge into cold water to set the color. Squeeze dry and chop coarsely. Mix with ground pork. Heat butter in a small skillet, and simmer onion for 5 minutes, until softened. Combine onion with spinach mixture and add nutmeg, thyme, oregano, salt, pepper, bread crumbs, and eggs.

130 CONVECTION CUISINE

Spread stuffing over bottom half of veal and cover with top flap, forming a long sausage shape. Place skin side up on a work surface, and tie with string, looping it at 2-inch intervals. Turn meat over and twist string over each loop before tying off at one end. Transfer to a shallow roasting pan, skin side up. Sprinkle with salt and pepper to taste, and smear with softened butter. Roast for 30 minutes, then turn meat over and add vegetables, rolling them around in the pan juices. Continue roasting for a further 40 minutes. Remove meat and vegetables to a warm platter, and place roasting pan over medium-high heat. Add chicken stock, bring to a boil, and deglaze. Taste for seasoning and strain into a sauceboat.

PREPARATION TIME: 30 MINUTES / OVEN TIME: 1 HOUR AND 10 MINUTES

VEAL SHANKS WITH GINGER AND GREEN PEAS

A satisfying family-style dish that doesn't require much attention. The ginger root adds a lively, fresh note and the meat is nice and tender. Don't be tempted to simply throw the peas in at the last minute—they must be blanched or they will lose their appetizing bright green color. Boiled rice cooked in chicken stock makes a good accompaniment for soaking up the pan juices.

2 *tablespoons vegetable oil*

4 *pounds sliced veal shanks*

Salt and pepper

Flour for dredging

1 *red bell pepper, seeded, de-ribbed, and sliced*

1 *onion, sliced*

3 *tomatoes, quartered*

6 *slices peeled ginger root, ⅛ inch thick*

2 *cups (approximately) White Veal Stock (page 301) or canned chicken broth*

1 *cup peas, fresh or frozen*

Preheat convection oven to 400 degrees. Pour oil into a metal baking pan just large enough to hold the sliced veal shanks in one layer, and place pan in oven to get very hot. Sprinkle veal with salt and pepper to taste, and dredge with flour. Brown in hot baking pan for 30 minutes, turning meat over after 15 minutes. Reduce heat to 350 degrees and add bell pepper, onion, tomato, and ginger to pan. Add enough veal stock to almost cover the meat. Season to taste with salt and pepper. Bake uncovered for 1½ hours, until very tender. (If there is too much sauce at the end, pour it off and reduce by rapid boiling, then return to meat.)

Blanch peas in boiling salted water for 1 minute, then drain and plunge into cold water to set the color. Five minutes before you are ready to serve veal, remove ginger and scatter with peas.

PREPARATION TIME: 15 MINUTES / OVEN TIME: 2 HOURS / EASY

VEAL SHANKS WITH LEMON AND TOMATO

Veal shanks are low in cost (and in fat) and have a wonderful flavor and texture when slowly braised with vegetables. This very light version of a typical northern Italian dish goes well with orzo, the small rice-shaped pasta.

1 tablespoon olive oil

4 pounds sliced veal shanks

Salt and pepper

All-purpose flour for dredging

2 onions, chopped

2 carrots, chopped

½ cup white wine

1 can Italian plum tomatoes, 28 ounces

Pinch sugar

½ teaspoon aniseeds or fennel seeds

Pinch thyme

½ stalk celery, de-stringed and very finely chopped

1 tablespoon chopped fresh parsley

1 teaspoon grated lemon peel

Preheat convection oven to 400 degrees. Pour oil into a metal baking pan large enough to hold the sliced veal shanks in one layer, and place in the oven to get very hot. Season veal with salt and pepper to taste, and dredge with flour. Brown veal in baking pan for 15 minutes, then turn meat over and add onions and carrots. After a further 15 minutes, reduce heat to 350 degrees, and add wine, chopped-up tomatoes with their juice, sugar, aniseeds, and thyme. Cover and bake for 1½ hours, until very tender. Combine celery, parsley, and lemon peel, and sprinkle on top before serving.

PREPARATION TIME: 15 MINUTES / OVEN TIME: 2 HOURS / EASY

BEEF CROSSRIBS BRAISED IN RED WINE

Half of this roast with its tasty garnish of vegetables will serve four. If you like, you can save the other half and the remaining sauce for the Jellied Braised Beef on page 135.

2 tablespoons butter

½ tablespoon onion juice (purée onion in food processor and strain)

1 tablespoon Cognac

1 teaspoon Herbes de Provence, or 3 sprigs thyme

6 peppercorns
   Pinch salt

1 bay leaf

1 boneless beef crossrib roast, 4½ to 5 pounds, rolled and tied

1 tablespoon olive oil

1 carrot, coarsely chopped

1 onion, coarsely chopped

3 cloves garlic, unpeeled, lightly mashed

1 bottle Cabernet Sauvignon or other dry red wine

2 cups Brown Veal Stock (page 302), or 14-ounce can double-strength beef broth plus ¼ cup water

GARNISH

2 turnips, 8 ounces each

4 small carrots

8 ounces slender young green beans

1 package frozen peas, 10 ounces

In a small saucepan, melt butter and add onion juice, Cognac, Herbes de Provence, peppercorns, salt, and bay leaf. Simmer very slowly for 5 minutes. Holding the herbs back in the pan, transfer the flavored butter to a bulb baster fitted with an injector needle. (Or use a syringe with a very large needle from a veterinary supply or farmers' feed store.) Reserve the herbs and peppercorns. Inject butter at intervals throughout meat for tenderness and extra flavor.

Preheat convection oven to 325 degrees. In a large enameled cast-iron casserole, heat oil and brown meat on all sides, about 5 minutes altogether. Add carrot, onion, and garlic cloves and cook for 5 minutes. Add reserved herbs and peppercorns, wine, and stock. Bring to a boil, cover, and transfer to the oven. Bake for 3 hours.

Peel turnips, cut them in half, and then into ¼-inch-thick slices. Peel carrots, and cut into rounds. Top and tail green beans, and destring if necessary. Cook vegetables separately in boiling salted water until just tender, about 10 minutes. Blanch peas in boiling salted water for 1 minute and drain.

Remove meat from juices and keep warm. Strain juices into a large glass measure and remove fat. (Let stand for a few minutes and fat will rise to the surface. Remove clear juices from below this level with a bulb baster; trail paper towels across the surface to soak up fat; or place in freezer until fat solidifies and then lift it off. Then reheat sauce.) Slice the meat, cutting across the grain to make round slices. Place on heated dinner plates, top with sauce, and surround with little heaps of turnips, carrots, beans, and peas.

PREPARATION TIME: 30 MINUTES / OVEN TIME: 3 HOURS

SERVES 4

JELLIED BRAISED BEEF

A colorful summer dish that's a welcome change from cold cuts, this is an inspired use of leftover Beef Crossrib Braised in Red Wine. It's made by enclosing the meat in a vegetable-studded aspic, which creates a beautiful pattern when the meat is sliced.

½ *Beef Crossrib Braised in Red Wine (recipe above), in one piece*

Meat juices from leftover roast

White Veal Stock (page 301) or canned chicken broth

2 *packages unflavored gelatin*

2 *turnips, 8 ounces each*

4 *small carrots*

1 *package frozen peas, 10 ounces*

Set meat aside and measure juice, adding enough veal stock to make 4 cups. Bring to a boil, add gelatin, and stir until gelatin is completely dissolved. Set aside to cool.

Peel turnips; cut in half, and then into ¼-inch slices. Peel and slice carrots. Cook turnips and carrots separately in boiling salted water until just tender, about 10 minutes. Blanch peas in boiling salted water for 1 minute and drain.

In the bottom of a bowl slightly larger than the round of beef, arrange a layer of peas. Surround with a wide band of carrot and turnip slices. Pour in just enough stock to cover the peas without making them float. Freeze until set, about 10 minutes. Carefully set the meat on top and cover with remaining vegetables. Fill bowl with remaining stock, which should just cover the contents. Chill for at least 4 hours, until set.

Dip bowl in very hot water, wipe dry, and turn mold out onto a flat platter. Cut in slices to serve.

PREPARATION TIME: 20 MINUTES / OVEN TIME: NONE

LEMON POT ROAST

SERVES 8 TO 10

Pot roast is a family dish that most people remember fondly from their childhood. This version is made extra-special with the addition of lemon. Serve with boiled potatoes, pickles, and a selection of mustards.

1 tablespoon olive or vegetable oil

1 tablespoon butter

1 top sirloin of beef, 5 pounds

Flour for dredging

½ cup fresh lemon juice

½ cup water

Grated peel of 1 lemon

2 tablespoons finely chopped onion

1 clove garlic, mashed and chopped

1 teaspoon chopped fresh thyme, or ½ teaspoon dried

1 teaspoon salt

½ teaspoon pepper

Preheat convection oven to 300 degrees. Heat oil and butter in an enameled cast-iron casserole just large enough to hold the meat. Dredge meat with flour, and brown to a deep rich color on all sides, about 10 minutes.

Combine lemon juice, water, lemon paste, onion, garlic, thyme, salt, and pepper. Spread over and around meat, cover, transfer to the oven, and bake for 3½ to 4 hours, or until meat is very tender. Remove meat to a warm platter. Skim fat off meat juices, taste for seasoning, and serve with pot roast.

PREPARATION TIME: 15 MINUTES / OVEN TIME: 3½ TO 4 HOURS / EASY

SERVES 2

FILET MIGNON IN PHYLLO

This updated version of Beef Wellington serves two people and can be prepared in under 30 minutes. (Remember to transfer the frozen phyllo dough to the refrigerator the night before.) If you have time, Stuffed Pattypan Squash (page 196) make an attractive and colorful vegetable garnish; if not, serve asparagus spears or broccoli florets.

2 *filet mignons, 4 ounces each, trimmed of all fat or silvery membrane*

Salt and pepper

1 *tablespoon butter*

1 *shallot, chopped*

1 *clove garlic, chopped*

2 *sheets phyllo dough, thawed if frozen*

1 *ounce imported Swiss cheese, in paper-thin slices (use a cheese plane or a wide-bladed vegetable peeler)*

6 *spinach leaves, rinsed well and dried*

¼ *cup white wine*

¼ *cup heavy cream*

1 *tablespoon Dijon mustard*

½ *teaspoon green peppercorns in brine, drained*

Preheat convection oven to 400 degrees. Season filets with salt and pepper to taste. Heat butter in a heavy skillet and sauté the steaks quickly on both sides and on the edges, about 2 minutes. Allow to cool for a few minutes. In the same skillet, sauté shallot and garlic very briefly, about 30 seconds.

Spread out sheets of phyllo and brush lightly with butter from the skillet. Fold in half and brush again with butter. Place a few slices of cheese in the center of each and top with a steak. Cover each steak with half the sautéed shallot and garlic, the remaining cheese, and the spinach leaves. Fold the phyllo over the steaks, forming a loose package with all the folds on top, and transfer to a baking sheet. Brush with butter and bake for 8 minutes.

In the meantime, add white wine to the skillet and deglaze. Stir in the cream, mustard, and green peppercorns, and taste for seasoning. Serve sauce alongside the golden-brown phyllo packages.

PREPARATION TIME: 15 MINUTES / OVEN TIME: 8 MINUTES / EASY

OXTAIL WITH
RED WINE AND ORANGE PEEL

Oxtail has a wonderful flavor, but requires long cooking to make it succulent and tender. A traditional country dish, it is at its best when cooked one day and eaten the next, as the flavor improves if allowed to mellow. Also, chilling the meat allows you to lift the congealed fat off the surface. Serve it with crusty bread to mop up the juices. If you don't want to serve this dish with the bones (and inelegantly sucking on these is half the enjoyment!), strip the meat off, place in a pie dish with the sauce, top with puff pastry, and bake until golden. (Follow directions and timing for making a Honeyed Apple Pie, page 249.)

4 *pounds oxtail, cut up*
1 *tablespoon olive oil*
1 *onion, chopped*
1 *carrot, chopped*
2 *cloves garlic, chopped*
2 *strips orange peel, 3 inches each, slivered*
1 *tablespoon tomato paste*

Pinch thyme
Salt and pepper
1½ *cups Brown Veal Stock (page 302) or canned beef broth*
1½ *cups dry red wine*
2 *teaspoons cornstarch*

Preheat convection oven to 325 degrees. Trim excess fat from pieces of oxtail. Heat olive oil in a large, enameled cast-iron casserole and brown meat on all sides, about 10 minutes. Scatter onion, carrot, garlic, orange peel, tomato paste, thyme, and salt and pepper to taste over the meat. Add stock and wine and bring to a boil. Cover, transfer to the oven, and bake for 3 to 4 hours, until meat is very tender and almost falling off the bones, adding a little more stock or water if necessary. Let cool, and refrigerate overnight.

Lift congealed fat from surface and discard. Reheat oxtail for 10 to 15 minutes until heated through—try a piece of the meat to make sure. Dissolve cornstarch in a little water and stir into sauce. Boil until sauce thickens and clears, about 30 seconds.

PREPARATION TIME: 15 MINUTES / OVEN TIME: 3 TO 4 HOURS / EASY

PRIME RIB OF BEEF
WITH YORKSHIRE PUDDING

Prime rib roasted in a convection oven is particularly succulent, as the juices remain inside the meat. To reheat any leftovers, cover the surface of the meat with two large lettuce leaves, then heat at 325 degrees for 15 minutes.

1 *prime rib of beef (standing rib roast), 5 pounds*
Salt and pepper

YORKSHIRE PUDDING

¾ *cup (3½ ounces) all-purpose flour*
¼ *teaspoon salt*
Pinch nutmeg
2 *large eggs, beaten*
¾ *cup milk*

SAUCE

2 *pounds meaty beef bones, cut into 2-inch lengths*
1 *onion, chopped*
1 *carrot*
1 *stalk celery*
1 *bay leaf*
½ *teaspoon thyme*
Few sprigs parsley
Salt and pepper
Cornstarch dissolved in 1 tablespoon cold water

Preheat convection oven to 325 degrees. Place a 9-inch cast-iron skillet inside a shallow roasting pan, and rest a flat rack across the sides of the pan, over the skillet. (This is so that the flavorful beef fat will drop into the skillet.) Rub roast with salt and pepper to taste, and place on rack, bone side up. Roast for 20 minutes per pound for medium-rare meat, a total of 1 hour and 40 minutes. Halfway through roasting time, turn the meat fat side up. Test the internal temperature with a meat thermometer after 1½ hours. When it reachs 120 degrees, remove meat from the oven; the internal temperature will continue to rise another 5 or 10 degrees as the meat stands. This is for rare beef. See temperature chart on page 13 for medium rare or medium. (Another test for doneness is that the meat will have retracted up the bones by about 1 inch when it is medium-rare.) Remove beef to a heated platter and keep warm for 15 to 20 minutes so the juices can settle.

While the meat is roasting, make the sauce (which can be reheated and thickened at the last minute): Arrange the bones, vegetables, and herbs in a separate roasting pan and roast (along with the beef) for 45 minutes, turning the bones once. Transfer to a saucepan and cover with water. Boil until reduced by half, about 15 minutes. Strain into another saucepan, pressing down on bones and vegetables, and taste for seasoning. Add salt and pepper to taste. Just before serving, stir in any accumulated juices from the roast platter and heat to boiling. Stir in dissolved cornstarch and boil for a few seconds until the sauce clears and thickens.

While the roast is resting, prepare the Yorkshire Pudding, which is a giant crispy popover that puffs up around the edges: Increase oven heat to 400 degrees. About 4 ounces of fat will have rendered from the meat and dripped into the cast-iron skillet. Pour this off into a jug; carefully wipe the hot skillet out with paper towels, and return it to the oven so it can get very hot. In a mixing bowl, combine flour, salt, and nutmeg. Add eggs and stir well; then whisk in the milk. Pour ¼ cup of the reserved beef fat into the skillet and allow to get very hot in the oven. Add the batter, and bake for 20 minutes, until well puffed and browned.

PREPARATION TIME: 20 MINUTES / OVEN TIME: 2 HOURS

SCALLOPS OF BEEF IN BEER

SERVES 4

An easy, family-style way of cooking a lean cut of meat. Serve with buttered noodles or spaetzle and green beans.

2 *tablespoons butter*

2 *onions, 8 ounces each, sliced*

1 *pound boneless eye of round beef steaks, about 3 by 4 inches, ½ inch thick*

Salt and pepper

Flour for dredging

1 *tablespoon vegetable oil*

1 *clove garlic, minced*

1 *bay leaf*

1 *teaspoon fresh chopped thyme, or ½ teaspoon dried*

½ *tablespoon brown sugar*

1 *tablespoon cider vinegar*

1 *cup beer*

1 *cup Brown Veal Stock (page 302) or canned beef broth*

Preheat convection oven to 325 degrees.

Heat butter in a skillet and sauté onions for 5 minutes, until softened and starting to turn brown. Transfer onions to an ovenproof casserole with a tight-fitting lid.

Flatten the steaks slightly with the flat side of a cleaver, sprinkle with salt and pepper to taste, and dredge in flour. Add oil to the same skillet and brown beef quickly on both sides. Transfer the steaks to the casserole and bury them in the onions; add the garlic, bay leaf, and thyme.

Add brown sugar to the skillet and stir in vinegar. Then add beer and bring to a boil. Deglaze skillet. Add veal stock, bring to a boil again, and pour over beef and onions. Cover casserole and bake for 1¾ hours.

PREPARATION TIME: 15 MINUTES / OVEN TIME: 1¾ HOURS / EASY

LAMB "SAUSAGES" WITH EGGPLANT PURÉE

This Middle Eastern–style recipe makes exceptionally good use of ground lamb and is fast and easy to prepare. Serve it with Bulgur Pilaf (page 205), which can bake along with the eggplant mixture.

EGGPLANT PURÉE

3 tablespoons olive oil

1 onion, chopped

2 cloves garlic, chopped

1 eggplant, 6 ounces, peeled and diced

2 large tomatoes, peeled, seeded, and chopped

½ teaspoon ground coriander

Juice of ½ lemon

Salt

1 pound ground lamb

1 onion, chopped

2 cloves garlic, chopped

1 egg, beaten

½ cup bread crumbs made from day-old white bread

2 tablespoons chopped fresh parsley

2 tablespoons chopped fresh mint

Salt

Cayenne pepper

½ tablespoon olive oil

Make eggplant purée first, as it takes longer: Preheat convection oven to 350 degrees. Heat 1 tablespoon of the olive oil in an ovenproof casserole and sauté onion for 2 minutes. Add garlic, eggplant, and tomatoes and stir well. Cover, transfer to the oven, and bake for 20 minutes. Let cool, and then transfer to a food processor. Reduce to a purée, and add remaining 2 tablespoons oil, coriander, lemon juice, and salt to taste. Mix well, and serve at room temperature.

In the bowl of a food processor, combine lamb, onion, garlic, egg, bread crumbs, herbs, and salt and cayenne pepper to taste. Process to a fairly smooth paste, but do not purée. Wet your fingers with water and form mixture into finger-length sausages about 1 inch in diameter. Heat oil in a heavy ovenproof skillet and brown lamb rapidly, about 2 minutes. Transfer the skillet to the oven, and bake at 350 degrees for 7 minutes. Serve sausages with room-temperature eggplant.

PREPARATION TIME: 20 MINUTES / OVEN TIME: 20 MINUTES; 7 MINUTES / EASY

LAMB SHANKS WITH LENTILS

A tasty one-dish meal that is very comforting on a cold night, and more or less cooks itself after the shanks have been browned. This method seals the lamb and adds a great deal of flavor to the dish.

4 *lamb shanks, 10 to 12 ounces each*
Salt and pepper
1 *tablespoon butter*
1 *onion, chopped*
1 *clove garlic, chopped*
1 *stalk celery with leaves, chopped*

2 *cups Chicken Stock (page 300) or canned chicken broth*
14 *ounces brown lentils*
1 *tablespoon tomato paste*
2 *cups water*
Celery leaves, for garnish

Preheat convection oven to 350 degrees. Trim any excess fat off lamb shanks, and sprinkle with salt and pepper to taste. Heat butter in an enameled cast-iron casserole and brown the meat slowly, covered, for 15 minutes. Add onion and garlic and cook for 5 minutes. Add celery and chicken stock. Transfer to the oven and bake, covered, for 1 hour.

Add lentils, tomato paste, and water. Cover pot and bake for another hour, cooking 2 hours in all. Check for seasoning and serve in deep plates. Garnish with celery leaves.

PREPARATION TIME: 25 MINUTES / OVEN TIME: 2 HOURS / EASY

LAMB SHANKS WITH POTATOES AND MINT JELLY

Mint has a natural affinity for lamb but can be hard to find in cold weather, when this savory, inexpensive family-style dish would be most appreciated. Mint jelly solves the problem.

4 *lamb shanks, 10 to 12 ounces each*	4 *all-purpose potatoes, peeled in neat ovals*
1 *tablespoon vegetable oil*	1 *bay leaf*
Salt and pepper	*Pinch thyme*
16 *boiling onions, peeled*	*Pinch rosemary*
2 *cloves garlic, unpeeled*	1½ *cups water*
	1 *tablespoon mint jelly*

Preheat convection oven to 350 degrees. Trim any excess fat off lamb shanks and place in a shallow baking pan. Sprinkle with oil, season with salt and pepper to taste, and roast for 30 minutes. Add onions and unpeeled garlic, turn lamb shanks, and roast for another 30 minutes. Add potatoes, bay leaf, thyme, rosemary, and water, and roast for another hour, a total of 2 hours altogether.

Transfer lamb shanks to a cutting board and take the meat off the bones. Arrange lamb, onions, and potatoes on heated plates. Strain cooking juices into a saucepan and squeeze garlic pulp out of the husks into the sauce. Reduce by rapid boiling to 1 cup, about 7 minutes, and stir in mint jelly. Spoon sauce over lamb.

PREPARATION TIME: 20 MINUTES / OVEN TIME: 2 HOURS / EASY

LEG OF LAMB MARINATED IN HONEY AND SOY SAUCE

Honey and soy sauce combine to create a special flavor and a wonderful brown glaze on this leg of lamb. Be sure to let the lamb rest for 10 to 15 minutes before carving as it makes a big difference to the tenderness and juiciness of the meat, which should still be pink in the middle to be at its succulent best. A Gratin of Potatoes with Cream (page 195) is ideal with it.

1 *leg of lamb, 4 to 5 pounds (see below)*	4 *cloves garlic, mashed and minced*
⅓ *cup honey*	1 *cup soy sauce*
½ *cup boiling water*	½ *cup dry red wine*

Have your butcher remove the hip joint and femur from the lamb, leaving a small cavity. (Save the bones.) This makes the lamb much easier to carve, and the seasoning can penetrate from the inside. Remove fell (papery skin) and all but a very thin layer of fat from the meat.

The day before, place honey in a bowl just big enough to hold the lamb, and add boiling water. Stir until honey dissolves. Add garlic and soy sauce, and mix well. Add lamb and turn to coat well, making sure that plenty of the mixture goes inside the cavity. Add bones. Cover, and refrigerate for 24 hours.

The next day, preheat convection oven to 375 degrees. Tie lamb into a compact shape with kitchen string. Rest a flat rack across a shallow baking pan and place the lamb on top (to allow for maximum air circulation around the meat). Put the bones inside the pan. (Reserve marinade.) Roast for 45 minutes or until internal temperature reaches 145 degrees for medium-rare meat. Remove lamb from oven and let rest in a warm place for 10 to 15 minutes, so juices can redistribute.

To make the sauce, pour off fat and place roasting pan, with bones, over medium-high heat. Stir in wine and remaining marinade, and boil briskly for 5 minutes. The blood from the lamb will clarify the juices, but the foam that collects on top should be skimmed off. Taste for seasoning, strain into a bowl, and serve with the lamb.

PREPARATION TIME: 20 MINUTES; OVERNIGHT MARINATING /
OVEN TIME: 45 MINUTES / EASY

MARINATED LEG OF LAMB WITH JUNIPER BERRIES

SERVES 8

A tender, juicy leg of lamb cooked with hardly any fat comes as a wonderful surprise to those who think they don't like lamb, and in fact when you offer people lamb cooked this way they often cannot recognize it. (Lamb fat has a flavor that many people dislike.) Having the butcher remove the upper bone makes it very easy to carve, and in this case a classic game marinade (often used for venison) adds a tantalizing flavor.

1 *leg of lamb, 6 pounds (see below)*	*Salt and pepper*
¼ *cup red wine vinegar*	3 *tablespoons butter, softened*
2 *tablespoons olive oil*	3 *cups Brown Veal Stock (page 302) or canned beef broth*
2 *slices onion*	
1 *bay leaf*	
1 *sprig parsley*	2 *teaspoons cornstarch*
1 *clove garlic, crushed*	1 *tablespoon cold water*
2 *sprigs fresh thyme, or pinch dried*	1 *tablespoon red currant jelly*
5 *juniper berries*	*Pinch dry mustard powder*

Have your butcher remove the hip joint and femur from the lamb, leaving a small cavity. This makes the lamb much easier to carve, and the seasoning can penetrate from the inside. Remove fell (papery skin) and all but a very thin layer of fat from the meat.

The day before, combine vinegar, oil, onion, bay leaf, parsley, garlic, thyme, juniper berries, and salt and pepper to taste in a large dish. Place the lamb in the marinade, and turn to coat it well, making sure some marinade goes inside the cavity. Cover, and refrigerate for 24 hours. Turn meat occasionally.

The next day, preheat convection oven to 375 degrees. Drain meat and reserve marinade. Pat meat dry and tie into a compact shape with kitchen string. Rub with butter, and sprinkle lightly with salt and pepper. Place on a rack, and rest rack across roasting pan so air can circulate. Roast for 1 hour or until internal temperature reaches 145 degrees for medium-rare meat. Remove lamb from oven and let stand in a warm place for 20 minutes so juices can redistribute, which makes the meat easier to carve. Place roasting pan over medium-high heat. Strain marinade, reserving the liquid, and fry the onion slices and herbs in the roasting pan for 1 minute. Spoon off and discard fat. Add marinade liquid and beef broth, and boil until reduced by one third, about 15 minutes. Strain into a saucepan.

Just before serving time, return sauce to boiling point. Dissolve cornstarch in water, stir into sauce, and add currant jelly and mustard. Cook for 1 minute, until clear and slightly thickened. Taste for seasoning.

PREPARATION TIME: 30 MINUTES; OVERNIGHT MARINATING   /
OVEN TIME: 1 HOUR   /   EASY

RACK OF LAMB WITH ROSEMARY AND BREAD CRUMBS

Unfailingly delicious, this classic herb-and-breadcrumb-coated rack of lamb is the kind of entrée you can enjoy at a good restaurant—for a hefty price. There are only two secrets to success: One is that the butcher must "French cut" the rack so that the rib bones are exposed, the fat is all shaved off, and the chine bone is cut out to simplify carving. The other is that you must not overcook the meat.

1 *rack of lamb, 8 to 9 ribs, prepared by butcher in a "French cut" with rib bones exposed (see below)*

Salt and pepper

1 *teaspoon fresh rosemary, or ½ teaspoon dried*

1 *tablespoon chopped fresh parsley*

½ *teaspoon chopped fresh thyme, or pinch dried*

1 *clove garlic, chopped*

½ *cup bread crumbs made from day-old white bread*

1 *tablespoon butter, softened*

½ *cup water*

Have your butcher prepare the rack of lamb by removing chine bone, cutting between rib bones, and trimming off *all* the fat. Save bones for sauce.

Preheat convection oven to 375 degrees. Season lamb with salt and pepper to taste, and place in a shallow roasting pan, surrounded by the bones. Roast for 15 minutes.

While lamb is cooking, combine rosemary, parsley, thyme, garlic, bread crumbs, and butter into a paste and flatten into a postcard size rectangle. Lay paste on top of lamb and continue roasting for a further 15 minutes. Remove meat and keep warm. Pour fat off roasting pan and place pan, with bones, over high heat. Add water and boil for 2 minutes, scraping the pan with a wooden spoon. Taste for seasoning and strain. Serve with lamb.

PREPARATION TIME: 10 MINUTES / OVEN TIME: 30 MINUTES / EASY

RACK OF LAMB
WITH HERBED YOGURT SAUCE

This rack of lamb could not be easier to prepare, and the elegant sauce is light, fresh tasting, and very simple to make. It's best to buy the lamb from a butcher who will "French cut" it. Packaged racks of lamb at the meat counter in a supermarket are almost invariably left with the chine bone and all the fat intact, and are simply sawed through at intervals. Quite aside from any health considerations, lamb fat has a rather strong flavor, and the chops tend to spread apart during roasting when cut this way. This means that they both exude their juices and get overcooked, which is a criminal thing to do to a fine cut of meat.

1 *rack of lamb, 8 to 9 ribs, prepared by butcher in a "French cut" with rib bones exposed (see below)*

1 *large clove garlic, unpeeled, cut in half*

Salt and pepper

1 *tablespoon olive oil*

1½ *cups plain yogurt (creamy Continental style preferred)*

2 *tablespoons finely chopped peeled, seeded tomato*

2 *tablespoons finely chopped onion*

2 *tablespoons finely chopped scallions, white bulb and half of green tops*

2 *tablespoons finely chopped peeled, seeded cucumber*

1 *tablespoon finely chopped fresh mint*

Have your butcher prepare the rack of lamb by removing the chine bone, cutting between and exposing the rib bones, and trimming off *all* fat.

Preheat convection oven to 375 degrees. Rub lamb with garlic, and season with salt and pepper to taste. Heat oil in a heavy ovenproof skillet and brown the meat very quickly, about 5 minutes. (This seals in the juices.) Transfer skillet to the oven and roast for 25 minutes. Let stand for 10 minutes before carving.

Heat the yogurt, but do not allow to boil. Spread a pool of yogurt on each heated dinner plate and scatter with tomato, onion, scallion, cucumber, and mint. Top with two or three lamb chops.

PREPARATION TIME: 15 MINUTES / OVEN TIME: 25 MINUTES / EASY

SHOULDER LAMB CHOPS WITH EGGPLANT AND LEMON

SERVES 4

The Bulgur Pilaf on page 205 goes well with this Middle Eastern family-style dish, which makes good use of eggplant, tomatoes, garlic, and lemon.

1 *tablespoon butter*

1 *tablespoon olive oil*

4 *shoulder lamb chops, 6 to 8 ounces each, trimmed of any excess fat*

1 *leek, white part and some green, rinsed well and diced*

1 *onion, chopped*

2 *eggplants, 1 pound each, peeled and diced*

2 *lemons, peel and pith removed, cut into sections between membranes*

4 *tomatoes, peeled, seeded, and quartered*

2 *cloves garlic, chopped*

1 *teaspoon fresh chopped thyme, or ½ teaspoon dried*

1 *bay leaf*
   Salt and pepper

2 *tablespoons chopped fresh parsley*

1 *cup water*

Preheat convection oven to 350 degrees. Heat butter and olive oil in a large ovenproof casserole. Brown chops quickly, about 1 minute on each side, and add all the remaining ingredients, except the water. Stir well, and simmer for 10 minutes. Add water and bring to a boil. Cover pan and transfer to the oven. Bake for 1¼ hours, until very tender.

PREPARATION TIME: 15 MINUTES / OVEN TIME: 1¼ HOURS / EASY

SHOULDER LAMB CHOPS WITH LEEKS AND POTATOES

A French country dish that can be kept warm almost indefinitely, the combination of meltingly tender lamb, mild-tasting leeks, and sliced potatoes that have taken up lots of herb flavors and meat juices is irresistible. Very easy to prepare, it's the kind of dish that gave French housewives their great culinary reputation.

4 *shoulder lamb chops, 8 ounces each*

1 *tablespoon vegetable oil*

1 *leek, white part and some green stem, rinsed well and chopped*

1 *onion, chopped*

2 *stalks celery, chopped*

2 *cloves garlic, mashed and chopped*

4 *all-purpose potatoes, 7 ounces each, peeled and thickly sliced*

Pinch thyme

1 *bay leaf*

Salt and pepper

2 *cups water (approximately)*

Preheat convection oven to 350 degrees. Trim any excess fat off lamb chops. Heat oil in an enameled cast-iron casserole and brown chops very quickly, two at a time, about 1 minute on each side. Remove and reserve.

In the same pan, sauté leek, onion, celery, and garlic until lightly colored. Add sliced potatoes and mix well. Add thyme, bay leaf, and salt and pepper to taste. Bury lamb chops under the vegetables and barely cover with water. Bring to a boil. Cover surface with a circle of buttered baking parchment, or use the paper wrappers from three sticks of butter, and place lid on pan. Transfer to the oven and bake for 1¼ hours.

PREPARATION TIME: 15 MINUTES / OVEN TIME: 1¼ HOURS / EASY

SIRLOIN OF LAMB WITH PESTO-MUSHROOM STUFFING

This tender cut of meat provides an excellent small roast for four—or two depending on appetites—in a little over half an hour. Pesto, a savory paste of basil, garlic, and Parmesan cheese, is generally used as a sauce for pasta but goes with lamb extremely well.

1 *boneless loin of lamb,*
  1½ pounds

1 *tablespoon butter,*
  softened

½ *small onion, finely*
  chopped

2 *mushrooms, finely*
  chopped

½ *cup bread crumbs made*
  from day-old white
  bread

2 *tablespoons Genoese*
  Pesto Sauce (page 304)
  or store-bought pesto
  sauce

Salt and pepper

1 *cup water*

1 *tablespoon honey*

1 *tablespoon cider vinegar*

1 *tablespoon chopped fresh*
  mint or parsley

Preheat convection oven to 400 degrees. Trim any skin and all fat from lamb and completely sever the piece of filet, if this is present. (Reserve the filet, cutting off any membrane.) Butterfly-cut the loin: Place meat skin side down on a work surface. Make a cut down the center without going all the way through the meat. Next make a horizontal cut on either side, starting from the first cut, stopping short of the edge. Open meat out flat into four "panels." It may look a little uneven.

Heat half the butter in a skillet and simmer onion for 5 minutes, until soft. Add mushrooms and simmer until liquid has evaporated, about 5 minutes. Remove skillet from the heat and add bread crumbs and pesto. Taste to see if salt is necessary (the pesto is salty), and add pepper to taste. Spread the stuffing on the meat, place the filet in the center, and roll up. Tie meat with string, and place in a shallow roasting pan. Spread with remaining butter and roast for 30 minutes.

Remove meat and let stand for 10 minutes in a warm place. Place baking pan over high heat, add the water, bring to a boil and deglaze, scraping up any coagulated brown juices.

Combine honey and vinegar in a saucepan, bring to a boil, and allow to caramelize, which will take about 3 minutes. Add liquid from roasting pan and reduce by half, about 5 minutes. Add mint, and salt and pepper to taste. Carve meat into slices (it should be pink in the middle), and serve on heated plates with the sauce.

PREPARATION TIME: 20 MINUTES / OVEN TIME: 30 MINUTES

SIRLOIN OF LAMB
WITH PROSCIUTTO AND MINT
SERVES 4

Just the right size for a small roast for two or four (depending on appetites and the rest of the menu), sirloin of lamb is beautifully tender and very easy to carve. The prosciutto adds a piquant flavor and combines well with the herb stuffing.

1 *boneless loin of lamb,*
  1½ to 2 pounds
1 *tablespoon butter*
2 *tablespoons chopped*
  onion
1 *clove garlic, mashed*
  and chopped
1 *tablespoon chopped fresh*
  mint
1 *tablespoon chopped fresh*
  parsley

1 *cup bread crumbs made*
  from day-old white
  bread
  Salt and pepper
1 *large egg, beaten*
4 *ounces prosciutto, very*
  thinly sliced
½ *onion, unpeeled,*
  roughly chopped
1 *cup water*
  Mint sprigs, for garnish

Preheat convection oven to 400 degrees. Trim any skin or fat from lamb, and completely sever the piece of filet, if this is present. Trim membrane from filet, and reserve meat. Butterfly-cut the loin: Place meat skin side down on a work surface. Cut along center without going all the way through; then make a horizontal cut on either side starting from the center cut, stopping short of the edge. Open meat out flat in four "panels." It may look a little uneven.

Heat butter in a skillet and sauté onion and garlic for 5 minutes, until softened. Remove from the heat and combine with mint, parsley, bread crumbs, salt and pepper to taste, and egg.

Lay meat out flat, skin side down, and spread with a layer of stuffing. Top with a layer of prosciutto slices and then another layer of stuffing. (If you have the extra filet, wrap this in stuffing and then in prosciutto, and place in center.) Wrap the meat around the stuffing and turn it over. Lay slices of prosciutto around and on top of the meat, and tie with string. Place in a shallow baking pan with chopped unpeeled onion (this adds color to sauce), and roast for 30 minutes.

Remove meat and let stand for 10 minutes in a warm place. Place baking pan over high heat, add water, and deglaze, scraping up the coagulated dark brown juices. Reduce by one third, which will take about 5 minutes. Strain sauce, and taste for seasoning. Carve meat into ¾-inch-thick slices. Place on hot plates with a little of the sauce and a mint sprig.

PREPARATION TIME: 20 MINUTES / OVEN TIME: 30 MINUTES

PAELLA WITH RABBIT

This is a superb one-dish meal that is authentically Spanish. Paella can contain rabbit or chicken or sausage or seafood, or sometimes a mixture of ingredients, depending on what happens to be available in that particular part of Spain. Be sure to use imported Valencia or Italian short-grain rice, as it has a very special quality: When cooked, the grains retain their shape and yet stay creamy. Ordinary rice would go mushy here.

1 *fresh frying rabbit, 3 pounds*
Flour for dredging
1 *to 2 tablespoons olive oil*
1 *tablespoon butter*
1 *onion, chopped*
2 *cloves garlic, chopped*
1 *red bell pepper, cut into julienne*
1 *green bell pepper, cut into julienne*

1 *cup Italian Arborio or Spanish short-grain rice*
2½ *cups Chicken Stock (page 300) or canned chicken broth*
Pinch saffron
Dash chili powder
1 *teaspoon salt*
Black pepper

Preheat convection oven to 325 degrees. Cut rabbit into serving pieces, discarding back and reserving liver for another purpose (see illustration). Just before frying, dredge with flour (if allowed to stand, the flour will become soggy and the rabbit pieces will not brown appetizingly). Heat olive oil and butter in a large skillet and brown rabbit on all sides, about 10 minutes. Set aside.

In the same skillet, adding a little more olive oil if necessary, cook the onions for 5 minutes. Add garlic and julienned bell peppers and sauté for 2 minutes. Add rice, stirring to coat all the grains with oil. Stir in chicken stock, saffron, chili powder, salt, and pepper to taste. Bring to a boil and then transfer to a shallow baking dish. (One of Spanish earthenware is nice, but not essential.) Bury the pieces of rabbit in the rice, and bake for 30 minutes, until rice and rabbit are tender.

PREPARATION TIME: 30 MINUTES / OVEN TIME: 30 MINUTES / EASY

To cut a frying rabbit into serving portions, first cut off the back legs. Cut off and discard the end of the backbone with the hip joints. Remove and discard any loose fat as you work; it has a "gamey" taste. Cut off front legs. Cut the meaty saddle crossways in two or three pieces. The neck and rib sections can be included while cooking the rabbit, as they will add flavor to the sauce, but should not be served as there is so little meat on them. A serving portion should consist of a back leg, or a front leg and a piece of the saddle. The kidneys and liver can be added to the sauce at the last minute, but should not be overcooked.

RABBIT WITH LIME, MUSTARD, AND CREAM SAUCE

The tender white meat of rabbit is becoming increasingly popular in the United States. In this recipe, which is quick and easy to prepare, the mild meat is combined with lime, mustard, garlic, and cream for an exceptionally tasty result. Serve with rice or crusty French bread to take up the good sauce.

1 *fresh frying rabbit, 3 pounds*

2 *limes*

3 *shallots, peeled*

3 *cloves garlic, peeled*

2 *tablespoons olive oil*
  Salt and pepper

1 *tablespoon sugar*

1 *tablespoon Dijon mustard*

¼ *cup white wine vinegar*

1 *cup Chicken Stock (page 300) or canned chicken broth*

1 *cup heavy cream*

½ *cup sour cream*

Preheat convection oven to 350 degrees. Cut rabbit into serving pieces (see illustration on page 157), reserving liver for another use. Pare skin off limes and simmer lime peel in water for 10 minutes; then cut into julienne. Place rabbit pieces in a shallow baking dish large enough to hold them in a single layer. Add shallots, garlic, olive oil, salt and pepper to taste, sugar, mustard, and juice from the 2 limes. Combine well, turning rabbit to coat well. Roast for 30 minutes, turning meat over halfway through to absorb seasonings.

Remove baking dish from the oven and stir in vinegar, chicken broth, cream, and julienned lime zest. Return dish to the oven and bake for 30 minutes, turning meat over halfway through. Just before serving, stir in sour cream.

PREPARATION TIME: 20 MINUTES / OVEN TIME: 1 HOUR

RECIPES FOR THE BRAVE

SERVES 8
AS A FIRST COURSE
OR 4 AS AN ENTRÉE

MEDALLIONS OF MONKFISH WITH BROCCOLI PURÉE AND BEET SAUCE

Rounds of monkfish are placed on a small mound of broccoli purée and surrounded with a ribbon of wine-colored beet sauce. Monkfish has a wonderful flavor and a texture not unlike lobster, but it can be tough and chewy if it is not expertly trimmed, so it's best to pay a little more and buy it from a knowledgeable fish dealer.

2 *beets, 8 ounces total*

2 *tablespoons red wine vinegar*

1 *cup bottled clam juice*

1½ *pounds broccoli, heads only*

Salt and pepper

Pinch nutmeg

1 *tablespoon butter*

1 *tablespoon olive oil*

1 *filet of monkfish, 1 to 1¼ pounds, as short and thick as possible, very well trimmed*

Preheat convection oven to 350 degrees. Trim beets and bake on oven rack for 1½ hours, or until they give to light pressure. (Time depends on variety and age of beets.) Peel, chop, and place in a food processor with vinegar and clam juice. Purée. Strain into a saucepan and set aside.

Cook broccoli heads in boiling salted water until tender, about 7 minutes. Drain, and place in food processor with salt and pepper to taste, nutmeg, and butter. Purée, then transfer to a separate saucepan and reserve for up to 2 hours.

Raise oven heat to 375 degrees. Place olive oil in a small oval ovenproof dish and heat in oven for 2 minutes. Add monkfish to dish, turning to coat with the hot oil. Bake for 10 to 12 minutes, turning once, until fish is firm and white.

Gently reheat broccoli purée and beet sauce. Transfer monkfish to a chopping board, and slice into thick medallions. Stir the fish cooking juices into the beet sauce. On each heated dinner plate arrange a mound of brilliant green broccoli purée. Top with a medallion of monkfish, and grind some black pepper over it. Surround broccoli with a ribbon of beet sauce.

PREPARATION TIME: 30 MINUTES / OVEN TIME: 1½ HOURS; 10 TO 12 MINUTES

SOLE AND SALMON WITH BASIL IN BAKED TOMATOES

Looking for a luxury three-star presentation? This one is worth the time and trouble and will dazzle your guests. It can be prepared ahead and baked at the last minute, leaving only the sauce to assemble.

8 *small filets of sole, 1 pound total*

8 *large spinach leaves*

1 *pound filet of salmon, cut into 8 thin slices*

32 *small fresh basil leaves*

1 *tablespoon butter*

1 *tablespoon chopped shallots*

8 *ounces mushrooms, finely diced*

Salt and pepper

½ *cup dry white wine*

8 *large tomatoes*

½ *cup heavy cream*

Beurre manié (1 teaspoon soft butter mixed with 1 teaspoon flour)

1 *tablespoon chopped fresh chives or parsley*

Preheat convection oven to 350 degrees. Flatten the filets of sole slightly with a cleaver. Cover each one with a spinach leaf and top with a slice of salmon filet. Arrange four basil leaves in a row on top, then roll up and fasten with a toothpick. Spread butter in an ovenproof skillet or sauté pan, and scatter with shallots and mushrooms. Place fish rolls on top, and season lightly with salt and pepper. Add wine and bring to a boil. Cover, transfer to the oven, and bake for 5 minutes.

While the fish is cooking, peel tomatoes (dip in boling water for a few seconds to loosen skin). Cut the tops off the tomatoes and discard. Scoop out and discard seeds and core. Sprinkle inside of tomatoes with salt and pepper. Place tomato shells in a buttered heatproof serving dish.

Remove toothpicks from rolled filets, and place fish rolls inside tomatoes—they will be slightly higher than the tomato shells. (Reserve pan with mushrooms and shallots.) Bake for 5 minutes. Cut tops off fish rolls to show pinwheel design, reserving the cut pieces.

While filled tomatoes are baking, add cream to sauté pan containing shallots and mushrooms. Bring to a boil and reduce to ¾ cup, about 5 minutes. Add the beurre manié, stirring with a whisk, and cook for 1 minute, until thickened. Add chives.

Pour a little sauce on each heated plate. Top with stuffed tomato, laying the cut piece of fish roll alongside, flat side up and leaning against the tomato.

PREPARATION TIME: 20 MINUTES / OVEN TIME: 10 MINUTES

HALIBUT WITH AVOCADO MOUSSE IN PUFF PASTRY

SERVES 4

An avocado mousse mixture, made in a food processor, is spread on a piece of halibut filet and sandwiched between two sheets of puff pastry. These are sealed together and cut into a simple fish shape, which is decorated with "scales" cut with the edge of a large, plain pastry tip. The pastry puffs up dramatically in the oven into a flaky golden fish, which is presented at the table with a simple Lemon Butter Sauce. Don't serve fish or seafood for a first course, or more pastry or lemon in the dessert.

12 ounces filet of halibut
1 tablespoon Cognac
½ teaspoon chopped fresh tarragon, or ¼ teaspoon dried
½ avocado, about 3 ounces
1 large egg yolk
1 cup heavy cream
1 teaspoon fresh lemon juice

Salt and pepper
Dash cayenne pepper
Dash nutmeg
8 ounces Quick Puff Pastry dough (page 244), or ½ package frozen puff pastry sheets, thawed
1 egg, beaten
1 cup Lemon Butter Sauce (page 306)
Tarragon sprigs, for garnish

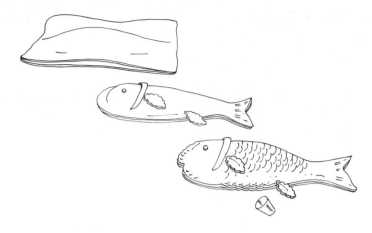

Remove any skin from halibut. Trim into an oval shape measuring approximately 7 by 3 inches, weighing about 8 ounces. Sprinkle with Cognac and tarragon. Cover and marinate for 1 hour in the refrigerator.

Place leftover halibut trimmings (about 2 to 3 ounces) in the bowl of a food processor and grind until smooth. Add avocado, egg yolk, cream, lemon juice, salt and pepper to taste, cayenne, and nutmeg. Process to form a smooth purée. Cover and chill for 1 hour.

On a lightly floured surface, roll puff pastry out ⅛ inch thick and cut into two strips, one slightly wider than the other. Place halibut filet on the smaller one and cover filet with avocado mousse. Brush edges of pastry with cold water and cover with the second strip. Press around the edges of the fish to seal; then form fins and a tail by cutting away excess pastry with a knife. Use pastry trimmings to outline the head and eye (see illustration). Chill until ready to use.

Preheat convection oven to 400 degrees. Brush pastry with beaten egg, and form fish scales in the dough by making shallow overlapping cuts with the large end of a pastry tube held at an angle. Bake for 20 to 25 minutes, until well puffed and golden brown. Present baked fish on a platter with a few sprigs of tarragon for decoration, and serve Lemon Butter Sauce separately.

PREPARATION TIME: 30 MINUTES; 1 HOUR MARINATING AND CHILLING /
OVEN TIME: 20 TO 25 MINUTES

ORANGE ROUGHY WITH POTATO GALETTE

This is a novel way to present fish: overlapping "scales" of thinly sliced golden brown potatoes cover the filets, which are served with a tasty leek sauce. A small quantity of rendered duck fat is the best fat to use here, as it is flavorful and browns the potatoes beautifully without danger of scorching. (Save the rendered fat when cooking any of the duck recipes in this book; then strain and refrigerate or freeze.)

3 *long oval white potatoes (preferably White Rose), 5 ounces each*

Salt

2 *filets of orange roughy, 8 ounces each*

White pepper

1 *tablespoon rendered duck fat or butter*

1 *leek, white part and some green stem, rinsed well and shredded*

Pinch sugar

2 *tablespoons water*

Juice of ½ lemon

4 *tablespoons unsalted butter, softened*

Preheat convection oven to 400 degrees. Peel potatoes, and slice very thin on a mandoline or in a food processor. Do not wash slices; the starch holds them together. Sprinkle with salt. Cut fish filets in half to make four equal-sized wedges, and season with white pepper to taste. Arrange "scales" of overlapping potato slices on both sides of the fish filets, turning them over with a metal spatula. (The potatoes will stick to the fish because of the potato starch drawn out by the salt.)

Heat duck fat in an ovenproof nonstick skillet, and brown the pieces of potato-covered fish on one side, about 2 minutes. Carefully turn them over and transfer the skillet to the oven. Bake for 8 minutes.

While fish is baking, place shredded leek, salt to taste, sugar, and water in a skillet. Bring to a boil, cover, and cook for 1 minute. Remove leek with a slotted spoon and keep warm. Add lemon juice to skillet and bring to a boil. Whisk in butter a little at a time.

Turn fish over onto heated dinner plates so that the best browned side is uppermost. Surround with sauce, and scatter sauce with shredded leek.

PREPARATION TIME: 20 MINUTES / OVEN TIME: 8 MINUTES

SHRIMP WITH SOUFFLÉ TOPPING

SERVES 4 TO 6

A three-star presentation for very special occasions, this consists of sautéed shrimp in a delicious wine sauce, topped with a soufflé mixture. The soufflé can be simply smoothed on with a spatula, or you can pipe it out of a pastry bag fitted with a large star tube, forming decorative swirls.

1 *pound large fresh shrimp, unshelled*
1 *tablespoon butter*
1 *tablespoon olive oil*
2 *cloves garlic, chopped*
2 *shallots, chopped*
2 *tablespoons chopped carrot*
1 *tablespoon chopped celery*
5 *tablespoons chopped onion*
1 *tablespoon chopped fresh tarragon, or 1½ teaspoons dried*
  Salt and pepper
2 *tablespoons Cognac*
2 *teaspoons all-purpose flour*

½ *cup white wine*
½ *cup water*
1 *tablespoon tomato paste*
  Pinch cayenne pepper
½ *cup heavy cream*

SOUFFLÉ TOPPING

1 *tablespoon butter*
2 *tablespoons all-purpose flour*
½ *cup milk*
  Salt and pepper
  Pinch cayenne pepper
2 *large egg yolk*
½ *cup grated imported Swiss cheese*
4 *large egg whites*

Shell and devein shrimp, reserving the shells. (If possible, get shrimp with heads, as they add flavor to the sauce.) Butter a shallow 2-cup oval or round ovenproof baking dish, one attractive enough to bring to the table. Tin-lined copper is the best, as it holds heat so well.

Heat butter in a heavy skillet and sauté shrimp for 2 minutes. Remove and place in prepared pan. Heat olive oil in the same skillet and add shrimp shells, and heads if available. Sauté over medium-high heat for 2 minutes, then add garlic, shallots, carrots, celery, onions, and tarragon. Season with salt and pepper to taste and cook, stirring often, for 10 minutes. Add Cognac, bring to a boil, stirring well, and carefully set ablaze. When flame dies down, stir in flour. Add wine, water, and tomato paste, and simmer for 10 minutes. Strain mixture into a sauce pan, pressing down hard on the shells to extract all the good juices. Stir in cayenne and cream, bring to a boil, and taste for seasoning. Pour ¼ cup of this sauce over the shrimp, and keep the remainder warm.

Preheat convection oven to 350 degrees. Prepare topping: Melt butter in a small saucepan, and stir in flour. Then add milk, season with salt and pepper to taste and cayenne, and stir over medium heat until smooth and thick, about 1 minute. Remove from the heat, and whisk in egg yolks and cheese. Beat egg whites until stiff and fold into mixture. Spread over shrimp and smooth the top. Bake for 10 minutes, until puffed and golden brown. Serve from the pan at the table, pouring a little of the sauce around each portion.

PREPARATION TIME: 30 MINUTES / OVEN TIME: 10 MINUTES

WARM SHRIMP AND SOLE PÂTÉ WITH DILL

A spectacular first course for special occasions. Use whatever size shrimp you like, but make sure they're fresh.

There is enough pâté here to serve twelve, or you can halve the amount of Creamy Lemon Sauce and serve the remaining pâté cold with Yogurt Herb Sauce, below (the pâté will keep in the refrigerator for two or three days).

1 *pound fresh shrimp, peeled and deveined*

1 *pound very fresh filet of sole*

2 *large eggs*

¾ *teaspoon salt*

  Pinch cayenne pepper

  Pinch nutmeg

2 *cups heavy cream, well chilled*

2 *tablespoons finely chopped peeled red bell pepper*

1 *tablespoon chopped fresh tarragon*

CREAMY LEMON SAUCE

2 *cups heavy cream, at room temperature*

  Juice of 2 lemons

  Salt and white pepper

2 *tomatoes, peeled, seeded, and julienned*

  Fresh dill sprigs

Preheat convection oven to 300 degrees. Butter a 1-quart rectangular terrine or glass loaf pan, and set out a baking pan large enough to contain it.

Grind the shrimp and sole together in a food processor. Add eggs and process for 1 minute, then add salt, cayenne, and nutmeg. With motor running, add cream through the feed tube and process until smooth, scraping down the bowl with a rubber spatula as necessary. Do not overmix or pâté will turn to butter—it should just hold its shape. Stir in bell pepper and tarragon.

Pack mixture into prepared terrine and smooth top with a rubber spatula dipped in cold water. Cover surface with buttered baking parchment, placing the buttered side directly on top of pâté. (Or use two paper wrappers from butter packages.) Place terrine in baking pan. Add enough hot water to reach halfway up sides of terrine. Bake for 30 minutes, or until a knife blade inserted in the center of the pâté comes out clean. Allow to cool for 5 minutes, and meanwhile warm the required number of serving plates.

Prepare sauce: Whip cream lightly, until it just starts to hold its shape, and season with the lemon juice. Add salt and white pepper to taste.

Unmold pâté and cut into ½-inch-thick slices. Spread ¼ cup of sauce on each plate, and top with a slice of pâté. Place strips of tomato and sprigs of dill on top of the sauce, around the pâté.

PREPARATION TIME: 15 MINUTES / OVEN TIME: 30 MINUTES

YOGURT HERB SAUCE   *SERVES 6*

2 *sprigs parsley, stems*
   trimmed
2 *leaves fresh chervil*
6 *leaves fresh tarragon*

½ *cup dry white wine,*
   such as Chardonnay
¼ *cup mild vegetable oil*
1 *cup plain yogurt*
   Salt
   White pepper

In a blender or food processor, combine all ingredients except the yogurt. Blend well. Add the yogurt and mix until smooth. Season to taste with salt and pepper.

TERRINE OF SPINACH
AND MUSHROOM CRÊPES

Tender French crêpes are used to line a loaf pan, and more crêpes are rolled up with a filling of spinach before being layered in the pan with thinly sliced prosciutto and a creamy mushroom sauce. The terrine should be lukewarm when unmolded, not hot, or it might not hold its shape. When sliced, the circles of crêpes with their green filling are divided by layers of red prosciutto—very attractive.

8 *Basic French Crêpes*
  (page 298)
1 *pound small, young,*
  tender spinach leaves
2 *tablespoons butter*
  Salt and pepper
  Dash nutmeg
1 *shallot, chopped*

10 *ounces mushrooms,*
   sliced
   Juice of ½ lemon
1 *tablespoon all-purpose*
  flour
½ *cup heavy cream*
2½ *ounces thinly sliced*
   prosciutto
1 *cup plain yogurt*

Line an 8½ by 4½ by 3-inch loaf pan with a sheet of baking parchment large enough to cover the top as well. (The short ends of the pan need not be lined.) Overlap two crêpes inside, letting the top third of each crêpe hang over the side of the pan.

Rinse the spinach well and chop off the roots, but leave stems attached. Blanch for 1 minute in boiling salted water, and chop coarsely. Melt 1 tablespoon of the butter in a skillet and let it brown a little. Add spinach, and season with salt, pepper, and nutmeg. Sauté for 1 minute and set aside.

In a separate skillet, melt remaining butter and simmer shallot for 1 minute. Add mushrooms and lemon juice, and stir in flour. Season lighly with salt, pepper, and nutmeg. Then add cream, bring to a boil, and cook for 2 minutes. Reserve for filling crêpes.

Preheat convection oven to 300 degrees. Fill remaining six crêpes with spinach mixture, and roll into cigar shapes. Place three spinach

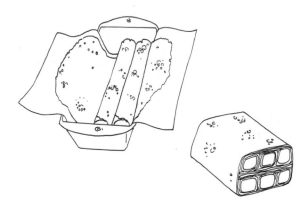

rolls in the bottom of the loaf pan. Cover with half the prosciutto and top with the mushroom mixture. Cover with remaining three spinach rolls and remaining prosciutto. Fold the ends of the overhanging crêpes over the top. Butter the baking parchment flaps, and fold them over the top of the mold. (Terrine can be prepared ahead to this point, covered, and refrigerated.) Bake for 10 minutes.

Let terrine cool for 20 minutes before turning it out upside down on a platter.

While the terrine is cooling, warm (but do not boil) the yogurt. Cut terrine into 1- to 1½-inch slices, and arrange on hot dinner plates with warm yogurt sauce to one side.

PREPARATION TIME: 45 MINUTES / OVEN TIME: 10 MINUTES

QUAIL WITH CRACKED CORIANDER AND WILTED SPINACH SALAD

A festive and appetizing first course: boned quail served on a bed of vinaigrette-dressed spinach tossed with hot, crisp bacon. They take only 6 minutes to roast, so all the other ingredients are prepared ahead. It is perfectly acceptable to eat certain foods with your fingers—these crisp little birds are a case in point. Offer Baguettes (page 210) or other French bread to mop up the good juices.

4 *quail, 4 ounces each*

3 *teaspoons coriander seeds*

3 *tablespoons olive oil*
   Salt and pepper

1 *tablespoon Cognac*

4 *strips lean bacon*

2 *cups small spinach leaves*

¼ *cup Vinaigrette (page 308)*

Bone the quail (see illustration on page 93) and cut each one in half, or buy them ready-boned. Crack the coriander seeds coarsely, using a mortar and pestle or the base of a heavy skillet. Heat 1 tablespoon of the olive oil in a heavy skillet and sauté coriander for 3 to 4 minutes. Place quail halves in a shallow baking pan. Sprinkle with coriander, the remaining 2 tablespoons of olive oil, salt and pepper to taste, and Cognac. Turn to coat well, and marinate at room temperature for 1 to 2 hours, covered with plastic wrap.

Cut bacon into julienne. Rinse and dry spinach leaves. Just before serving, fry bacon and toss with spinach leaves and vinaigrette.

Preheat convection oven to 400 degrees. Roast quail for 6 minutes. Divide spinach salad among four plates. Cut each quail half into a leg and breast portion, then reassemble on the beds of spinach and serve at once.

PREPARATION TIME: 30 MINUTES; 1 TO 2 HOURS MARINATING / OVEN TIME: 6 MINUTES

CORNISH GAME HEN "PEARS" WITH BRAISED CABBAGE AND BACON SERVES 4

In this recipe, boned hen halves are stuffed and formed into pear shapes, with the drumstick bone forming the stalk. It's a very elegant and impressive presentation for a dinner party, and not all that hard to do. Gnocchi Parisian style (page 57) is a good choice for a first course, and Peaches Stuffed with Coconut and Vanilla Wafers (page 285) would make a suitable dessert.

2 *Cornish game hens,*
  1¼ pounds each
  Salt and pepper
6 *scallions, chopped,*
  white bulb and half of
  green tops
½ *clove garlic, minced*
1 *cup bread crumbs*
  made from day-old
  white bread
  Pinch thyme
  Pinch oregano

1 *large egg*
4 *strips lean bacon*
1¼ *pounds green cabbage*
  (curly open-leaf type if
  possible)
2 *to 3 teaspoons butter,*
  softened
¾ *cup Chicken Stock*
  (page 300) or canned
  chicken broth
½ *cup heavy cream*

Preheat convection oven to 375 degrees. Remove giblets from hens and reserve. Chop off wing tips. Bone birds, leaving only the drumstick in place, and cut in half. (See illustration on page 93.) Reserve bones. Lay meat skin side down on a work surface, and sprinkle with salt and pepper to taste.

To make stuffing, combine scallions, garlic, trimmed livers from game hens, bread crumbs, salt and pepper to taste, thyme, oregano, and egg in the bowl of a food processor. Process very briefly, until just mixed. There should be about 6 tablespoons. Divide among the four hen halves and form into pear shapes as shown in the illustration.

Stack bacon and cut into 1-inch pieces. Quarter cabbage, remove and discard core, and chop coarsely. Bring a pot of salted water to a boil. Blanch cabbage for 1 minute and drain.

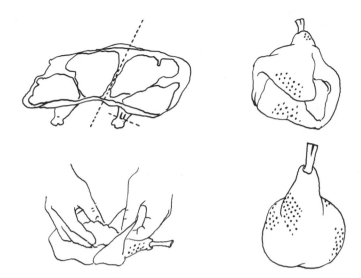

In a large deep enameled cast-iron casserole, heat bacon until the fat starts to run, about 3 minutes. Add cabbage, and season with salt and pepper to taste. Place game hen "pears" on top, pushing them into the cabbage slightly so that they will stand bone up. Rub meat with softened butter. Place reserved bones and giblets around and between game hens, and add chicken broth. Bake, uncovered, for 25 minutes. Then add cream and continue cooking for another 10 minutes.

Remove game hens and keep warm. Pick out and discard bones and giblets. Place casserole over high heat and reduce liquid slightly, about 5 minutes. Make a bed of cabbage on each heated dinner plate, and spoon cream sauce around the edge. Top with a game hen "pear," "stalk" pointing upward.

PREPARATION TIME: 30 MINUTES   /   OVEN TIME: 35 MINUTES

CORNISH GAME HENS
WITH KUMQUATS

Game hen halves are served on a bed of sherry-flavored wild rice surrounded with a truly memorable sauce and caramelized kumquats —those miniature oval Chinese oranges that are now raised in Texas and California, among other states.

2 *Cornish game hens, 1¼ pounds each*

½ *onion, unpeeled, quartered*

1 *small carrot, cut up*

Salt and pepper

Pinch thyme

4 *teaspoons olive oil*

1 *teaspoon butter*

Wild Rice Pilaf (page 207)

1 *tablespoon Dry Sack sherry*

SAUCE

6 *ounces kumquats*

Pinch nutmeg

Pinch cinnamon

2 *tablespoons sugar*

2 *cups Chicken Stock (page 300) or canned chicken broth*

1 *tablespoon sherry wine vinegar*

Preheat convection oven to 375 degrees. Cut game hens in half, and cut out breastbone, wishbone, and backbone. Trim off wing tips. Make a little slit in the skin near the tail, and tuck knob of drumstick inside, to keep meat flat while roasting. Chop bones and giblets and place in a shallow roasting pan with onion and carrot. Lay game hen halves bone side up on top. Season with salt and pepper to taste and thyme, and sprinkle with olive oil. Roast for 30 minutes, turning skin side up after 15 minutes. Remove game hens from pan and keep warm.

Prepare the sauce: Wash kumquats and remove stems, if any. Place in a small heavy saucepan with nutmeg, cinnamon, and sugar. Cover with water and boil for 15 minutes, or until liquid has evaporated and kumquats are lighly caramelized. Remove fruit with a slotted spoon, reserving liquid in pan. Place kumquats in a sieve and set over the pan.

174 CONVECTION CUISINE

Pour fat off roasting pan and place pan over high heat. Add chicken stock and deglaze, stirring up bones and vegetables. Reduce to 1 cup, about 7 minutes. Heat the caramelized kumquat liquid, and add vinegar. Strain the pan sauce into the kumquat glaze, and reduce to ¾ cup. When ready to serve, add kumquats to the sauce and heat through, about 1 minute.

Heat butter in a nonstick skillet and add cooked rice pilaf. When very hot, stir in sherry and cook for 1 minute. Pull the rib bones off each game hen half—they will come away very easily. For each serving, arrange a bed of pilaf on a warmed dinner plate and top with a hen half. Spoon a band of sauce around the rice, and arrange six or seven kumquats in it at equal intervals.

PREPARATION TIME: 35 MINUTES / OVEN TIME: 30 MINUTES

SQUAB WITH GARLIC, PEA PURÉE, AND STUFFED MUSHROOMS

Squab (farm-raised young pigeon) is an expensive delicacy, and must be cooked just right to be at its best. The breast should always be served rare. It is perfectly all right to eat squab with your fingers, and in this instance diners are expected to squeeze the mellow garlic paste out of the husks with a fork, which is also a little messy but very enjoyable. When preparing this dish, you will find that a microwave oven is handy for reheating the purée and the stuffed mushrooms without changing their textures.

2 *squab, 1 pound each*

2 *teaspoons chopped fresh thyme*

Salt and pepper

16 *fat garlic cloves, unpeeled*

1 *tablespoon mild vegetable oil*

1 *tablespoon sherry wine vinegar*

½ *cup Brown Veal Stock (page 302) or canned beef broth*

PURÉE

8 *ounces green peas*

Pinch chopped fresh thyme

Salt

Pinch sugar

4 *leaves fresh mint*

1 *teaspoon butter*

STUFFED MUSHROOMS

3 *tablespoons butter*

16 *mushroom caps, 1½ inches across*

1 *shallot, finely chopped*

1 *tablespoon Cognac*

Pinch thyme

Pinch oregano

Pinch marjoram

¼ *cup bread crumbs made from day-old white bread*

1 *clove garlic, crushed*

2 *teaspoons chopped fresh parsley*

Salt and pepper

To prepare squab, cut off and reserve wing tips, and reserve livers for the stuffing. To hold legs in place while squab are roasting, make two little slits in the skin near the tail and insert ends of legs. Season with thyme, and salt and pepper to taste, sprinkling the birds inside and out. Place unpeeled garlic cloves in a roasting pan along with wing tips, neck, and giblets. Put squab on top, sprinkle with oil, and set aside

Make purée: Cook peas in boiling salted water for 1 minute. Plunge into cold water to set the color, and drain. Place in a food processor with thyme, salt, sugar, and mint, and purée. When almost ready to serve, heat the butter in a small pan, add the purée, and warm through.

Prepare mushrooms: Heat 1 tablespoon of the butter in a skillet and sauté mushroom caps for 5 minutes. Set them aside.

Dice reserved squab livers into sixteen pieces. Heat remaining 2 tablespoons of butter in another skillet, and sauté shallot for 2 minutes, until softened. Add diced livers and sauté very quickly, about 30 seconds. Add Cognac, and carefully set aflame. When the flame has died, stir in herbs, bread crumbs, garlic, parsley, and salt and pepper to taste, and cook for 30 seconds. Divide this mixture among the mushroom caps, and arrange on a baking sheet. When almost ready to serve, heat the stuffed mushroom caps in a 325-degree oven until just warmed through, about 3 minutes.

Preheat convection oven to 400 degrees. Roast squab for 25 minutes, and then transfer birds from the pan to a carving board. Cut off breast (which must be pink) and wing portions and keep warm. Cut off legs and return them to roasting pan along with the carcasses. Roast legs for a further 10 minutes. Remove squab legs and garlic cloves, and keep warm. Pour off any fat in roasting pan and place pan over high heat. Add sherry vinegar and deglaze pan. Stir in veal stock and bring to a boil. Taste for seasoning, and strain—there should be about ½ cup of sauce. Reduce by rapid boiling if necessary.

To serve, mound one quarter of the pea purée in the center of each heated dinner plate. Top with breast and leg portions of squab. Spoon a little sauce around each, and surround with mushrooms and garlic cloves.

PREPARATION TIME: 30 MINUTES / OVEN TIME: 35 MINUTES

TURKEY CUTLETS WITH ASPARAGUS AND ORANGE SAUCE

A sophisticated way to present boneless breast of turkey that is really very simple to prepare: The breaded cutlets cook in the oven while you make a sauce from puréed asparagus stalks, egg yolk, and butter.

To obtain orange segments without any membrane, peel the orange down to the flesh, taking off all the skin and white pith. Holding the orange cupped in one hand, cut between the membranes and let the segments fall free onto a plate, rotating the orange as you go.

1 *pound asparagus*
Juice of 1 lemon
Juice of ½ orange
2 *tablespoons olive oil*
4 *slices turkey breast, 5 ounces each*
Salt and pepper

Flour for dredging
1 *egg, beaten*
2 *cups fine dry white bread crumbs*
Pinch nutmeg
1 *large egg yolk*
4 *tablespoons butter*

Trim the asparagus, peeling the stalks if they are tough. Poach asparagus in boiling salted water until just tender, which can be as little as 5 minutes, depending on size. Cut off 3-inch tips and set aside for garnish. Purée remaining stalks in a food processor with lemon and orange juices.

Preheat convection oven to 400 degrees, and at the same time heat a rimmed baking sheet spread with olive oil. Sprinkle turkey cutlets with salt and pepper to taste, and dredge lightly in flour, shaking off the excess. Dip in beaten egg, and then in crumbs. (Do this just before cooking, so the coating does not get soggy.) Place cutlets on the heated baking sheet, and bake for 10 minutes, turning once.

While cutlets are baking, transfer asparagus purée to a saucepan and gently heat. Season with salt, pepper, and nutmeg. Whisk in the egg yolk and then the butter, little by little. The sauce should emulsify like a mayonnaise, so do not let the butter get too hot or it will "break" and liquify.

Reheat the asparagus tips gently by immersing in very hot water for 1 minute. Serve cutlets on heated dinner plates garnished with sauce and asparagus tips.

PREPARATION TIME: 20 MINUTES / OVEN TIME: 10 MINUTES

SERVES 4, OR 8
AS AN APPETIZER

SWEETBREADS
WITH RED SWISS CHARD

This is a spectacular contemporary recipe. There is no need to use veal sweetbreads, which are sought after by top-flight restaurants and are usually very expensive. Frozen and defrosted beef sweetbreads, which most butchers keep though you will have to ask for them, will do very well.

1 *pound beef sweetbreads*
12 *to 16 ounces red Swiss chard*

4 *tablespoons butter*
Salt and pepper
1 *clove garlic*

The day before they are to be cooked, rinse sweetbreads well. Place in a saucepan, cover with cold water, and bring to a boil. Drain, and plunge into cold water. Pull off as much of the membrane and connecting tissue as possible. Put sweetbreads on a plate, cover with plastic wrap, and press down with a plate weighted with a can of tomatoes or something similar. Leave in the refrigerator overnight.

Preheat convection oven to 350 degrees. Separate chard leaves from stems and rinse both well. Blanch leaves in boiling salted water for 1 minute, then squeeze dry and chop coarsely. Set aside.

Cut stems into 2-inch lengths. In a small ovenproof skillet, heat 1 tablespoon of the butter, add the shallots and the chard stems. Sauté for 1 minute and remove skillet from heat.

Cut the sweetbreads into eight equal pieces and lay on top of the chard stems. Sprinkle with salt and pepper to taste, and dot with 1 tablespoon butter. Bake for 45 minutes, turning the sweetbread pieces halfway through.

In a sauté pan, heat remaining 2 tablespoons of butter with the garlic clove until the butter turns golden brown and smells nutty. Discard garlic, add chard leaves, and sauté for 1 minute.

To serve, arrange a small mound of chard leaves on each heated dinner plate. Top with red chard stems and a portion of sweetbreads. Surround with the reddish gold sauce from the baking pan.

PREPARATION TIME: OVERNIGHT WEIGHTING; 15 MINUTES / OVEN TIME: 45 MINUTES

TWO-WAY RABBIT

This does take a little time and trouble, but it is a delicious way to make one small rabbit serve eight to twelve people—depending on the rest of the two meals, of course. The two dishes are prepared simultaneously—you can chop all the vegetables and herbs at the same time and divide them up. The boneless stuffed saddle is served hot, with wine sauce taken from the Rabbit Confit, which in turn can be served the next day as a cold appetizer.

1 *fresh frying rabbit, 3 pounds*
3 *tablespoons pork sausage meat*
1 *tablespoon butter*
½ *small carrot, chopped fine*
1 *shallot, chopped*
½ *clove garlic, chopped*
2 *mushrooms, diced*
1 *cup fresh white bread crumbs*

1 *large egg*
1 *tablespoon fresh parsley, chopped*
Salt and pepper
½ *teaspoon chopped fresh thyme*
1 *teaspoon chopped fresh basil*
2 *strips lean bacon*
1 *cup sauce from Rabbit Confit*
1 *teaspoon cornstarch*

Cut rabbit into serving pieces (see illustration on page 157), leaving the saddle and extending flaps of flank in one piece. Use saddle and one hind leg for this recipe; reserve remainder for Rabbit Confit. Carefully remove backbone from rabbit saddle without cutting through skin, and butterfly the meat so that it is as flat as possible. (Slice horizontally from center without cutting all the way through the meat; then open out like a book.) Grind meat from hind leg in a food processor, saving the bones for Rabbit Confit. Mix ground rabbit with pork sausage.

Heat butter in a skillet and sauté carrot, shallot, and garlic for 2 minutes. Add mushrooms and cook for 5 minutes, until liquid has evaporated. Transfer to a bowl and stir in bread crumbs, egg, parsley, and salt and pepper to taste. Let cool, and then add ground meat, thyme, and basil.

Preheat convection oven to 350 degrees. Place stuffing mixture on top of saddle of rabbit, enclosing it within the flaps of skin and making a neat rectangular package. Cover sides with 1½ strips of bacon, and lay the remaining ½ strip of bacon on top—they will stick in place. Lay package on a small sheet of aluminum foil, and fold up the edges to form a shallow case that will also help to hold the meat in shape. Transfer to a baking sheet and roast for 45 minutes.

When ready to serve, heat the reserved cup of sauce from the Rabbit Confit (see recipe) and stir in cornstarch dissolved in a little cold water. Boil for a few seconds, until sauce thickens and clears.

PREPARATION TIME: 40 MINUTES / OVEN TIME: 45 MINUTES

RABBIT CONFIT WITH PRUNES SERVES 4 TO 6

Serve this appetizer over a green salad dressed with Vinaigrette, and garnish the plates with cornichons.

1 *tablespoon olive oil*
1 *onion, chopped*
½ *small carrot, chopped*
1 *shallot, chopped*
1½ *cloves garlic, chopped*
  Rabbit pieces reserved from Roast Saddle of Rabbit
  Salt and pepper
1 *teaspoon chopped fresh basil*
1 *teaspoon chopped fresh thyme*
1 *tablespoon chopped fresh parsley*

1 *tablespoon Cognac*
½ *bottle dry red wine*
1 *cup Chicken Stock (page 300) or canned chicken broth*
1 *package unflavored gelatin*
14 *soft pitted prunes, about 5 ounces total*
  Lettuce or young spinach leaves for salad
  Vinaigrette (page 308)
  Cornichons (French pickled gherkins)

Preheat convection oven to 350 degrees. In an ovenproof skillet, heat oil and add onion, carrot, shallot, and garlic. Sauté for 3 minutes, then add rabbit pieces (reserve liver for another use) and brown on all sides, about 10 minutes. Season with salt and pepper to taste, and add herbs. Deglaze pan with Cognac, and carefully set ablaze. When flame has died, add wine and chicken stock and bring to a boil. Transfer to the oven and bake, uncovered, for 45 minutes, until meat is tender.

Strain cooking juices into a saucepan, and reserve half (about 1 cup) for the Roast Saddle of Rabbit. Pull the meat off the bones; there should be about 2 cups. Combine remaining 1 cup of sauce, gelatin, and prunes in a saucepan and simmer gently for 6 to 7 minutes. Add rabbit meat and taste mixture for seasoning. Pour into a glass loaf pan, cover, and refrigerate overnight. Serve confit in slices over salad greens dressed with vinaigrette, and garnish with cornichons.

PREPARATION TIME: 30 MINUTES; OVERNIGHT CHILLING   /   OVEN TIME: 45 MINUTES

FILET OF PORK WITH LEEKS IN PUFF PASTRY

An eye-catching, very contemporary way to present a tender cut of meat. With its center of prunes, the juicy meat contrasts well with the leek purée and crisp pastry crust, and it is further enhanced by the orange-accented sauce. The pork can be prepared several hours ahead. The sauce can also be prepared ahead, and reheated just before serving.

If you have no veal stock, substitute 1 cup of double-strength canned chicken broth and ½ cup canned beef broth. It won't be quite as good, but will make a very acceptable sauce.

2 *filets of pork, 12 ounces each*
Salt and pepper
1 *tablespoon butter*
12 *soft pitted prunes*
2 *leeks, white part and some green stem, chopped*
½ *cup heavy cream*
1 *large egg*
½ *teaspoon ground sage*
8 *ounces Quick Puff Pastry (page 244), or ½ package frozen puff pastry sheets, thawed*
1 *egg, beaten*

SAUCE

1 *teaspoon green peppercorns, drained*
1 *tablespoon Cognac*
1 *orange*
2 *tablespoons sugar*
1 *tablespoon red wine vinegar*
1 *cup Chicken Stock (page 300) or canned chicken broth*
1 *cup Brown Veal Stock (page 302)*
1 *teaspoon tomato paste*
½ *cup Dry Sack sherry*
1 *teaspoon cornstarch*

Trim the pork filets, cutting off any fat and silver membrane. Chop off tapered ends (6 ounces total), and reserve for stuffing. Open up pork filets by making a cut along the center, then make two horizontal cuts on either side, starting from the original cut and stopping short of the edge. Open the meat out flat in four "panels," and sprinkle with salt and pepper to taste. Heat butter in heavy skillet and brown filets on both sides very quickly, about 1 minute. Set filets aside.

Sauté prunes in the same pan for 2 minutes, and arrange close together on top of one filet; then cover with the other.

In the same pan, sauté leeks for 2 minutes, then add cream and season with salt and pepper to taste. Cover, and simmer slowly for 10 minutes, cooking mixture until almost dry. Set aside to cool. Then combine reserved pork filet ends, leek mixture, and egg in a food processor, and purée. Season the purée with a little salt and pepper and the sage.

Preheat convection oven to 375 degrees. Roll puff pastry dough into a 12 by 16-inch rectangle, and cut off a 12 by 2-inch strip for the top decoration. Spread a band of stuffing along the center of the rectangle, and place meat on top. Cover with remaining stuffing, spreading it with a spatula to completely enclose the meat. Brush edge of dough with some of the beaten egg, and enclose meat and stuffing inside the pastry. Flatten ends of dough slightly with a rolling pin, brush with egg, and fold against the package. Turn package over and place on a baking sheet. Brush the surface with egg glaze. Make 1-inch diagonal cuts at 1-inch intervals along both sides of the reserved pastry strip, and place it on top, tucking the ends underneath. Brush with egg. Bake for 45 minutes. Let stand for a few minutes before carving.

While the pork is baking, prepare the sauce: Reduce veal stock to ½ cup by boiling rapidly for about 8 minutes. Steep peppercorns in Cognac for 20 minutes.

Peel zest (colored part only) from orange and cut it into julienne. Cover with cold water in a small saucepan, and bring to a boil. Simmer for 10 minutes and strain.

In a separate saucepan, cook sugar and vinegar until caramelized. Squeeze juice from orange and add to caramelized mixture. Add chicken stock, reduced veal stock, and tomato paste, and reduce by one third.

Place peppercorns and Cognac in a small saucepan, heat gently, and then carefully flame. When the flame has died, add sherry and reduce to a glaze in the bottom of the pan, about 2 minutes. Stir sauce into this glaze, and add julienned zest. Dilute cornstarch with a little water and stir into sauce. Boil for a few seconds, until thickened and clear.

To serve, make a "mirror" of sauce on each heated dinner plate. Cut off and discard end of pastry package. Cut into 1-inch-thick slices, and place on top of the sauce.

PREPARATION TIME: 30 MINUTES / OVEN TIME: 45 MINUTES

DOUBLE RIB LAMB CHOPS
WITH HERB STUFFING IN PHYLLO

SERVES 4

The success of this recipe depends on having very well trimmed lamb chops, without fat and with only one long curved bone. It is actually very simple to prepare: You make an herb stuffing, spread it on the lightly browned chops, and then wrap each one in a sheet of ready-prepared phyllo dough. The chops and sauce can be prapared several hours ahead of time, which makes it a convenient dish for serving to guests.

4 double rib lamb chops,
  6 ounces each

3 tablespoons butter

1 small onion, finely
  diced

2 large mushrooms, finely
  diced

½ cup bread crumbs made
  from day-old white
  bread

¼ cup grated Swiss cheese

½ teaspoon chopped fresh
  thyme, or ¼ teaspoon
  dried

¼ teaspoon fresh chopped
  rosemary, or pinch dried

1 tablespoon chopped fresh
  parsley

Salt and pepper

4 sheets phyllo dough,
  thawed if frozen

1 tablespoon melted butter

SAUCE

1 tablespoon butter

1 small onion, chopped

1 carrot, chopped

1 stalk celery, chopped

1 sprig fresh rosemary, or
  pinch dried

  Few parsley stems

1 small bay leaf

  Salt and pepper

1 teaspoon cornstarch

1 tablespoon water

Have your butcher trim the lamb chops, leaving just the nugget of meat and one rib bone, and flatten the meat slightly with the flat side of a large knife. (If you are doing this yourself, remove all fat, the chine bones, and one of the rib bones from each chop.) Save the bones and trimmings.

Melt 1 tablespoon of the butter in a heavy skillet and brown the lamb for 1 minute on each side. Allow to cool.

RECIPES FOR THE BRAVE   187

In a saucepan, melt the remaining 2 tablespoons of butter, and simmer onion very slowly until softened, about 5 minutes. Add mushrooms and simmer for 2 minutes. Remove from heat and stir in bread crumbs, cheese, thyme, rosemary, parsley, and salt and pepper to taste. Mix well. The stuffing should just hold together.

Spread one sheet of phyllo dough out on a work surface. Cover surface of one lamb chop with stuffing, packing it down, and place the chop stuffing side down in the center of the phyllo. Spread the other side with a layer of stuffing. Bring two ends of phyllo around lamb bone (like a shawl) and gather the edges together. Twist lightly to form a loose rosette on top of the meat—the dough will stay in place with the bone sticking out to one side. Repeat with remaining three chops. Place on a greased baking sheet, and brush tops of phyllo lightly with melted butter. Refrigerate, covered, until required (can be prepared several hours ahead of time).

To make the sauce, heat butter in a sauté pan and brown reserved bones and trimmings (no lamb fat) with onion, carrot, celery, and herbs, about 8 minutes. Pour off any butter, and season with salt and pepper to taste. Add water to cover, and simmer for about 25 minutes, until reduced by half. Strain into a saucepan and taste for seasoning. Just before serving, reheat sauce. Blend cornstarch with 1 tablespoon water, and stir into sauce. Boil for a few seconds, until slightly thickened.

Preheat convection oven to 375 degrees. Bake chops for 10 minutes. To serve, divide sauce among four heated dinner plates, and top with a phyllo-wrapped lamb chop.

PREPARATION TIME: 1 HOUR / OVEN TIME: 10 MINUTES

WHOLE CALF'S LIVER BAKED IN PUFF PASTRY

A whole calf's liver is surprisingly inexpensive, and makes an elegant and festive dish when presented in puff pastry with a wine sauce. It will be popular with anyone who enjoys pâté.

1 *whole calf's liver, 2 pounds*
Salt and pepper
2½ *tablespoons butter*
1 *tablespoon chopped fresh thyme, or 1½ teaspoons dried*
12 *ounces mushrooms*
½ *onion, chopped*

2 *tablespoons Cognac*
8 *ounces Quick Puff Pastry dough (page 244), or ½ package frozen puff pastry sheets, thawed*
1 *egg, beaten*
1 *cup Cabernet Sauce (page 304)*

Preheat convection oven to 375 degrees. Cut tubes and membranes out of the liver, and cut off and reserve the lobe that projects on one side. Pull off the membrane covering the liver. (This is a bit tedious, but must be done as it tightens and toughens when cooked.) Season liver with salt and pepper to taste. Heat 1 tablespoon of the butter in a heavy skillet, and quickly sauté liver on both sides, about 3 minutes, to firm it up. Remove and let cool.

Chop mushrooms in a food processor. Heat 1 tablespoon butter in the same skillet, and sauté onion for 1 minute. Add thyme and mushrooms, and cook, stirring often, until mixture is dry—about 5 minutes. Allow to cool. Return mushroom mixture to the food processor.

Chop the reserved lobe of liver. Add remaining ½ tablespoon of butter to the skillet, and sauté chopped liver for 1 minute. Then add Cognac and deglaze pan, scraping it with a wooden spoon. Scrape this mixture into the food processor and run machine briefly, until well mixed with mushrooms.

Roll puff pastry into a 14-inch square, and cut off a 2-inch strip. Spoon half the mushroom mixture onto the center of the pastry dough, and top with liver. Cover with remaining mushroom mixture. Brush edge of dough with water, and fold it over the liver. Flatten both overlapping ends of dough slightly with a rolling pin, and fold them over the top. Turn package over and place on a baking sheet. Brush top with beaten egg. Make a series of diagonal cuts along both edges of the reserved strip of pastry. Place it on top of the package and brush with egg. Bake for 25 minutes, until well browned. The liver will cook inside the pastry, but should be pink inside when sliced. Let it cool on a rack for 10 minutes before slicing, so that the juices can settle. Serve Cabernet Sauce in a sauceboat.

PREPARATION TIME: 30 MINUTES / OVEN TIME: 25 MINUTES

SIDE DISHES

BEET MOUSSE

This purée goes very well with duck or game. Beets should always be baked, never boiled, as they can develop a muddy taste when cooked in water. The length of baking time depends on the variety and age of the beets—they are far more dense than potatoes and take longer to cook.

3 *beets, 4 ounces each*
1 *tablespoon butter*
1 *onion, sliced*
1 *clove garlic, chopped*
1 *teaspoon red wine vinegar*

¼ *cup Chicken Stock (page 300) or canned chicken broth*
¼ *cup heavy cream, warmed but not boiling*
Salt and pepper

Preheat covection oven to 350 degrees. Trim tops off beets, rinse and dry beets, and bake on an oven rack for 1½ hours. When done, they should yield to light pressure. Peel and slice the beets.

Heat butter in a skillet and sauté onion for 5 minutes, until soft. Add sliced beets, garlic, vinegar, and chicken stock. Simmer until all the liquid has evaporated, about 3 minutes. Transfer beet mixture to a food processor and with the motor running, add warm cream through the feed tube. Process to a smooth purée, and season to taste with salt and pepper. Keep warm in a double boiler until ready to serve.

PREPARATION TIME: 20 MINUTES / OVEN TIME: 1½ HOURS / EASY

CARROT, RUTABAGA, AND POTATO MOUSSE

Somewhere between a mousse and a soufflé, the delicious combination of three root vegetables makes an attractive and out-of-the-ordinary alternative to plain potatoes or carrots. Be sure to drain the vegetables very well. If the puréed mixture looks the least bit watery, transfer it to a heavy saucepan and stir over medium-heat for a few seconds, until the excess liquid has evaporated.

2 carrots, 8 ounces each
2 all-purpose potatoes, 6 ounces each
1 rutabaga, 8 ounces
Salt
3 tablespoons butter, softened

2 tablespoons grated Parmesan cheese
½ teaspoon salt
Black pepper
Pinch nutmeg
3 large egg yolks
2 large egg whites

Pare the skin off the potatoes and carrots, and cut into ¼-inch-thick slices. Peel rutabaga with a knife (the skin is usually too thick and fibrous for a vegetable peeler), cut in half, and then cut into ¼-inch-thick slices. Place vegetables in a pot, cover with water, add a little salt, and boil until tender, about 15 minutes.

Preheat convection oven to 350 degrees. Grease a 1-quart soufflé dish with 1 tablespoon of the butter, and dust with Parmesan cheese.

Drain vegetables well and place in the bowl of a food processor. Add remaining 2 tablespoons butter, salt, pepper to taste, and nutmeg. Process until smooth and transfer to a bowl. (Or mash by hand.) Stir in egg yolks. Beat egg whites until stiff, adding a tiny pinch of salt, and stir one quarter into vegetable mixture. Gently fold in the remaining egg whites. Pile mixture into the prepared dish, smooth the top, and bake for 25 minutes, until well puffed and browned. Serve immediately.

PREPARATION TIME: 25 MINUTES / OVEN TIME: 25 MINUTES / EASY

GRATIN OF
CORN WITH SPINACH

This is a good combination that goes well with chicken or turkey. The blanched spinach is quickly sautéed in browned butter before being combined with the corn, cream, and Swiss cheese, and of course the dish can be prepared ahead of time.

2 *cups corn kernels (approximately 3 ears of fresh corn)*

12 *ounces fresh spinach, well rinsed and stems removed*

1 *cup heavy cream*

1 *large egg yolk*
Salt and pepper
Pinch nutmeg

1 *tablespoon butter*

1 *cup grated Swiss Gruyère cheese*

Preheat convection oven to 350 degrees. Grease an 8 by 10-inch shallow baking dish with butter. Bring 2 large pots of salted water to the boil. In one pot, blanch corn kernels for 2 minutes, or until tender. (If using very fresh corn, 2 minutes will be sufficient. Frozen mature corn kernels take longer.) Drain.

In the other pot, blanch spinach leaves for 1 minute. Drain, plunge into cold water to refresh, then drain again. Squeeze out excess water and chop coarsely.

Heat cream in a small saucepan, and pour over egg yolk, whisking briskly. Season with salt, pepper, and nutmeg. Heat butter in a skillet and allow to turn golden brown. Sauté spinach for 30 seconds, and season with salt and pepper to taste. Arrange spinach in the prepared baking dish, and cover with half the grated cheese. Top with corn kernels and remaining cheese. Pour cream over the top, and bake for 20 minutes.

PREPARATION TIME: 15 MINUTES / OVEN TIME: 20 MINUTES / EASY

GRATIN OF EGGPLANT, MUSHROOMS, AND TOMATOES

SERVES 4 TO 6

A typically Mediterranean combination of vegetables cooked with olive oil, this gratin is good with lamb or grilled fish.

¾ cup olive oil

1 onion, finely chopped

4 mushrooms, diced

2 cloves garlic, minced

2 tablespoons chopped fresh parsley

1 tablespoon chopped fresh marjoram, or 1½ teaspoon, dried

1 tablespoon chopped fresh thyme, or 1½ teaspoons dried

4 tomatoes, peeled, seeded, and quartered

1 pound eggplant, peeled and diced

Salt and pepper

2 to 3 tablespoons bread crumbs made from day-old white bread

Preheat convection oven to 350 degrees. Heat ½ cup of the oil in a skillet and sauté onion for 3 minutes, until softened. Add mushrooms and garlic, and sauté for 1 minute. Remove skillet from the heat, and stir in parsley, marjoram, thyme, tomatoes, and eggplant. Season with salt and pepper to taste. Grease a shallow casserole with oil and fill with the mixture. Top with crumbs, and sprinkle with the remaining ¼ cup olive oil. Bake for 45 minutes.

PREPARATION TIME: 15 MINUTES / OVEN TIME: 45 MINUTES / EASY

GRATIN OF
POTATOES WITH CREAM

As they cook, the sliced potatoes will absorb all the liquid and form into a tender cake with a golden brown topping. Cut the gratin in squares or triangles to serve.

To make a Gratin of Potatoes with Chicken Stock, substitute chicken stock for the cream, dot with a little butter, and bake at 350 degrees for approximately 40 minutes, until tender.

2 *pounds russet or all-purpose potatoes*	1 *cup grated Swiss cheese*
1 *clove garlic, unpeeled, cut in half*	1 *teaspoon salt*
	¼ *teaspoon pepper*
1 *tablespoon butter, softened*	¼ *teaspoon nutmeg*
	2 *cups half-and-half or light cream, boiling*

Preheat convection oven to 325 degrees. Peel potatoes and slice very thin on a mandoline or in a food processor. Rub a 2-quart shallow baking dish with garlic, and then smear with soft butter. Layer the potatoes in the dish, sprinkling each layer with a little of the cheese and seasonings. Cover with the hot half-and-half. Bake, uncovered, for approximately 50 minutes, until tender.

PREPARATION TIME: 15 MINUTES / OVEN TIME: 50 MINUTES / EASY

These little fluted squash make an exceptionally pretty vegetable accompaniment, and the coriander gives an intriguing flavor to the stuffing. They can be prepared ahead of time ready for baking, so it's a good dish to multiply for a large number.

6 *pattypan squash, 2½ inches across*

2 *strips lean bacon, chopped*

2 *shallots, chopped*

1 *clove garlic, mashed and chopped*

Pinch oregano

Pinch thyme

Salt and pepper

½ *cup bread crumbs made from day-old white bread*

¼ *cup dry white wine*

¼ *cup Chicken Stock (page 300) or canned chicken broth*

¼ *teaspoon coriander seeds*

2 *tablespoons olive oil*

Preheat convection oven to 350 degrees. Scoop out squash, reserving the centers, without breaking through the skin underneath. (One way to do this is to start by inserting a 1¾-inch round scalloped cookie cutter into the squash, without pushing it all the way through. Finish removing the center with a spoon.) Finely chop these trimmings.

Sauté bacon in a skillet until it starts to soften, about 2 minutes, then add one of the chopped shallots and cook for 2 minutes. Add garlic, oregano, thyme, salt and pepper to taste, and chopped squash centers. Cook for 3 minutes. Remove from the heat and stir in bread crumbs.

Combine wine, chicken stock, remaining shallot, and coriander seeds in a shallow ovenproof dish just large enough to hold the squash in one layer. Fill squash with stuffing, and place in dish. Drizzle with olive oil and bake for 30 minutes.

PREPARATION TIME: 15 MINUTES / OVEN TIME: 30 MINUTES / EASY

GRATIN OF GREEN BEANS WITH ALMONDS

SERVES 4 TO 6

The crunchy almonds make a nice contrast to the green beans in this dish, and the gratin can be prepared ahead of time, which is always handy. If you can find them, Chinese "yard-long" string beans are excellent prepared this way—they have good flavor and texture.

1 *pound young green beans*

½ *cup sliced almonds, with skins*

Salt and pepper

1 *cup heavy cream*

2 *tablespoons grated Parmesan cheese*

Preheat convection oven to 350 degrees. Top and tail beans and remove strings, if any. Cut on the diagonal into 1-inch pieces. Simmer in boiling salted water for about 10 minutes, until just tender. (Length of cooking time depends on age and variety, so check often.) Butter a 9-inch baking dish and fill with beans. Add almonds, salt and pepper, and cream. Sprinkle with Parmesan, and bake for 12 minutes.

PREPARATION TIME: 15 MINUTES / OVEN TIME: 12 MINUTES / EASY

OVEN-FRIED POTATOES
WITH GARLIC AND PARSLEY

This is a very easy way to make "fried" potatoes in a small amount of fat. The garlic is left unpeeled so that it doesn't scorch—you can add more cut cloves if you want a more pronounced flavor. These potatoes go well with roast meats or poultry.

1 *pound russet or all-purpose potatoes*

2 *tablespoons butter*

1 *tablespoons olive or vegetable oil*

2 *cloves garlic, unpeeled, cut in half*

Salt

1 *tablespoon chopped fresh parsley*

Preheat convection oven to 400 degrees, heating a shallow roasting pan or jelly roll pan at the same time. Peel potatoes, slice them, and dry on paper towels. Combine butter and oil in a small saucepan and add the garlic. Heat until butter melts. Dip each slice of potato in this mixture and arrange on the heated pan in a single layer. Add the garlic. Bake for 25 minutes, until crisp, golden, and tender. (There is no need to turn.) Discard garlic, season to taste with salt, and sprinkle with parsley.

PREPARATION TIME: 10 MINUTES / OVEN TIME: 25 MINUTES / EASY

POTATO PATTIES WITH
GOAT CHEESE AND PARSLEY

An out-of-the-ordinary accompaniment for any white meat—veal, chicken, or pork. Mashed baked potato is combined with goat cheese and seasonings and formed into a roll. The roll is chilled, then cut into thick rounds, brushed with egg, and baked.

2 baking potatoes, 10 ounces each

4 ounces goat cheese

4 tablespoons unsalted butter

Salt and pepper

Pinch nutmeg

Scant ⅓ cup (2 ounces) all-purpose flour

1 large egg yolk

2 tablespoons chopped fresh parsley or chives

1 egg, beaten

Preheat convection oven to 375 degrees. Bake potatoes for 45 minutes, or until soft. Split in half, scoop out interior, and put pulp through a potato ricer or push through a coarse sieve into a bowl. Add goat cheese and butter to hot potatoes, and season with salt, pepper, and nutmeg. Beat in flour and egg yolk to make a stiff mixture. Add parsley last.

On a lightly floured surface, roll mixture into a 2-inch-diameter "sausage." (At this point, roll can be enclosed in plastic wrap and chilled until required.) Slice into twelve equal pieces, and form into ½-inch-thick patties. Place on a buttered baking sheet, and brush with egg. Bake at 375 degrees for 15 minutes.

PREPARATION TIME: 15 MINUTES / OVEN TIME: 45 MINUTES; 15 MINUTES

CRISP BUTTERED POTATO CAKE   SERVES 4 TO 6

Potatoes are prepared like this at Maxim's in Paris. The crunchy texture and buttery flavor are impossible to resist. Don't let the amount of butter bother you: Most of it is poured off after cooking and can be saved for another use.

8 *tablespoons butter*   *Salt and pepper*
1 *pound all-purpose*
   potatoes

Preheat convection oven to 350 degrees. Melt butter and skim off foam. Peel potatoes and slice very thin on a mandoline or in a food processor. Blot dry on paper towels. Brush a 10 by 16-inch baking dish with melted butter, and spread with potatoes. Brush potatoes liberally with butter and season with salt and pepper to taste. (The potatoes are meant to be spread out thinly so they will get crisp.) Bake for 20 minutes, or until golden brown and tender. Pour off butter, reserving it for another use, and blot the surface with paper towels. Cut into squares to serve.

PREPARATION TIME: 10 MINUTES / OVEN TIME: 20 MINUTES / EASY

POTATO AND ZUCCHINI TART

Sliced potatoes, zucchini, garlic, and herbs are packed into a cast iron skillet and baked until tender. The golden brown cake is cut into wedges to serve. It goes well with any roast meat.

3 tablespoons olive oil

4 tablespoons butter, melted

2 pounds all-purpose potatoes, thinly sliced

¼ cup mixed chopped fresh herbs: parsley, thyme, and oregano

4 cloves garlic, chopped

Salt and pepper

1¼ pounds zucchini, thinly sliced

Preheat convection oven to 375 degrees. Combine the olive oil and butter, and pour 2 tablespoons of the mixture into a 9-inch cast-iron skillet. Cover the bottom of the skillet with one third of the sliced potatoes in a neat spiral pattern. Brush with oil and butter, and sprinkle with some of the herb mixture and a little of the garlic. Season with salt and pepper to taste. Cover with an even layer of half the zucchini. Brush with oil and butter, and top with herbs, garlic, salt and pepper. Repeat layers, finishing with potatoes, and press down gently. Brush top with oil and butter, and bake for 35 minutes, until top is browned and potatoes are tender. Invert onto a platter and cut into wedges to serve.

PREPARATION TIME: 15 MINUTES / OVEN TIME: 35 MINUTES / EASY

STUFFED BAKED POTATOES WITH CHIVES

The classic accompaniment for steak, these potatoes can be prepared and left at room temperature for an hour or two before returning to the oven to heat through.

4 baking potatoes, 8 ounces each

1 tablespoon butter, softened

1 to 1¼ cups sour cream

2 egg yolks

½ cup grated Swiss Gruyére cheese

2 tablespoons chopped fresh chives

Dash nutmeg

Salt and pepper

Preheat convection oven to 375 degrees. Rinse and dry potatoes, and place on an oven rack. Bake for 45 minutes, or until tender. Cut in half and scoop out the pulp into a bowl, leaving a thin shell. Put pulp through a potato ricer or push through a coarse sieve, and mash until very smooth. (Do not be tempted to use a food processor; it will turn the mixture to glue.) Beat in the butter, sour cream, egg yolks, cheese, chives, nutmeg, and salt and pepper to taste. Add extra sour cream if necessary to make the mixture light and fluffy.

Using a pastry bag and a large open star tip, fill the potato skins; or simply pile the mixture back into the skins and mark the tops decoratively with a fork. Place in a greased pan. (Potatoes can be prepared ahead to this point and left at room temperature for an hour or so covered.) Bake for 15 minutes at 350 degrees to heat through.

PREPARATION TIME: 15 MINUTES / OVEN TIME: 45 MINUTES; 15 MINUTES / EASY

PUMPKIN
PANCAKE WITH SCALLIONS

This big, fluffy golden-orange pancake is baked in the oven, then flipped into a skillet to brown the other side. If fresh pumpkin is unavailable, substitute 1 cup of unflavored, unsweetened canned pumpkin purée. It should be lukewarm when combined with the other ingredients. Serve with turkey, or with eggs and bacon for a late weekend breakfast.

12-ounce piece of raw pumpkin or other yellow winter squash

2 scallions, chopped, white bulb and half of green tops

Salt and pepper

Pinch nutmeg

Heaping ¼ cup (1 ounce) all-purpose flour

1 tablespoon heavy cream

2 large eggs, separated

1 tablespoon butter

½ tablespoon vegetable oil

Preheat convection oven to 350 degrees. Wrap pumpkin in foil and bake for 1 hour, until tender.

Discard pumpkin peel and purée pulp in a food processor; there should be 1 cup. Combine warm pumpkin purée with scallions, salt and pepper to taste, nutmeg, flour, cream, and egg yolks. Beat until smooth. Beat egg whites until stiff and fold them into mixture.

Heat butter in a heavy ovenproof 9-inch skillet and add the batter. Bake for 10 minutes, until very puffy. While pancake is baking, heat oil in a second skillet (it doesn't matter if it is slightly bigger than the first one). Flip the baked pancake into it. Cook on top of the stove for 2 minutes to brown the underside. Cut pancake in wedges to serve.

PREPARATION TIME: 10 MINUTES / OVEN TIME: 1 HOUR; 10 MINUTES / EASY

GRATIN OF
TURNIP, POTATO, AND LEEK

Serve this gratin where you might normally serve plain potatoes.

Always rinse leeks very well—they tend to harbor sand inside the tightly furled leaves. Trim off the root and the coarse green leaves, then cut the leeks in half lengthways and wash under running water. Chop to the required size, and rinse the pieces again, always scooping them up from the water so that any sand stays in the bottom of the bowl.

1 *turnip, 5 ounces*
12 *ounces white potatoes (preferably White Rose)*
1 *small leek, rinsed well and finely chopped*
1 *clove garlic, minced*

Salt and pepper
Dash nutmeg
2 *cups half-and-half, or a mixture of milk and heavy cream*
1 *tablespoon butter*

Preheat convection oven to 375 degrees. Butter a 9-inch shallow baking dish. Peel turnip and potatoes, and slice very thin. Cover bottom of the baking dish with half the potatoes, and sprinkle with half the leek and garlic. Season lightly with salt, pepper, and nutmeg. Cover with a layer of turnip, sprinkle with remaining leek and garlic, season as before, and finish with remaining potatoes. Pour half-and-half on top and dot with butter. Bake for 45 minutes.

PREPARATION TIME: 10 MINUTES / OVEN TIME: 45 MINUTES / EASY

GRATIN OF SAVOY CABBAGE

Simple to make, with a good fresh taste, a cabbage gratin goes well with almost any pork dish.

2 *pounds Savoy (green curly) cabbage*
Salt and pepper
Dash nutmeg
1 *cup heavy cream, heated*

¼ *cup grated Gruyére cheese*
2 *tablespoons bread crumbs made from day-old white bread*

Preheat convection oven to 350 degrees. Butter a shallow 2-quart baking dish. Bring a large pot of salted water to a boil. Cut cabbage in quarters and remove core. Shred cabbage leaves and blanch in boiling salted water for 1 minute. Remove cabbage with a skimmer or slotted spoon, so that any sand will remain in the bottom of the pot. Place in prepared baking dish and season to taste with salt, pepper, and nutmeg. Add cream, and bake for 20 minutes. Sprinkle with cheese and bread crumbs, and bake for a further 10 minutes.

PREPARATION TIME: 10 MINUTES / OVEN TIME: 30 MINUTES / EASY

BULGUR PILAF

Bulgur makes an interesting alternative to rice and has a pleasantly nutty flavor. It goes particularly well with lamb dishes, and can be reheated.

1 *tablespoon olive oil*
1 *tablespoon butter*
1 *onion, chopped*
1 *red bell pepper, seeded and diced*

1 *cup bulgur (cracked wheat)*
1 *clove garlic, chopped*
Salt and pepper
2 *cups Chicken Stock (page 300) or canned chicken broth*

Preheat convection oven to 350 degrees. In an ovenproof sauté pan, heat oil and butter. Add onion and bell pepper and cook for 5 minutes, covered, until softened but not browned. Add bulgur and stir well to coat the grains. Cook for 2 minutes, stirring often. Add garlic, salt and pepper to taste, and chicken stock. Bring to a boil, cover pan, and transfer to the oven. Bake for 20 minutes.

PREPARATION TIME: 10 MINUTES / OVEN TIME: 20 MINUTES / EASY

RICE PILAF WITH SHIITAKE MUSHROOMS
SERVES 4

The woody stems of shiitake (Japanese forest mushrooms) are very tough, so discard them. If fresh shiitake are unavailable, use dried ones, which can be found in the Oriental section of most supermarkets. Soak them in warm water for 20 minutes, then drain and blot dry with paper towels, gently squeezing out the excess moisture. Six 1-inch dried shiitake mushrooms will make ½ cup of sliced mushrooms when reconstituted.

1 *tablespoon butter*
1 *tablespoon finely chopped onion or shallot*
½ *cup sliced fresh shiitake mushrooms*
1 *cup long-grain rice*

2½ *cups Chicken Stock (page 300) or canned chicken broth, boiling*
Salt
¼ *teaspoon pepper*
½ *cup grated Parmesan cheese*

Preheat oven to 350 degrees. Heat butter in a 1½ quart ovenproof saucepan or enameled cast-iron casserole. Add onion and sauté for 3 minutes. Add sliced shiitake, and sauté for 2 minutes more. Rinse rice to remove any loose starch, drain, and stir into pan. Add the boiling chicken stock, salt to taste, and pepper. Cover, transfer to the oven, and bake for 18 minutes. Stir in the Parmesan cheese and serve at once.

PREPARATION TIME: 10 MINUTES / OVEN TIME: 18 MINUTES / EASY

WILD RICE PILAF

Wild rice is technically not a rice at all, but the seed of a grass that grows in shallow water. It is expensive, but when combined with brown or white rice, wild rice will impart its distinctive flavor to the other grain. (Cook rices separately, then combine and reheat if necessary so that both grains are cooked for the proper length of time.)

1 *tablespoon butter*
½ *onion, finely chopped*
½ *cup wild rice*

1½ *cups Chicken Stock (page 300) or canned chicken broth*
Salt and pepper

Preheat convection oven to 350 degrees. Heat butter in an ovenproof saucepan and sauté onion for 5 minutes, until softened. Stir in rice, and add chicken stock. Season with salt and pepper to taste. Cover pan, transfer to the oven, and bake for 1 hour.

PREPARATION TIME: 8 MINUTES / OVEN TIME: 1 HOUR / EASY

*B*READS AND MUFFINS

*B*RAIDED EGG BREAD WITH SAFFRON (CHALLAH)

MAKES 2 LOAVES

The traditional Jewish Sabbath loaf, this golden bread is delicious for breakfast, or it can be served in thin buttered slices with afternoon tea. Stale, it makes excellent toast.

1 *package dry yeast*

6 *cups (1¾ pounds) unbleached bread flour (approximately)*

1 *cup warm water, 110 degrees*

   Pinch saffron

1 *tablespoon hot water*

4 *tablespoons butter, softened*

4 *large eggs, lightly beaten*

2 *teaspoons salt*

1 *egg, beaten*

1 *to 2 teaspoons poppy seeds*

In a small bowl, mix yeast with 1 tablespoon of the flour. Stir in ½ cup of the warm water and let proof for 10 minutes, until bubbly. Dissolve saffron in hot water.

Measure 5 cups flour into the bowl of an electric mixer. Using a wooden spoon, stir in remaining warm water, yeast mixture, butter, lightly beaten eggs, dissolved saffron, and salt. Set bowl on mixer stand and knead for 15 minutes, adding more flour if required to make a soft, silky, elastic dough.

Preheat oven to 85 degrees, or barely warm. Turn dough onto a lightly floured surface and knead by hand for 1 minute. Place in a well-buttered bowl, and turn dough to coat on all sides. Cover bowl with a hot, damp terry-cloth towel. Place in the oven and let dough rise for about 1 hour, until doubled in bulk. (The moist warmth will encourage rising; redampen towel occasionally.)

Turn dough out onto a lightly floured surface and punch down. Cut in half and form into two balls. Let rest for 5 minutes. Divide each ball of dough in half, and cut each half into two unequal pieces: one third and two thirds. Divide one of the larger pieces into thirds, and roll into 12-inch ropes. Braid together, pinch ends to seal, and place on a baking sheet. Divide one of the smaller pieces into thirds, and roll into 10-inch ropes. Braid together and place on top of larger braid. Seal braids together at the ends. Repeat with remaining dough to form a second loaf. Cover loosely with a clean kitchen towel and return to the warm oven. Let rise for 1 hour, until doubled in bulk.

Remove loaves from the oven and increase heat to 375 degrees. Brush loaves with beaten egg and sprinkle with poppy seeds. Bake for 30 minutes, and cool on a rack.

PREPARATION TIME: 25 MINUTES; 2 HOURS RISING / OVEN TIME: 30 MINUTES

BAGUETTES
("DISHWASHER BREAD")   MAKES 4 BAGUETTES

It takes a little practice to make light French bread with an airy crumb and a crispy yet chewy crust, but even the first effort will be very rewarding, and a convection oven is of inestimable help in getting good results. Alas, French bread does not keep—it should be enjoyed within 4 hours of coming out of the oven. However, it freezes well: Wrap in aluminum foil as soon as it cools, and either reheat in the foil or let thaw at room temperature.

When developing this recipe we rarely had an oven to spare for proofing the bread (letting it rise), so we used the dishwasher instead, running a short cycle, without soap of course, to create a warm, moist atmosphere. You can do this with any yeast dough. (Do not cover the bowl; let the steam get at the dough.) However, don't follow our example if your dishwasher always smells of detergent, for obvious reasons. This bread was much in demand after cooking sessions for finishing up all the good sauces, so we made it often, and it was always known as dishwasher bread.

1 *package dry yeast*
5 *cups (1½ pounds) unbleached bread flour (approximately)*

2 *cups warm water, 110 degrees*
2 *teaspoons salt*
   Cornmeal
1 *egg white, beaten*

In a small bowl, mix yeast with 1 tablespoon of the flour. Stir in ½ cup of the warm water and let proof for 10 minutes, until bubbly. Measure 4½ cups of flour into the bowl of an electric mixer, and add salt. Using a wooden spoon, stir in remaining 1½ cups warm water and the yeast mixture. Set bowl on mixer stand and knead with the dough hook at medium speed for 15 minutes, adding more flour if required to make a supple and elastic dough.

Preheat oven to barely warm, about 85 degrees. Turn dough out onto a lightly floured surface and knead by hand for 1 minute. Rinse and dry mixer bowl, and place dough in it. Dust lightly with flour. Cover bowl with a hot, damp terry-cloth towel. Place in the oven and

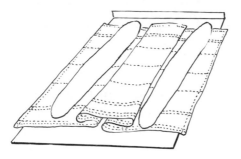

let dough rise for about 1¼ hours, until very puffy and trebled in bulk. (The moist warmth will encourage rising; redampen towel occasionally.)

Lay clean cotton kitchen towels on two 17 by 12-inch baking sheets. Bunch up most of the fabric to the center, and rub the remainder with flour, so the loaves won't stick (see illustration). Turn dough out, punch it down, and cut into four equal pieces. Form into balls and let rest for 5 minutes. Then pat each one out flat and roll it up into a 16-inch-long loaf, jelly-roll fashion, with pointed ends. Place on floured areas of towels, seam side facing up. Cover loaves loosely with another kitchen towel and let rise in the barely warm oven for about 45 minutes, until almost trebled in bulk. Remove dough from the oven and increase heat to 400 degrees. One at a time, pull the loaves toward the center of the baking sheet by pulling on the towel. Sprinkle exposed area with cornmeal. Flip loaves over onto the cornmeal so that the soft underside is uppermost. Brush loaves with egg white (which helps to create a shiny brown surface), and slash diagonally three times with a razor blade. Bake for 20 to 25 minutes, until golden brown and crusty. Remove baguettes from baking sheets and return them to the oven for 2 minutes, laying them upside down on the oven rack. Then set aside to cool, with plenty of air circulation to preserve the crisp crust.

PREPARATION TIME: 25 MINUTES; 2 HOURS RISING / OVEN TIME: 20 TO 25 MINUTES

Brioche, the lightest and most delicate of all breakfast breads, is worth your time and effort for a special brunch. It is not very difficult to make if you have an electric mixer (it requires a lot of kneading to achieve the right airy texture), and a convection oven makes a big difference in the final results. Cut in wedges or slice straight across to serve.

If you prefer, you can make twelve individual 3-inch brioches instead of one large one, and bake for only 25 to 30 minutes. Like all breads, brioche can be frozen, but be sure to thaw and reheat before serving.

1 *package dry yeast*	4 *large eggs, lightly beaten*
4 *cups (1¼ pounds) unbleached bread flour (approximately), sifted*	1 *teaspoon Orange Paste (page 295), or grated peel of ½ orange*
½ *cup warm water, 110 degrees*	1 *cup unsalted butter, softened*
2 *teaspoons salt*	1 *egg, beaten*
2 *tablespoons sugar*	

One day ahead, mix yeast with 1 tablespoon of the flour in a small bowl. Stir in warm water and let proof for 10 minutes, until bubbly. Place remaining flour in the bowl of an electric mixer and add salt and sugar. Using a wooden spoon, stir in lightly beaten eggs, yeast mixture, and Orange Paste. Set bowl on mixer stand and knead with the dough hook for 15 minutes, adding more flour or water if necessary to make a smooth and elastic dough. With dough hook turning at low speed, add softened butter a little at a time until all is incorporated. Continue kneading at medium-high speed until the dough becomes smooth, shiny, and supple, about 10 minutes. (It should slap the sides of the bowl vigorously.)

Heat oven to 85 degrees, or barely warm. Transfer dough to a clean 5-quart bowl and cover with a hot, damp terry-cloth towel. Place in the oven and let dough rise for about 1 hour, until very puffy and more than doubled in bulk. (The moist warmth will encourage rising;

redampen towel occasionally.) Turn out on a lightly floured surface, pat flat, and form into a ball. Return dough to the bowl, cover loosely with buttered plastic wrap, and refrigerate overnight.

The next day, heat oven to 85 degrees. Turn chilled dough out onto a lightly floured surface, pat flat, and knead for 2 minutes. Form into a ball and let rest for 5 minutes. Grease an 8-inch fluted brioche mold with butter. To form the brioche, cut off one fifth of the dough. Form the remainder into a ball, place it in the mold, and use your fingers to make an indentation in the center of the dough. Form the small piece of dough into a teardrop shape, and insert the smaller end in the hole. Let dough rise in the oven until doubled in bulk, uncovered, about 1 hour.

Remove dough from the oven and increase heat to 350 degrees. Brush dough with beaten egg. Bake for 50 minutes, or until well risen and golden brown. Cool on a rack and serve slightly warm.

PREPARATION TIME: 45 MINUTES; 1 HOUR INITIAL RISING; OVERNIGHT RISING; 1 HOUR FINAL RISING / OVEN TIME: 50 MINUTES

MAKES
2 LOAVES

FRENCH SANDWICH OR TOASTING BREAD (PAIN DE MIE)

This fine-textured milk bread is ideal for canapés, sandwiches of all kinds, and toast. It also makes very good crumbs for use in cooking. It should be wrapped and stored overnight before slicing, and will keep in the refrigerator for several days, or in the freezer for 3 months.

1 *package dry yeast*
4 *cups (1½ pounds) unbleached bread flour (approximately)*
½ *cup warm water, 110 degrees*

2 *tablespoons unsalted butter*
1½ *cups milk, warmed to 110 degrees*
½ *tablespoon salt*

In a small bowl, mix yeast with 1 tablespoon of the flour. Stir in warm water, and let proof for 10 minutes, until bubbly. Melt 2 tablespoons of the butter in warm milk. Measure 4 cups of flour into the bowl of an electric mixer and add salt. Using a wooden spoon, stir in milk and yeast mixtures. Set bowl on mixer stand and knead at medium speed for 15 minutes, adding more flour or water if necessary to make a supple and elastic dough.

Preheat oven to barely warm, about 85 degrees. Turn dough out onto a lightly floured surface and knead by hand for 1 minute. Grease a clean bowl with butter and place dough in it, turning to coat all sides. Cover bowl with a hot, damp terry-cloth towel. Place it in the oven and let dough rise for about 1¼ hours, until trebled in bulk. (The moist warmth will encourage rising; redampen the towel with hot water occasionally.) Turn the dough out, punch it down, and knead for 2 minutes. Form it into a ball and return it to the bowl. Cover as before and return to the warm oven. Let rise until doubled in bulk, about 45 minutes.

Have ready two well-buttered 8½ by 4½ by 2½-inch loaf pans, a sheet of buttered plastic wrap large enough to fit over both of them, and a heavy baking sheet. Turn dough out and punch it down. Cut it in half, form into two balls, and let rest for 5 minutes. Form each ball into an even loaf shape, jelly-roll fashion, and place inside buttered pans. Return pans to the warm oven, place them side by side, and cover with plastic wrap. Let rise until pans are three-quarters full, about 40 minutes.

Remove pans from the oven, and increase heat to 375 degrees. Discard plastic wrap and brush tops of loaves with butter. Return pans to the oven, placing them side by side, and cover with baking sheet. (This way, the bread dough will rise into a square shape instead of having a rounded top.) Bake for 45 minutes. Turn out and test loaves for doneness; they should sound hollow when tapped on the underside. If they require more baking or need more browning, return them to the oven for a few minutes without the pans. Let cool on a rack.

PREPARATION TIME: 30 MINUTES; 2¾ HOURS RISING / OVEN TIME: 45 MINUTES

All children love raisin bread, and this loaf has a much better texture than any you can buy. It also makes outstanding toast.

1 *package dry yeast*

6 *cups (1½ pounds) unbleached bread flour (approximately), sifted*

½ *cup warm water, 110 degrees*

1½ *cups milk*

3 *tablespoons butter*

1 *tablespoon sugar*

1½ *teaspoons salt*

1 *teaspoon Lemon Paste (page 295), or grated peel of 1 lemon*

1 *cup raisins*

½ *cup currants*

¼ *teaspoon ground cardamom, or ¼ teaspoon cinnamon*

1 *egg, beaten*

In a small bowl, combine yeast with 2 tablespoons of the flour. Stir in the warm water, and let stand until bubbly, about 10 minutes. Heat milk and butter together (butter should melt) and let cool to 110 degrees. Measure 5 cups of the flour into the bowl of an electric mixer, and add sugar and salt. Using a wooden spoon, stir in milk and yeast mixtures. Place bowl on mixer stand and knead with the dough hook for 15 minutes, adding more flour if required to make a soft, silky, and elastic dough. Add Lemon Paste, raisins, currants, and cardamom.

Preheat convection oven to 85 degrees, or barely warm. Turn dough out onto a lightly floured surface and knead by hand for 1 minute. Clean mixer bowl, grease with butter, and place dough inside, turning it to coat on all sides. Cover bowl with a hot, damp terry-cloth towel. Place bowl in the oven and let dough rise for about 1 hour, until very puffy and more than doubled in bulk. (The yeast will thrive in the warm, moist atmosphere; redampen towel occasionally.)

Remove dough from bowl, punch down, and pat flat. Form into two balls and let rest for 5 minutes. Grease two loaf pans with butter. Pat each ball of dough into a flat rectangle and form into a loaf, jelly-roll fashion. Place in pans seam side down and cover loosely with buttered plastic wrap. Return to the warm oven and let rise for 1 hour, until dough has risen above level of pans.

Remove pans from oven and increase heat to 350 degrees. Brush loaves with egg and bake for 35 minutes, until well risen and golden brown. Loaves should sound hollow when tapped on the underside. Let cool on a rack.

PREPARATION TIME: 30 MINUTES; 2 HOURS RISING / OVEN TIME: 35 MINUTES

RYE BREAD
WITH CARAWAY SEEDS

MAKES 2 LOAVES

Few things will establish a cook's reputation more securely than a freshly baked loaf of good bread, and if you add two or three different kinds of cheese, a bowl of sweet butter, some soup and a salad, you have the perfect light meal.

If you don't like the assertive flavor of caraway seeds, you can also use sesame seeds or aniseeds in this bread.

1 *package dry yeast*
3 *cups (1 pound) unbleached bread flour (approximately)*
2 *cups warm water, 110 degrees*

2 *cups (12 ounces) rye flour (approximately)*
1 *tablespoon salt*
1 *tablespoon caraway seeds Cornmeal*

In a small bowl, mix yeast with 2 tablespoons of the bread flour. Stir in ½ cup of the warm water and let proof for 10 minutes, until bubbly. Measure remaining bread flour and rye flour into the bowl of an electric mixer. Add salt. Add remaining 1½ cups of warm water and the yeast mixture, and stir with a wooden spoon. Set bowl on mixer stand and knead with the dough hook at low to medium speed for 15 minutes, until dough is smooth and elastic. (If dough rises up dough hook, switch off machine briefly and push it down, repeating as necessary.) Add a little more bread flour or water if the dough looks either sticky or dry—different flours absorb different amounts of water. Add caraway seeds during the last few minutes of kneading. Dough should be silky and elastic.

Preheat oven to barely warm, about 85 degrees. Turn dough out onto a lightly floured surface and knead by hand for 1 minute. Form into a ball. Grease a clean bowl with mild vegetable oil and place the dough in it, turning it over to grease all sides. Cover bowl with a hot, damp terry-cloth towel. Place bowl in the oven and let dough rise until doubled in bulk, about 1 hour. (The moist warmth will encourage rising; redampen towel occasionally.)

Remove dough from bowl, punch it down, and knead for a few seconds. Cut in half and let rest for 5 minutes. Dust a baking sheet with cornmeal. Form dough into two long ovals and place on the baking sheet. Cover with a clean kitchen towel. Return to the barely warm oven and let rise until doubled in bulk, about 45 minutes.

Remove loaves from oven and increase heat to 375 degrees. Slash tops of loaves with a razor blade, making three diagonal cuts. Bake for 25 to 30 minutes, until well risen and crusty. Loaves should sound hollow when tapped on the underside. Let cool on racks.

PREPARATION TIME: 30 MINUTES; 1¾ HOURS RISING   /   OVEN TIME: 25 TO 30 MINUTES

RYE BREAD
WITH WALNUTS

Like the Rye Bread with Caraway Seeds on page 216, this is a wonderful bread to serve with cheese. In fact, there are few things more inviting than a big basket of assorted homemade breads, and they are really easy to make with the help of a heavy-duty electric mixer and a convection oven.

5 *to 6 ounces Baguette dough (page 210), or ½ tube commercial refrigerated French bread dough*

1 *package dry yeast*

2 *cups warm water, 110 degrees*

4 *cups (1¼ pounds) unbleached bread flour (approximately)*

⅔ *cup (4 ounces) rye flour (approximately)*

2 *teaspoons salt*

1 *cup finely chopped walnuts*

Place the bread dough in a bowl and let rise until puffy, about 20 minutes. (If using homemade dough, it should have completed the first rising.) Dissolve the yeast in ½ cup of the warm water and let stand until bubbly, about 10 minutes. Combine flours and salt in the bowl of an electric mixer. Add remaining 1½ cups warm water, and mix with a wooden spoon to blend thoroughly. Add French bread "sponge" (risen dough) and the yeast mixture. Place bowl on mixer stand and knead with the dough hook at medium speed for 15 minutes, adding a little more bread flour or water if necessary to make a smooth and elastic dough. Add walnuts at the end of the kneading.

Preheat oven to barely warm, about 85 degrees. Turn dough out onto a lightly floured surface, knead lightly by hand (it will be quite soft), and place in a large bowl. Cover with a hot, damp terry-cloth towel. Place in the warm oven and let dough rise for about 1 hour, until more than doubled in bulk. (The moist warmth will encourage rising; redampen towel occasionally.)

Turn dough out onto a lightly floured surface and punch it down. Cut in half and form into balls. Let rest for 5 minutes. Form into two oval or round loaves. Place loaves on a baking sheet and return to the barely warm oven. Cover loosely with a kitchen towel and let rise until doubled in bulk, about 45 minutes.

Remove loaves from oven and increase heat to 350 degrees. Slash tops of loaves with a razor blade (three diagonal slashes for long oval loaves, a crisscross pattern for round ones), and bake for 1¼ hours. The loaves should sound hollow when tapped on the underside. Let cool on a rack. Store for 24 hours before slicing. This is a country bread that keeps well, and in fact the flavor and texture are best after a couple of days.

PREPARATION TIME: 40 MINUTES; 1¾ HOURS RISING / OVEN TIME: 1¼ HOURS

SLOW-RISING COUNTRY LOAVES WITH ANISEEDS

MAKES 2 LOAVES

This is a true country bread of great character. It is unusual in that it is made in a food processor—you don't have to knead it. The dough must be started the night before in order to develop a good flavor, but it is so little trouble that you will want to make it often. The recipe came from a German friend, Inge Roberts, who grew up in Westphalia and who now casually combines Old World baking traditions with modern technology. Whole-wheat bread flour or part rye flour can be substituted for a completely different flavor.

DAY 1

½ teaspoon dry yeast

2 cups (11 ounces) unbleached bread flour

¼ cup warm water, 110 degrees

1½ to 2 cups cold water

DAY 2

3 cups (1 pound) unbleached bread flour (approximately)

1 tablespoon salt

3 tablespoons sesame seeds

2 tablespoons aniseeds

1½ to 2 cups warm water, 110 degrees

Day 1: Blend yeast and 1 tablespoon of the flour in a small bowl. Add the warm water and let stand until bubbly, about 10 minutes. Add remaining flour, and stir in enough cold water to make a soft dough. Cover, and let stand at room temperature for 8 to 24 hours.

Day 2: Measure 3 cups flour into the bowl of a food processor. Add salt, sesame seeds, and aniseeds. Add the dough from day before (it is known as a sponge) and just enough warm water to make a kneadable mixture. Process until the dough clears the sides of the workbowl, about 1 minute. Transfer dough to a bowl, cover, and let rise until doubled in bulk, about 2 hours in a warm kitchen. (Or place bowl in an 85-degree oven and cover with a hot, damp terry-cloth towel. Dough will rise in about 1 hour.)

Remove dough from the bowl, punch it down, and cut in half. Let rest for 5 minutes. Line a baking sheet with a clean kitchen towel rubbed with flour. Form dough into two round flat loaves, and place them on the prepared baking sheet. Cover loosely with a clean kitchen towel. Let rise until doubled in bulk, 1 to 1½ hours.

Preheat convection oven to 375 degrees. Flip loaves off the kitchen towel and back onto the baking sheet upside down, so that the air-dried side is underneath. Make deep indentations with three fingers twice on each loaf, almost all the way through the dough. Bake for 40 minutes. Loaves are done if they sound hollow when tapped on the underside. Cool on a rack.

PREPARATION TIME: 20 MINUTES; OVERNIGHT RISING; 3½ RISING   /
OVEN TIME: 40 MINUTES   /   EASY

WHOLE WHEAT BREAD WITH ROSEMARY AND BLACK PEPPER

Another good bread to serve with cheese, and one that complements lamb dishes beautifully. Be sure to use fresh rosemary leaves—the dried variety can be very spiky and hard.

1 *package dry yeast*

2 *cups (12 ounces) unbleached bread flour (approximately)*

2 *cups warm water, 110 degrees*

3 *cups (1 pound) whole-wheat bread flour (approximately)*

1 *tablespoon salt*

¼ *cup olive oil*

1 *teaspoon chopped fresh rosemary*

1 *teaspoon cracked black pepper*

In a small bowl, mix yeast with 1 tablespoon of the flour. Stir in ½ cup of the warm water and let proof for 10 minutes, until bubbly. Measure remaining white and whole-wheat bread flour into the bowl of an electric mixer. Add salt. Using a wooden spoon, stir in remaining warm water, olive oil, and the yeast mixture. Set bowl on mixer stand and knead with the dough hook at medium speed for 15 minutes, adding more flour or water if necessary to make a supple and elastic dough. Add rosemary and cracked black pepper at the end.

Preheat oven to barely warm, about 85 degrees. Turn dough out onto a lightly floured surface and knead by hand for 1 minute. Grease a clean bowl with olive oil and place dough in it, turning to coat all sides. Cover bowl with a hot, damp terry-cloth towel. Place in the oven and let dough rise for about 1 hour, until puffy and doubled in bulk. (The moist warmth will encourage rising—redampen towel with hot water occasionally.)

Turn dough out onto a lightly floured surface. Punch it down and cut in half. Form into two balls and let rest for 5 minutes. Place a clean kitchen towel on a baking sheet and rub some flour into it, to prevent loaves from sticking. Form balls of dough into two round, flat loaves. Place them on the floured towel and cover loosely with a second kitchen towel. Return to the warm oven. Let rise for 1 hour, or until doubled in bulk. Remove baking sheet from the oven, and increase heat to 375 degrees. Flip loaves off the towel and back onto the baking sheet, air-dried side down. Bake for 45 minutes, until loaves sound hollow when tapped on the underside. Let cool on a rack.

PREPARATION TIME: 30 MINUTES; 2 HOURS RISING / OVEN TIME: 45 MINUTES

BLUEBERRY-
LEMON MUFFINS

MAKES 12 MUFFINS

These muffins are exceptionally light and tender. Adding the blueberries by hand instead of stirring them into the batter prevents them from staining the baked muffins with their juice.

2 *cups (10 ounces) cake flour, sifted*

Scant ⅓ cup sugar

4 *teaspoons baking powder*

½ *teaspoon salt*

2 *large eggs*

½ *teaspoon vanilla extract*

1 *teaspoon Lemon Paste (page 295), or grated peel of ½ lemon*

1 *cup milk*

4 *tablespoons unsalted butter, melted*

¾ *cup blueberries, thawed and well drained if frozen*

Preheat convection oven to 375 degrees. Grease a 12-cup muffin tin with butter, or line with cupcake papers. Blend flour, sugar, baking powder, and salt in a large bowl. Combine eggs, vanilla, Lemon Paste, and milk in another bowl. Make a well in the center of the dry ingredients, pour in the liquid ingredients, and mix very lightly, just enough to blend. Pour melted butter around the edge and fold it in. Fill muffin cups one-third full, and dot with blueberries. Cover berries with remaining batter. Bake for 25 minutes, until muffins spring back to light finger pressure. Serve warm.

PREPARATION TIME: 15 MINUTES / OVEN TIME: 25 MINUTES / EASY

HONEY BRAN MUFFINS

Keep these good muffins on hand in the freezer—they reheat well.

1 *cup (2¼ ounces) toasted natural wheat bran*

1 *cup (5 ounces) all-purpose flour*

½ *teaspoon salt*

1 *teaspoon baking soda*

2 *teaspoons baking powder*

3 *tablespoons butter*

2 *tablespoons honey*

1 *large egg*

1 *cup milk*

⅓ *cup coarsely chopped walnuts*

Preheat convection oven to 375 degrees. Butter and flour a 12-cup muffin pan, or line it with cupcake papers. (The metallic kind don't stick to the muffins.) Combine bran, flour, salt, baking soda, and baking powder in a large bowl. Melt butter in a saucepan and add honey, egg, and milk. Mix well. Add to the dry ingredients and blend lightly, just enough to moisten. Stir in nuts. Spoon batter into muffin pan and bake for 20 minutes, until muffins spring back to light finger pressure. Serve warm.

PREPARATION TIME: 10 MINUTES / OVEN TIME: 20 MINUTES / EASY

PECAN CORNBREAD

Warm, freshly made cornbread with a pat of sweet butter melting on top is even more tempting with the addition of pecans. This bread seems to have a natural affinity for turkey (it makes good stuffing) and is delicious for breakfast drizzled with wild honey.

1 *cup (5 ounces) all-purpose flour*

1 *cup (6 ounces) yellow cornmeal*

4 *teaspoons baking powder*

¾ *teaspoon salt*

1 *tablespoon sugar*

2 *large eggs*

1¼ *cups milk*

4 *tablespoons butter, melted*

½ *cup chopped pecans*

Preheat convection oven to 350 degrees. Grease an 8-inch square cake pan generously with butter. In a large bowl, sift together the flour, cornmeal, baking powder, salt, and sugar. Combine eggs, milk, and melted butter in another bowl, and beat well. Stir quickly into the dry ingredients. Add chopped pecans and pour into the prepared pan. Bake for 30 minutes. Unmold onto a rack, cut into squares, and serve warm, with butter.

PREPARATION TIME: 10 MINUTES / OVEN TIME: 30 MINUTES / EASY

COOKIES

ENGLISH MINCEMEAT COOKIES

Be sure to use homemade mincemeat here, because the texture as well as the quality of store-bought mincemeats varies widely. If you like slightly crisp cookies, bake and serve them on the same day. If you like moist ones, store them airtight—the fruit will soften them.

8 tablespoons unsalted butter, softened

½ cup sugar

1 teaspoon grated orange peel

1 large egg, beaten

1 cup (5 ounces) all-purpose flour

Pinch salt

½ teaspoon baking powder

¾ cup Mincemeat (page 296)

Preheat convection oven to 350 degrees. Cream butter and sugar together in a large bowl until very light and fluffy. Add orange peel, and beat in egg. Incorporate flour, salt, baking powder, and mincemeat. Arrange by rounded teaspoonfuls at 2-inch intervals on ungreased baking sheets. Bake for about 10 minutes, until the edges brown.

PREPARATION TIME: 10 MINUTES / OVEN TIME: 10 MINUTES / EASY

JELLY COOKIES

Simple jelly cookies are always popular, and the dough can be made in the food processor in seconds, even with cold butter.

4 tablespoons unsalted butter, softened

¼ cup sugar

½ teaspoon grated lemon peel

1 egg yolk

⅔ cup (3¼ ounces) all-purpose flour

½ teaspoon baking powder

Pinch salt

Red currant jelly

Preheat convection oven to 350 degrees. Cream butter and sugar together in a bowl until fluffy. (This can be done in a food processor with cold butter, cut up.) Add remaining ingredients except jelly, and blend well. Pinch off pieces of dough (it will be soft) and form into 1-inch balls. Place on an ungreased baking sheet, spacing well apart. Make an indentation across each cookie with the handle of a wooden spoon dipped in water, and pinch ends shut to make oval cookies. Fill with a spot of jelly. Bake for 10 minutes, and cool on rack. Add more jelly when cookies have cooled.

PREPARATION TIME: 10 MINUTES / OVEN TIME: 10 MINUTES / EASY

REAL VANILLA WAFERS

Packaged vanilla wafers are not bad, just uninteresting. The real thing, on the other hand, made with real butter and a real vanilla bean, is a revelation.

6 tablespoons unsalted butter, softened

¼ cup sugar

1 plump fresh vanilla bean, 6 inches

¼ teaspoon salt

1 large egg, beaten

A generous ⅔ cup (4 ounces) all-purpose flour

Preheat convection oven to 375 degrees. Line a baking sheet with baking parchment, or grease with butter and dust with flour. Beat butter and sugar together in a bowl until fluffy. Split the vanilla bean and scrape the inside pulp and seeds into the butter mixture. Add salt. Whisk in egg. Sift flour over the mixture, and fold it in. Transfer dough to a pastry bag fitted with a plain ½-inch tip, and pipe out 1-inch rounds. Flatten the tops gently with the back of a spoon dipped in water. Bake for 12 minutes, until gold at the edges.

PREPARATION TIME: 10 MINUTES / OVEN TIME: 12 MINUTES

MAKES 40 COOKIES

RICH BUTTER COOKIES

The big advantage to making your own simple cookies is that you can afford to use the very best ingredients, and they are fresh when you serve them. The taste and texture of a genuinely fresh butter cookie, made with a generous amount of sweet butter, comes as a wonderful surprise to many people!

1 *cup unsalted butter, cut into pieces*

⅞ *cup (3½ ounces) confectioners' sugar*

1 *large egg*

2 *cups plus 1 tablespoon (10½ ounces) all-purpose flour*

Pinch salt

½ *teaspoon vanilla extract*

1 *teaspoon grated lemon or orange peel (optional)*

Candied cherries or candied citrus peel

Preheat convection oven to 350 degrees. Fit a pastry bag with a large star tip. In the bowl of a food processor, cream together butter and sugar. Add egg, and process to mix. Add flour, salt, vanilla, and grated peel. Pulse machine on and off until mixture is smooth, about 30 seconds. Transfer to the pastry bag and pipe out 1-inch rosettes on an ungreased baking sheet. Top each one with half a cherry or some candied peel, pushing it in well. Bake for 12 to 15 minutes, until lightly colored. Cool on a rack.

PREPARATION TIME: 10 MINUTES / OVEN TIME: 12 TO 15 MINUTES / EASY

RUM RAISIN
AND CHOCOLATE COOKIES

These delectable cookies are at their crispy best when eaten on the day they are made; they will soften slightly if stored.

½ cup raisins

2 tablespoons dark rum

8 tablespoons unsalted butter, softened

½ cup sugar

2 large eggs

½ teaspoon vanilla extract

1 cup (5 ounces) all-purpose flour

Pinch salt

¼ teaspoon baking powder

1 tablespoon milk or heavy cream

½ cup semisweet chocolate chips

Preheat convection oven to 350 degrees. Combine raisins and rum in a saucepan, and heat gently. Carefully light with a match and stir until rum has evaporated. Let cool.

Beat butter and sugar together in a bowl until very creamy. Add eggs one at a time, beating well. Add vanilla, flour, salt, baking powder, and milk. Stir in raisins and chocolate chips. Transfer dough to a pastry bag fitted with a ½-inch plain tube, and pipe out 1-inch mounds at 2-inch intervals on an ungreased baking sheet. (Or drop by rounded teaspoonfuls.) Flatten with a fork dipped in cold water. Bake for 10 minutes, until brown at the edges.

PREPARATION TIME: 15 MINUTES / OVEN TIME: 10 MINUTES / EASY

ALMOND SPONGE
COOKIES WITH APRICOT

Meringue cookies can be crisp or chewy—these are the soft kind.

⅔ cup whole almonds,
    unpeeled

4 large egg whites

1 cup (4 ounces)
    confectioners' sugar,
    sifted

Pinch salt

1 tablespoon cornstarch,
    sifted

Apricot jam

Preheat convection oven to 325 degrees. Line a baking sheet with baking parchment. Fit a pastry bag with a large star tip. Grind almonds to a powder. (If possible use a nut grinder, as this makes fine flakes without releasing the nut oil.) Beat egg whites in a large bowl until they begin to hold their shape, then add half the confectioners' sugar and the salt. Beat at high speed until stiff. Combine powdered almonds, remaining confectioners' sugar, and cornstarch, and fold into egg whites very lightly, so as not to deflate the mixture. Transfer to the pastry bag and pipe out 1-inch rosettes onto the prepared baking sheet. Bake for 15 minutes, until crisp.

Remove the baking sheet from the oven, and pour a little water under the parchment. This will create steam and loosen the cookies. Leave cookies for 2 minutes before peeling them off the paper, then cool on a rack. When completely cooled, sandwich together with apricot jam.

PREPARATION TIME: 15 MINUTES / OVEN TIME: 15 MINUTES

CORNMEAL ALMOND COOKIES

Quick to make in a food processor and not unlike Chinese almond cookies (they make a good dessert after a Chinese meal, with tea), these crunchy cookies keep well.

⅓ cup whole almonds, unpeeled

¼ cup sugar

Heaping ¾ cup (4 ounces) all-purpose flour

¼ cup (1 ounce) cornmeal

¼ teaspoon salt

Dash almond extract

8 tablespoons unsalted butter, chilled, cut into pieces

30 whole blanched almonds, for decoration

Preheat convection oven to 350 degrees. In the bowl of a food processor, combine almonds and sugar and process until evenly ground. Add flour, cornmeal, salt, almond extract, and butter. Process until a crumbly dough forms. Form into 1-inch balls and place on an ungreased baking sheet. Press a whole almond into each one, forming the cookie into a fat oval. Bake for 15 minutes, until lightly browned. Leave on baking sheet for 2 minutes to firm up, then remove and cool on a rack.

PREPARATION TIME: 10 MINUTES / OVEN TIME: 15 MINUTES / EASY

COCONUT MACAROONS

Unlike commercially made coconut macaroons, which are often cloyingly sweet and have a strange texture, these are light, crisp, and delectable. They are at their best eaten on the day they are made.

½ cup egg whites, about 4

½ cup sugar

Pinch salt

1 teaspoon vanilla extract

2 cups packaged lightly sweetened shredded coconut

Preheat convection oven to 300 degrees. Line a baking sheet with baking parchment. Beat egg whites until they start to hold their shape. Add half the sugar, the salt and vanilla, and beat until very stiff. Fold in remaining sugar and coconut. Using a large spoon, form mixture into tall mounds about 2 inches wide and 1½ inches high on the prepared baking sheet. Bake for 30 minutes. Leave on baking sheet for 5 minutes, then remove and cool on a rack.

PREPARATION TIME: 10 MINUTES / OVEN TIME: 30 MINUTES / EASY

CRUNCHY NUT DUNKING COOKIES WITH ANISE

This is an American version of a very crisp cookie that is traditional in the Limousin region of France. The cookies are delicious dipped in a cup of milky coffee—or in a glass of wine.

⅓ cup whole almonds, unpeeled

⅓ cup whole pecans

½ teaspoon aniseeds

Generous 1 cup sugar

Generous 1½ cups (8 ounces) all-purpose flour

1 tablespoon baking powder

½ cup milk

1 egg, beaten

In the bowl of a food processor, combine almonds, pecans, and aniseeds. Process until nuts are coarsely chopped. Add sugar, flour, baking powder, and milk, and process just enough to blend. Turn dough out onto a lightly floured surface and knead lightly for a few seconds. Form into a 15-inch-long sausage shape, roll in plastic or foil, and chill for at least 1 hour.

Preheat convection oven to 400 degrees. Grease two baking sheets with butter. Cut dough, which will be sticky, at a 45-degree angle into oval slices approximately ⅛ inch thick. Place on the prepared baking sheets about 1 inch apart, and brush with beaten egg. Bake for 10 minutes. Cookies will rise slightly and spread into 3¼-inch ovals. Cool on racks and store airtight.

PREPARATION TIME: 15 MINUTES; 1 HOUR CHILLING /
OVEN TIME: 10 MINUTES / EASY

HAZELNUT BUTTER COOKIES

MAKES
40 COOKIES

Austrian in origin, these cookies are irresistibly light and crunchy. They keep well if stored airtight, and make a much-appreciated gift. It is important to use cold butter—the tiny granules formed in the food processor melt as the cookies bake and form little air pockets. This makes the cookies rise, even though there is no leavening, and makes them light.

1 *cup whole hazelnuts,*
 with skins
1 *cup (5 ounces) all-*
 purpose flour
 Scant ⅓ cup sugar

½ *teaspoon vanilla extract*
12 *tablespoons butter,*
 chilled, cut into small
 cubes

Preheat convection oven to 350 degrees. Place hazelnuts in the bowl of a food processor and chop until quite finely ground. Add flour and sugar, and process until well mixed. Add vanilla and cold butter, and process until a dough forms. Pinch off pieces of dough and form into 1-inch balls. Flatten slightly and place on two ungreased baking sheets, allowing space for the cookies to expand. Bake for 15 minutes, until very lightly colored. (The bottoms should be light brown.) Let cool on racks.

PREPARATION TIME: 12 MINUTES / OVEN TIME: 15 MINUTES / EASY

MAKES 22
DOUBLE COOKIES

HAZELNUT SPONGE FINGERS WITH CHOCOLATE

The use of a nut grinder is recommended here, as it makes fine, powdery flakes without releasing the nut oil. (Oil or fat of any kind tends to deflate a meringue mixture.) If you are using a blender or food processor, which does release the nut oil, combine hazelnuts with a little of the sugar before grinding.

⅔ cup whole hazelnuts,
  with skins
4 large egg whites
1 cup (4 ounces)
  confectioners' sugar,
  sifted

Pinch salt
1 tablespoon cornstarch,
  sifted
2 ounces semisweet
  chocolate, melted

Preheat convection oven to 325 degrees. Line a baking sheet with baking parchment. Have ready a pastry bag fitted with a large star tube.

Grind hazelnuts to a powder. Beat egg whites in a large bowl until they begin to hold their shape, then add half the confectioners' sugar and the salt. Beat at high speed until stiff. In another bowl, combine powdered hazelnuts, remaining confectioners' sugar, and cornstarch, and fold into egg whites very lightly, so as not to deflate the mixture. Transfer to the pastry bag and pipe out 2-inch-long fingers onto the prepared baking sheet. Bake for 15 minutes, until crisp.

Remove baking sheet from the oven and pour a little water under the parchment, which will create steam and loosen the cookies. Leave cookies for 2 minutes before peeling them off the paper, then cool on a rack. When cold, sandwich cookies together with melted chocolate.

PREPARATION TIME: 15 MINUTES / OVEN TIME: 15 MINUTES

NUT LACE COOKIES   MAKES 48 COOKIES

These thin, crisp wafer cookies can be formed into attractive baskets by pushing them inside a cup while they are still hot from the oven. When they have cooled, fill the baskets with ice cream and garnish with fresh fruit. Even though several sheets of cookies can be baked at one time in a convection oven, don't make more than one sheetful of lace cookies at a time if you are forming baskets, or the cookies will harden before they can be molded.

Store lace cookies airtight, or they will lose their crispness.

1 cup (5 ounces) all-purpose flour, sifted	½ cup light corn syrup
⅔ cup finely chopped walnuts, pecans, or almonds	8 tablespoons butter
	⅔ cup brown sugar, firmly packed

Preheat convection oven to 350 degrees. Grease two large baking sheets.

Blend flour and chopped nuts in a bowl and set aside. In a saucepan, combine corn syrup, butter, and brown sugar and bring to a boil. Remove from the heat and stir in flour and nuts. Drop by rounded teaspoonfuls onto the baking sheets, 3 inches apart. Bake for 7 minutes. Leave on the baking sheets for 1 minute to firm up slightly, then remove with a spatula to a cooling rack. Repeat with remaining batter on a cold (not hot) baking sheet.

PREPARATION TIME: 20 MINUTES / OVEN TIME: 7 MINUTES / EASY

ORANGE TUILES, OR TILE COOKIES

Tuiles (curved wafer cookies) get their name from their resemblance to old-fashioned clay roofing tiles. Although you can bake two trays of cookies simultaneously in a convection oven, it is easier to work with one batch of tuiles at a time, as they turn crisp very quickly.

8 tablespoons unsalted butter, softened

½ cup sugar

½ orange

2 tablespoons fresh orange juice

2 large egg whites

½ cup (2½ ounces) all-purpose flour, sifted

Scant 1 cup sliced almonds, with skins

Preheat convection oven to 375 degrees. Grease a baking sheet generously with butter. Cream butter and sugar together in a bowl until fluffy. Grate the peel of the orange half directly into the mixture, and add orange juice. Whisk in egg whites, then flour, and finally add sliced almonds.

Drop batter by rounded teaspoonfuls onto the prepared baking sheet. Dip a fork in water and spread each mound into a 3¼-inch round. Bake for 6 or 7 minutes, until the edges turn golden brown. Immediately remove from the baking sheet with a spatula, and bend cookies over the back of a rolling pin or a bottle, or place inside a ring mold, to form a curve. Cookies will become crisp almost immediately—if they become too crisp to bend, return them to the oven briefly. Repeat with remaining batter, always using a cold baking sheet. Finish cooling cookies on a rack.

PREPARATION TIME: 20 MINUTES / OVEN TIME: 6 TO 7 MINUTES

PECAN CLOUD COOKIES

Quite easy to make but very fragile and delicate when baked, people tend to ask, "What holds them together?" as they reach for a second and a third. To make Walnut Cloud Cookies, substitute walnuts for the pecans.

10 tablespoons unsalted butter, chilled, cut into pieces
3 tablespoons sugar
2 cups ground pecans
1 cup (5 ounces) all-purpose flour

Tiny pinch salt
¼ teaspoon cinnamon
1 teaspoon vanilla extract
Confectioners' sugar

Preheat convection oven to 350 degrees. In the bowl of a food processor, combine butter, sugar, pecans, flour, salt, cinnamon, and vanilla. Process until dough forms. Handling it very lightly (it will be soft), pinch off pieces of dough and form into 1-inch balls. Place on an ungreased baking sheet and bake for 12 to 15 minutes. Let cool on baking sheet for 1 minute. Then sift confectioners' sugar onto a sheet of waxed paper or aluminum foil, and place warm cookies on top. Sift more confectioners' sugar over the cookies, and let cool.

PREPARATION TIME: 10 MINUTES / OVEN TIME: 12 TO 15 MINUTES

LADYFINGERS

Much nicer than any ladyfingers you can buy, these taste wonderful with tea or coffee, or you can serve them with any creamy dessert, including ice cream.

4 *large eggs, separated*
½ *cup sugar*
1 *teaspoon vanilla extract*
   Heaping ½ cup cornstarch

⅔ *cup (3½ ounces) cake flour*
Confectioners' sugar

Preheat convection oven to 325 degrees. Line a baking sheet with 5-inch-wide strips of baking parchment, securing them with a dab of butter under each corner. Have ready a pastry bag fitted with a plain round ½-inch tip.

Place egg yolks in a large bowl and add three fourths of the sugar. Beat until the mixture is thick, pale in color, and forms a slowly dissolving ribbon from a lifted beater. Add vanilla.

Combine cornstarch and flour, sift over the egg mixture, and fold in. Beat egg whites until they start to hold their shape, then add remaining sugar and beat until stiff and glossy. Fold into batter. Transfer batter to the pastry bag and form 3½-inch-long fingers across the width of the parchment strips. Sift confectioners' sugar lightly over the surface. Wet a pastry brush with water and shake it briskly in the air over the baking sheets, so that tiny drops of water fall on the ladyfingers. (This will ensure that sugar "pearls" form during baking.) Let stand for 5 minutes.

Bake ladyfingers for 15 minutes. Leave them on the baking sheet for 10 minutes before peeling them off the parchment. Cool on a rack, and store airtight.

PREPARATION TIME: 20 MINUTES / OVEN TIME: 15 MINUTES

MADELEINES

You will need a madeleine pan, with its shell-shaped indentations, to make these delicate sponge cookies. As they bake, a little "hump" should form on top of each one. When they have been unmolded and the pan is cold, wipe it thoroughly with paper towels but do not wash it. Cake pans should not be washed at all if possible; they will bake better and stick less.

4 *tablespoons unsalted butter, melted and cooled slightly*
1 *large egg*
3 *tablespoons sugar*

½ *teaspoon vanilla extract*
5 *tablespoons (1½ ounces) cake flour*
½ *teaspoon baking powder*
Pinch salt

Preheat convection oven to 350 degrees. Brush a 12-mold madeleine pan with some of the butter and sprinkle with flour. Rap the pan sharply upside down on the counter to leave a thin, even coating of flour in the molds.

Beat egg with sugar and vanilla in a bowl. Measure flour, baking powder, and salt onto a paper towel. Sift over the egg mixture and fold in. Pour butter around the edge of the bowl, and gently fold it in. Spoon batter into molds, and rap the pan sharply to spread the batter. Bake for 10 minutes. Upturn pan onto a rack; the madeleines should fall out easily.

PREPARATION TIME: 15 MINUTES / OVEN TIME: 10 MINUTES

PASTRY DOUGHS, PASTRIES, AND TARTS

PLAIN PASTRY SHELL

It saves time and effort to make two tart shells at once. The unused one can be frozen in the pan and baked without thawing. However, if you want to make only one tart shell, beat the egg with the water and use only half of it; save the remainder for an egg glaze in another recipe.

To make shortcrust pastry dough by hand, have the butter at room temperature. Place dry ingredients in a bowl, and rub butter in lightly with your fingers until the mixture resembles cornmeal. Make a well in the center, and add egg and water. Stir in and mix lightly until dough forms. (A few extra drops of water may be required; the food processor method requires very little.) Wrap and chill for 30 minutes before rolling out.

2 cups (10 ounces) all-
   purpose flour
½ teaspoon salt
10 tablespoons unsalted
   butter, chilled, cut into
   pieces

1 large egg
2 tablespoons cold water

Place flour, salt, and butter in the bowl of a food processor and process until evenly blended. With the motor running, add egg and water through the feed tube. Turn machine off as soon as the dough starts to form into a ball. Working with half the dough at a time, roll out on a lightly floured surface into an 11-inch circle. Fit into a 9-inch fluted tart pan with removable base, and trim the edge.

If the pastry shell is to be baked without a filling, push sides of dough very slightly above and over the edge of the rim. (This will prevent the sides of the pastry shell from shrinking and falling down.) Prick base and chill for at least 10 minutes before baking.

To bake without a filling, preheat convection oven to 350 degrees. Bake for 5 minutes, then check pastry and deflate any air bubbles with the tip of a knife. Continue baking for a further 10 to 15 minutes, until crisp and pale gold. (Then fill with required filling and continue baking according to recipe.) If a fully baked shell is required, continue baking until golden brown, about 10 minutes longer.

PREPARATION TIME: 10 MINUTES; 10 MINUTES CHILLING   /
OVEN TIME: 15 TO 20 MINUTES

SWEET PASTRY SHELL

Mixed in the food processor in seconds, this dough, made without egg, is exceptionally crisp and tender because it gets very little handling and stays cold. Should your dough be on the soft side and stick to the plastic wrap, place it in the refrigerator for a few minutes to firm up again.

Scant 1¼ cups (6 ounces) all-purpose flour

1 *tablespoon sugar*

8 *tablespoons butter, chilled, cut into pieces*

Dash vanilla extract

2 *tablespoons cold water*

In the bowl of a food processor, combine flour, sugar, butter, and vanilla. Process until evenly blended. With the motor running, add water. Turn machine on and off until dough forms. Immediately roll out between two sheets of plastic wrap into an 11-inch circle. Peel off top layer of plastic and reverse dough onto a 9-inch tart pan with removable base. Remove remaining plastic and fit the dough against the sides of the pan. Trim off edges and then, with your thumb and forefinger, extend the dough slightly above and over the rim. Prick bottom of shell, and chill for at least 10 minutes before baking.

To bake without a filling, preheat convection oven to 350 degrees. Bake for 5 minutes, then check pastry and deflate any air bubbles with the tip of a knife. Continue baking for a further 10 to 15 minutes, until crisp and pale gold. (Then add required filling and continue baking according to recipe.) If a fully baked shell is required, continue baking until golden brown, about 10 minutes longer.

PREPARATION TIME: 10 MINUTES; 10 MINUTES CHILLING   /
OVEN TIME: 15 TO 20 MINUTES

PASTRY SHELL
WITH LEMON PEEL

A good choice for a tart containing apples or citrus fruit. You can make a double batch and turn the remaining dough into lemon cookies: Roll dough out and cut into 3-inch circles with a cookie cutter, and bake at 350 degrees for 15 minutes or until light gold. Cool on a rack, and when cold spread with a light glaze of sifted confectioners' sugar beaten with enough lemon juice to make a thin icing.

1½ cups (7½ ounces) all-purpose flour

2 tablespoons sugar

8 tablespoons unsalted butter, chilled, cut into pieces

½ teaspoon salt

1 teaspoon grated lemon peel

1 large egg

1 to 2 teaspoons fresh lemon juice

In the bowl of a food processor, combine flour, sugar, butter, salt, and lemon peel. Process until evenly blended. With the motor running, add egg and lemon juice through the feed tube. Process until dough forms into a ball. (If the mixture remains crumbly, add more lemon juice.) Roll out on a lightly floured surface into an 11-inch circle. Fit into a 9-inch fluted tart pan with removable base, and trim the edge. If the pastry shell is to be baked without a filling, push sides of dough very slightly above and over the edge of the rim. (This will prevent sides of pastry shell from shrinking and falling down.) Prick base, and chill for at least 10 minutes before baking.

To bake without a filling, preheat convection oven to 350 degrees. Bake for 5 minutes, then check pastry and deflate any air bubbles with the tip of a knife. Continue baking for a further 10 to 15 minutes, until crisp and pale gold. (Then add required filling and continue baking according to recipe.) If a fully baked shell is required, continue baking until golden brown, about 10 minutes longer.

PREPARATION TIME: 10 MINUTES; 10 MINUTES CHILLING   /
OVEN TIME: 15 TO 20 MINUTES

PASTRY SHELL WITH ALMONDS

To make Pastry Shell with Walnuts, substitute ⅓ cup walnut meats for the almonds. As with any rich, sweet pastry dough, you can roll out any leftovers and bake them like cookies.

⅓ cup whole almonds, unpeeled

3 tablespoons sugar

Generous ¾ cup (4½ ounces) all-purpose flour

Pinch salt

6 tablespoons unsalted butter, chilled, cut into pieces

1 large egg yolk

Grind almonds and sugar together in a food processor until powdery (the sugar will prevent the nuts from becoming oily). Add flour and salt, and process to blend. Add butter and process until evenly incorporated. Add egg yolk and process, pulsing the machine on and off, just until dough forms. Roll dough out between sheets of plastic wrap into an 11-inch circle. (This makes the dough easier to handle, as it is quite soft. If it becomes difficult to work with, chill for a few minutes, plastic and all.) Peel off top layer of plastic and invert dough over a 9-inch tart pan with removable base. Fit the dough against the sides, and trim the edges. If pastry shell is to be baked without a filling, push sides of dough very slightly above and over edge of rim, which will prevent the sides from falling down. Prick base of tart shell, and chill for at least 10 minutes before baking.

To bake without a filling, preheat convection oven to 350 degrees. Bake for 5 minutes, then check pastry and deflate any air bubbles with the tip of a knife. Continue baking for a further 10 to 15 minutes, until crisp and pale gold. (Then add required filling and continue baking according to recipe.) If a fully baked shell is required, continue baking until golden brown, about 10 minutes longer.

PREPARATION TIME: 15 MINUTES; 10 MINUTES CHILLING /
OVEN TIME: 15 TO 20 MINUTES

QUICK PUFF PASTRY

There are five different methods for making puff pastry. This one, known in France as *Ecossaise*, or the Scottish method, is the easiest. Always let puff pastry rest in the refrigerator after rolling and shaping, so the gluten in the flour can relax. The pastry will then rise and bake more evenly. Unlike a classic puff pastry, which is a lot more complicated to make but which can be kept in the refrigerator for a few days, this one must be baked on the same day that it is made or it will not rise properly. However, it can be formed in the shape in which it is to be baked and then frozen. Transfer the frozen dough straight to the oven; there is no need to thaw it.

4⅓ cups (1 pound, 5½ ounces) all-purpose flour, sifted

1 teaspoon salt

1 cup cold water

1¾ cups plus 2 tablespoons (15 ounces) unsalted butter, chilled, cut into cubes

Combine flour, salt, and cold water in the bowl of an electric mixer. Stir until dough starts to form, then add butter and mix with the dough hook. Mix only enough to blend—the bits of butter should not disappear. This will take 1 minute or less. Gather dough together, crumbs and all, and turn out onto a lightly floured surface. Roll into a rectangle and fold in thirds like a business letter. (It will look a bit messy.) Roll lightly to seal. Give the dough a quarter turn to the left, so that you will now roll it in a different direction. Repeat the rolling and folding, dusting the dough lightly with flour and keeping the edges of your rectangle as straight as possible. Make two indentations in the dough with your fingers to indicate two "turns." Wrap dough in plastic and chill for 30 minutes. Repeat this whole process twice more, chilling between turns, making six turns in all. Chill for 30 minutes and then roll out for use.

PREPARATION TIME: 30 MINUTES; 2 HOURS CHILLING / OVEN TIME: NONE

BAKED APPLES IN
PUFF PASTRY WITH YOGURT SAUCE

Be sure to use Golden Delicious apples for this recipe; they have a good flavor and texture, and will not collapse when baked without skins.

4 *Golden Delicious apples,*
4 to 6 ounces each

½ *lemon*

2 *tablespoons sugar*

3 *tablespoons Mincemeat*
(page 296), or 1½
tablespoons raisins
mixed with 1½
tablespoons chopped
candied citrus peel

2 *teaspoons grated orange*
peel

1 *cup water*

2 *tablespoons honey*

8 *ounces Quick Puff*
Pastry (page 244), or
½ package frozen puff
pastry, thawed

1 *egg, beaten*

1 *cup plain yogurt*
Dash vanilla extract

Preheat convection oven to 350 degrees. Wash, peel, and core apples, and rub with the cut lemon to prevent discoloration. Place apple skins and cores in a saucepan, add sugar, and cover with water. Set aside.

Combine mincemeat with orange peel, and fill cavities of apples with this mixture. Arrange apples in a shallow baking dish, add water to the dish, and drizzle honey over apples. Bake for 45 minutes, basting several times, or until just tender.

While apples are baking, simmer skins and cores for 30 minutes, and then strain. Remove baked apples from baking dish and allow to cool completely. Combine baking juices with strained liquid and reduce over high heat to ¼ cup, about 5 minutes. Let cool.

Preheat convection oven to 375 degrees. On a lightly floured surface, roll pastry out ⅛ inch thick, and cut out four 6 by 6-inch squares. Transfer squares to a baking sheet and brush edges with beaten egg. Place an apple in the center of each square, and draw up the four corners of the pastry to meet at a point in the center, on top of the apple. Pinch points together to seal. Brush pastry with egg, and

bake for 30 minutes, until pastry is golden brown. To make the sauce, stir reduced apple glaze into yogurt, and add vanilla. Serve sauce alongside the pastries.

PREPARATION TIME: 30 MINUTES / OVEN TIME: 45 MINUTES; 30 MINUTES / EASY

MINCE PIES

MAKES 6 PIES
SERVES 6

Mince pies made with your own mincemeat are truly delicious and very different from the commercial variety. This is a very easy way to form them. The size and quantity of filling depends on the size of bowl used.

8 *ounces Quick Puff Pastry (page 244), or ½ package frozen puff pastry, thawed*

12 *tablespoons Mincemeat (page 296)*

1 *egg, beaten*
Confectioners' sugar

Preheat convection oven to 350 degrees. On a lightly floured surface, roll pastry out ⅛ inch thick into an 8 × 16-inch rectangle. Cut into six equal squares. Place one of the squares inside a small shallow bowl or teacup. Fill with 2 tablespoons of mincemeat, and brush sides of dough with egg wash. Fold points of pastry over filling, and seal together. Turn pie out of bowl, seam side down, and place on an ungreased baking sheet. Repeat with remaining dough. Brush tops of pies with egg wash, and mark lightly with a knife tip, starting at the center and making curved lines to the edge, like a flower. Bake for 20 to 25 minutes. Sprinkle with confectioners' sugar and serve warm.

PREPARATION TIME: 15 MINUTES / OVEN TIME: 20 TO 25 MINUTES / EASY

PEAR TARTS

These pear-shaped tarts are very easy to put together on short notice, using ingredients in the freezer and off the shelf. The contrast of the smooth, tender fruit and the crisp puff pastry is really excellent. Be sure to serve them straight from the oven or their charm will be lost —the pastry toughens as it cools.

4 *frozen puff pastry patty shells, thawed*

1 *tablespoon butter, chilled, cut into small dice*

1 *tablespoon sugar*

4 *poached or canned pear halves (in natural juice)*

1 *egg, beaten*
Apricot jam

Preheat convection oven to 375 degrees. On a lightly floured surface, roll patty shells into 6½ by 4½-inch ovals. With a knife, trim each into a pear shape with a stem at the top. (If this seems difficult to do freehand, make a pattern on cardboard first and cut around that.) Then score a border line all the way round each "pear," ½ inch from the edge. Do not cut all the way through the dough. Dot pastry with butter, sprinkle with sugar, and place on a greased baking sheet. Set in the freezer for 5 minutes to relax the dough, so pastry shells won't shrink in the oven and will rise properly.

Drain pear halves thoroughly. Place a pear half on each pastry base, flat side down. Brush edges of the dough with beaten egg. (Do not let it run down the sides, or the layers of puff pastry will stick together instead of rising.) Bake tarts for 20 minutes, until pastry is golden at the edges—the sides will rise and enclose the pear. Heat a little apricot jam, strain it through a sieve, and brush over the tarts. Serve warm.

PREPARATION TIME: 15 MINUTES / OVEN TIME: 20 MINUTES / EASY

APPLE AND ALMOND JALOUSIE

SERVES 8

A jalousie gets its name from a type of old-fashioned louvered window screen. The person inside could look out, but those outside could not look in, an arrangement that suited jealous husbands very well!

1 *tablespoon raisins*

1 *tablespoon dark rum*

1 *tablespoon unsalted butter*

1 *large tart green apple, 7 to 8 ounces, peeled, cored, and sliced*

1 *tablespoon brown sugar*

NUT FILLING

½ *cup whole almonds, with skins*

4 *tablespoons unsalted butter*

2 *tablespoons sugar*

1 *tablespoon all-purpose flour*

1 *large egg*

PASTRY

8 *ounces Quick Puff Pastry (page 244), or ½ package frozen puff pastry, thawed*

1 *egg, beaten Confectioners' sugar*

Soak raisins in rum while setting out other ingredients. Heat butter in a skillet and sauté apple slices with brown sugar for 3 or 4 minutes. Add raisins and rum, and carefully set alight. Cook for 2 minutes, shaking the pan, and allow to cool.

Make the filling: Grind almonds in a food processor. Add butter, sugar, and flour, and process until smooth. Add egg, and process until mixture is creamy. Combine with sautéed apple mixture.

Preheat convection oven to 375 degrees. On a lightly floured surface, roll puff pastry into a 12 by 14-inch rectangle. Cut into two strips, one about 1 inch wider than the other, and trim the edges. Place the narrower strip on an ungreased baking sheet, and brush the edges with water. Spread filling to within 1 inch of the edges. Fold remaining strip in half lengthways, and make small slices across the fold at ¼-inch intervals. Unfold strip and lay it on top of the filling, pressing edges down very well to seal. Make a scallop pattern along the edges by pushing with the back of a knife at regular intervals.

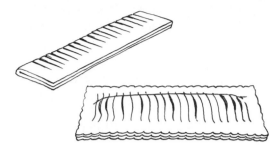

Brush top of tart with egg glaze, and bake for 30 minutes, until well puffed and golden brown. Sprinkle with confectioners' sugar and return to the oven for 5 minutes to glaze. Serve warm.

PREPARATION TIME: 25 MINUTES / OVEN TIME: 35 MINUTES

SERVES 6 TO 8   ## *HONEYED APPLE PIE*

There is no bottom crust to get soggy here, and the tart is very quick to put together. Placing a band of puff pastry dough on the rim gives the top crust a base to hold on to (tucking it under would prevent rising), and it can then rise in the most spectacular way. Be sure to serve this dessert straight from the oven, when it is still puffed and flaky. The dough will sink down and toughen as it cools.

4 *large crisp green apples,*
   about 2 pounds, Granny
   Smith or Pippins
¼ *cup raisins*
¼ *cup honey, or less if*
   apples are sweet
Nutmeg

Cinnamon
¼ *teaspoon salt*
8 *ounces Quick Puff*
   Pastry (page 244), or
   ½ package frozen puff
   pastry, thawed
1 *egg, beaten*

Preheat convection oven to 350 degrees. Peel apples, cut in half, and core. Lay apple halves flat side down and cut across into thin slices.

Fan an overlapping layer of apple slices around the edge of a 9-inch glass pie pan, forming a spiral and mounding the center with short end pieces. Sprinkle with raisins and drizzle with honey. Dust lightly with nutmeg, cinnamon, and a very little salt to bring out the flavors. Top with another overlapping layer of apple slices, mounding up the center. Drizzle with honey and season lightly as before.

Roll pastry out ⅛ inch thick and cut out a 10-inch circle. Cut a 2-inch-wide band from the trimmings, long enough to go round the edge, and some leaves or heart shapes for decoration. (It doesn't matter if the band is not all one piece.) Wet the rim of the pie pan with water, and lay the band of pastry on it, securing the dough under the rim. Brush the band with water, and lay the top crust in place, pressing the edges down well but not folding them under the rim. Brush the top with egg glaze. Make a hole in the center for steam to escape, and decorate the top of the pie with pastry cut-outs, glazing these also. Mark the rim of the pastry with the back of a knife placed at an angle. Bake for 30 minutes. Serve hot.

PREPARATION TIME: 20 MINUTES / OVEN TIME: 30 MINUTES / EASY

UPSIDE-DOWN PAPAYA TART

To make Upside-Down Apple Tart (Tarte Tatin) or Upside-Down Quince Tart, substitute peeled and sliced Golden Delicious apples or ripe quinces for the papaya. (The quinces will look hard and unpromising, but are delicious when cooked.) Always serve this tart hot, as the pastry will toughen as it cools.

2 tablespoons butter
½ cup sugar
2 firm ripe papayas, 8 to 10 ounces each

8 ounces Quick Puff Pastry (page 244), or ½ package frozen puff pastry, thawed
Crème fraîche, sour cream, or vanilla ice cream

Preheat convection oven to 375 degrees. Grease the bottom of a 9-inch cast-iron skillet (or other heavy ovenproof pan) with the butter, and sprinkle with sugar. Halve papayas and discard seeds. Peel, and cut into ¾-inch-thick slices. Starting at the outer edge of the skillet, arrange fruit in a spiral until pan is full. (The fruit will pack down as it cooks.) Place skillet over medium-high heat, and cook until sugar caramelizes on the surface and turns a deep golden brown, 7 to 10 minutes. Shake pan to distribute caramel, and remove from the heat. Press mixture down slightly with a spatula to make it as even as possible.

On a lightly floured surface, roll pastry dough out thin (¼ to ⅛ inch thick), and trim into a 10-inch circle. Place circle of dough on top of fruit, tucking edge *inside* pan. Prick top of dough to allow steam to escape. Bake for 18 minutes, until crust is brown and puffed. Place a large flat platter on top of the pan and invert quickly. Serve hot with crème fraîche, sour cream, or vanilla ice cream.

PREPARATION TIME: 20 MINUTES / OVEN TIME: 18 MINUTES / EASY

ALMOND TART WITH APRICOT-LEMON GLAZE

An excellent "off the shelf" tart that is quickly made in a food processor. The pastry is filled with a nut paste that rises in the oven and forms a rich sponge. The tart is finished with two layers of glaze: first a glaze of apricot jam, and then a lemon glaze. Unlike fruit tarts, this keeps well for 2 or 3 days, and is a great standby for picnics.

1 *recipe Plain Pastry dough (page 239)*
2 *cups Quick Nut-Paste Filling made with almonds (page 297)*
¼ *cup raspberry jam*

½ *cup apricot jam*
2 *tablespoons dry white wine*
2 *tablespoons fresh lemon juice*
⅓ *to ½ cup sifted confectioners' sugar*

Preheat convection oven to 350 degrees. On a lightly floured surface, roll out half the pastry dough and line a 9-inch tart pan with removable base. Roll out remaining dough ⅛ inch thick and place on a baking sheet. Chill tart shell and leftover dough for 10 minutes.

Cover bottom of tart shell with raspberry jam, and top with almond filling, smoothing it with a spatula. Cut chilled leftover pastry dough into ⅓-inch-wide strips. Brush edges of tart shell with water, and form a lattice top using the dough strips, securing the edges well. Bake for 35 minutes, until pastry is well browned and top is golden. (The filling will rise between the lattice strips.)

Combine apricot jam and wine in a small saucepan, and heat gently. Strain, and brush over tart while still warm. Let cool until the apricot glaze is no longer sticky. Then combine lemon juice with enough sifted confectioners' sugar to make a runny white glaze, and brush it over the tart, including pastry edges. Let cool completely and serve at room temperature.

PREPARATION TIME: 30 MINUTES / OVEN TIME: 35 MINUTES

252   CONVECTION CUISINE

APPLE-PECAN TART
WITH MERINGUE TOPPING

This is a variation on a traditional French recipe. We substituted pecans for the more usual almonds, and cut down on the sugar.

3 *tablespoons raisins*

2 *tablespoons dark rum*

1½ *tablespoons butter*

3 *tart green apples, 1 pound, peeled, cored, and diced*

1 *tablespoon brown sugar*

2 *cups Quick Nut-Paste Filling made with pecans (page 297)*

1 *Pastry Shell with Lemon Peel (page 242), unbaked*

MERINGUE TOPPING

2 *large egg whites*

2 *tablespoons sugar*

½ *teaspoon cornstarch*

2 *tablespoons apricot jam*

1 *tablespoon sliced almonds, with skins*

1 *tablespoon confectioners' sugar*

Soak raisins in rum for 30 minutes. Heat butter in a skillet and sauté diced apple with brown sugar for 5 minutes. Add raisins and rum, and carefully set alight. Cook for 2 minutes, and let cool.

Preheat convection oven to 350 degrees. Combine cooled apple mixture with pecan filling, and spread in pastry shell. Bake for 30 to 35 minutes, until top is brown and pastry shell is well cooked, and let cool.

An hour or two before serving time, preheat convection oven to 350 degrees. Beat egg whites with sugar and cornstarch until stiff. Whisk apricot jam in a bowl, and then whisk in the meringue. Spread over tart and sprinkle with sliced almonds. Sift confectioners' sugar on top, and bake for 10 minutes, until gilded. Serve at room temperature.

PREPARATION TIME: 30 MINUTES SOAKING; 10 MINUTES / OVEN TIME: 30 TO 35 MINUTES; 10 MINUTES

APRICOT TART
WITH CRÈME BRÛLÉE

This is an exceptional tart—the contrast of the crisp pastry, slightly acidic apricots, silky custard, and dark, crisp, caramelized topping is very seductive! The pastry shell, apricots, and custard can all be prepared a day ahead.

1 *Sweet Pastry Shell (page 241), unbaked*

8 *ounces dried apricots*

1 *cup water*

½ *cup white wine*

2 *tablespoons sugar*

2 *strips orange zest (colored part of peel only), each 3 inches long*

CUSTARD

3 *large egg yolks*

3 *tablespoons sugar*

1 *cup heavy cream*

¼ *cup dark brown sugar, firmly packed*

Preheat convection oven to 350 degrees. Bake pastry shell for 15 minutes. While it is baking, combine apricots, water, wine, sugar, and orange zest in a saucepan. Bring to a boil, simmer for 15 minutes, and let cool. Unmold pastry shell, and set aside to cool on a rack.

Make the custard: In the top of a double boiler (or metal bowl set over a saucepan), combine egg yolks, sugar, and cream. Whisk over simmering water until slightly thickened, 165 degrees on a candy thermometer, about 10 minutes. If you are not using the custard immediately, strain it into a bowl, dust with confectioners' sugar to prevent a skin from forming on the surface, and refrigerate.

Preheat convection oven to 350 degrees. Return cooled tart shell to tart pan. Drain apricots thoroughly, and lay them in the tart shell. Strain custard over the apricots. Bake for 20 minutes, until just set. Unmold and let cool.

Shortly before serving, sift brown sugar over custard. Place the tart briefly under a very hot broiler to caramelize the sugar and create a thin, brittle coating (watch it carefully as the sugar will melt and darken almost immediately). Alternatively, heat a heavy flat-bottomed cast-iron skillet until it is very hot and apply the underside to the sugar, rotating the pan slightly.

PREPARATION TIME: 40 MINUTES / OVEN TIME: 15 MINUTES; 20 MINUTES

SERVES 8

CHOCOLATE PECAN TART

Quick and easy to make, this has a very light, creamy filling and is not as sweet and dense as the standard chocolate pecan tart.

1 *Plain Pastry Shell (page 239), unbaked*

4 *tablespoons butter*

1 *ounce unsweetened chocolate, chopped*

½ *cup brown sugar, firmly packed*

1 *cup dark corn syrup*

Pinch salt

3 *large eggs, lightly beaten*

1 *tablespoon Cognac*

2 *cups pecan halves*

Preheat convection oven to 350 degrees. Bake pastry shell for 15 minutes, and set aside. Combine butter, chocolate, brown sugar, corn syrup, and salt in a metal bowl or the top of a double boiler. Heat over simmering water just until chocolate has melted, stirring gently. Cool to lukewarm.

Whisk eggs and Cognac into chocolate mixture, and stir in pecans. Pour mixture into pastry shell and bake for 35 minutes, covering edge of pastry shell with a "doughnut" of aluminum foil if necessary to prevent overbrowning. Cool on a rack, and serve at room temperature.

PREPARATION TIME: 15 MINUTES / OVEN TIME: 15 MINUTES; 35 MINUTES / EASY

FRESH STRAWBERRY TART

Unlike most strawberry tarts, which have a custard base, this one is all fruit, with a strawberry purée under the berries. As a result it has a wonderfully fresh and lively flavor.

1 *Pastry Shell with Almonds (page 243), unbaked*

5 *cups strawberries*

½ *cup sugar*

½ *cup white wine*

2 *tablespoons cornstarch*

1 *package unflavored gelatin*

1 *tablespoon red wine, burgundy or cabernet*

Preheat convection oven to 350 degrees. Bake pastry shell for 25 minutes, or until golden brown. Unmold and let cool on rack. Wash and hull the strawberries, and reserve 2 cups for the top of the tart. Crush remaining berries in a food processor, not too finely.

In a saucepan, blend the sugar and white wine. Mix cornstarch with a little water, and stir it into the mixture. Sprinkle with gelatin and stir it in. Bring to a boil, add the crushed berries, and simmer for 4 minutes. Pour 1 cup of the strawberry pulp into a small bowl, and blend with the red wine to make a glaze. Pour the remaining pulp into a shallow dish and cool in the refrigerator; when it has started to solidify, after about 15 minutes, pour into the prepared pastry shell. Slice reserved berries about ¼ inch thick. Arrange them on top of the filling like petals, pointed side outwards, starting at the outside. Brush with the glaze, coating all the fruit. Chill for 30 minutes to set up, but serve at cool room temperature, not icy cold.

PREPARATION TIME: 15 MINUTES; 1 HOUR CHILLING / OVEN TIME: 25 MINUTES

GOAT CHEESE AND LEMON TART

Traditional in the Vendée region of France, where I was born, this exceptional tart is known simply as "Le Tourteau Fromage" (Cheese Tart).

1 *Plain Pastry Shell (page 239), unbaked*

1 *tablespoon unsalted butter*

4½ *ounces fresh white goat cheese*

⅓ *cup sugar*

¼ *cup all-purpose flour*

Dash vanilla extract

½ *teaspoon Lemon Paste (page 295), or 1 teaspoon grated lemon peel*

1 *tablespoon milk*

4 *large eggs, separated*

Preheat convection oven to 350 degrees. Bake pastry shell for 15 minutes, until light gold. Remove shell from oven, leaving it in the tart pan.

Increase oven heat to 375 degrees. Combine butter, goat cheese, half the sugar, flour, vanilla, and Lemon Paste in the bowl of a food processor. Add milk and egg yolks, process until smooth, and transfer to a bowl. Whip egg whites until they start to hold their shape, add remaining sugar, and continue beating at high speed until stiff. Stir a little of this meringue into the cheese mixture, then lightly fold in the rest. Pour into the pastry shell, smooth the top, and bake for 18 minutes. The filling will rise into a golden brown dome, which will sink a little as it cools. Unmold tart onto a rack, and serve lukewarm or cold.

PREPARATION TIME: 30 MINUTES / OVEN TIME: 15 MINUTES; 18 MINUTES

GOAT CHEESE AND PEAR TART

Serve this tart in place of a cheese and fruit course after a meal; it is not a sweet pastry. Black pepper is of course simply a spice, though we are used to thinking of it solely as a seasoning for savory dishes. It brings out the flavor of the pears in the most wonderful way.

1 *Plain Pastry Shell (page 239), fully baked*

1 *pound firm ripe pears, 2 or 3*

½ *lemon*

Black pepper

2 *large eggs*

5 *ounces goat cheese*

¾ *cup heavy cream*

Preheat convection oven to 350 degrees. Let pastry shell cool for a few minutes, leaving the shell in the tart pan. Peel pears, core them, and cut in half. Then slice pears thinly and sprinkle with lemon juice to prevent discoloration. Lay the slices in the tart shell in an overlapping spiral. Season with a generous amount of freshly ground black pepper.

Beat eggs and add crumbled goat cheese. Work with a whisk until the mixture is very smooth, then whisk in cream. Pour custard mixture over pears, and bake tart for 20 minutes. Serve lukewarm or at room temperature.

PREPARATION TIME: 40 MINUTES / OVEN TIME: 20 MINUTES

LATTICE MINCEMEAT TART

The secret to success here it to use the homemade mincemeat, which is very different from the commercial variety. Its fresh taste and rich combination of flavors contrast beautifully with the tender, crumbly pastry crust.

1 *recipe Plain Pastry dough (page 239)*

1¾ *cups Mincemeat (page 296)*

¼ *cup sugar*

2 *large eggs*

4 *tablespoons unsalted butter, melted and cooled to lukewarm*

1 *egg, beaten*

Preheat convection oven to 350 degrees. On a lightly floured surface, roll out pastry dough and line a 9-inch tart pan with removable base. Roll out remaining dough ⅛ inch thick and place on a baking sheet. Chill tart shell and leftover dough while preparing filling.

In a bowl, combine mincemeat, sugar, eggs, and melted butter. Spread filling in tart shell, and brush edge of pastry with egg glaze. Cut remaining pastry dough into ⅓-inch-wide strips, and crisscross them over the tart, pressing the ends down well to seal. Brush the lattice with egg glaze, and bake tart for 45 minutes, until pastry is a deep gold. Let it cool in the pan for 2 minutes, then remove rim of pan. Remove base of pan, and let cool on a rack. Serve at room temperature.

PREPARATION TIME: 25 MINUTES / OVEN TIME: 45 MINUTES

LEMON SOUFFLÉ TART

The feather-light, creamy lemon filling requires a little effort, but it is worth every minute to achieve such a delicate and elegant tart.

1 *Sweet Pastry Shell (page 241), unbaked*

4 *large eggs, separated*

½ *cup sugar*

1 *teaspoon Lemon Paste (page 295), or grated peel of 1 lemon*

½ *cup fresh lemon juice*

¼ *cup heavy cream*

½ *teaspoon cornstarch*

Confectioners' sugar

Preheat convection oven to 350 degrees. Bake pastry shell for 20 minutes. Remove shell from the oven, leaving it in the tart pan, and reduce oven heat to 325 degrees.

Place egg yolks in a metal bowl or the top of a double boiler with three fourths of the sugar, and beat until the mixture is pale and light. Add Lemon Paste, lemon juice, and cream. Place the bowl over a pan of simmering water and whisk for 6 or 7 minutes until the mixture thickens slightly.

Using a separate bowl and clean, dry beaters, whisk egg whites until they start to hold their shape. Blend remaining sugar with cornstarch, and add to egg whites. Continue beating until meringue is stiff and glossy. Fold into egg yolk mixture. Pile mixture into prepared tart shell, and bake for 12 minutes. Serve at room temperature, dusted with confectioners' sugar.

PREPARATION TIME: 30 MINUTES / OVEN TIME: 20 MINUTES; 12 MINUTES

PEACH PECAN TART

A family-style tart with a southern flavor to make at the height of the season, when peaches are very sweet and juicy.

2 *pounds fresh peaches, peeled and sliced*

¾ *cup sugar*

¼ *cup all-purpose flour*

¼ *cup brown sugar, firmly packed*

4 *tablespoons unsalted butter*

⅓ *cup chopped pecans*

1 *Sweet Pastry Shell (page 241), unbaked*

1 *tablespoon peach brandy or bourbon (optional)*

Confectioners' sugar

Preheat convection oven to 350 degrees. Mix peaches and sugar in a bowl.

In a separate bowl, combine flour and brown sugar. Cut in butter until mixture forms crumbs, and then stir in nuts. Sprinkle one third of the flour-nut mixture in the bottom of the tart shell. Arrange peaches on top in a spiral pattern. Scatter remaining flour-nut mixture over the surface, and bake for 30 minutes. Remove the tart from the oven and sprinkle with peach brandy. (The easiest way to do this is to put your thumb over the opening and shake the bottle quickly over the tart; the exact quantity is not crucial.) Dust with confectioners' sugar before serving. Serve at room temperature.

PREPARATION TIME: 20 MINUTES / OVEN TIME: 30 MINUTES / EASY

PÉPÉ'S CITRUS
MERINGUE TART

A venerable French pastry chef fondly known to all as Pépé—"little grandfather"—gave this very old recipe to my good friend Udo Nechutnys when he was an apprentice. Pépé would make this tart for the kitchen crew on special occasions; it was his *spécialité*.

1 *Pastry Shell with Lemon Peel (page 242), unbaked*

2 *oranges*

2 *lemons*

4 *large eggs, separated*

½ *cup sugar*

Dash vanilla extract

1 *teaspoon confectioners' sugar*

Preheat convection oven to 350 degrees. Bake pastry shell for 20 minutes. Unmold, and let cool on a rack. Score the skin of 1 orange and 1 lemon and pull off the peel in quarters. Cover the peel with water, bring to a boil and drain, then repeat the process twice, which will take about 10 to 15 minutes in all. (This helps to remove any chemicals on the skin and reduces bitterness.) Peel both oranges and both lemons completely, cutting off the white pith and covering membrane. Cupping the fruit in one hand, cut between the membranes and let the segments fall into bowl. Place the segments in the bowl of a food processor and add blanched peel. Process to a purée. Add ¼ cup of the sugar, vanilla, and egg yolks, and process to blend. Transfer the mixture to a metal bowl or the top of a double boiler, and whisk over a pan of simmering water for 10 minutes, until custard thickens slightly and reaches 165 degrees. Do not let the water touch the underside of the bowl, or the eggs will curdle.

Preheat convection oven to 325 degrees. Return tart shell to tart pan. Pour custard filling into shell, and bake for 15 minutes, until just set. Let cool.

Preheat convection oven to 300 degrees. Beat egg whites until they start to hold their shape. Add the remaining ¼ cup of sugar and continue beating until stiff. Transfer meringue to a pastry bag fitted with a large star tube. Starting at the center of the tart, pipe a tight spiral of meringue over the entire surface. Decorate with rosettes around the edge and in the center. Sift confectioners' sugar over the surface, and bake for 8 minutes, until lightly colored. Serve tart at room temperature.

PREPARATION TIME: 40 MINUTES / OVEN TIME: 20 MINUTES; 15 MINUTES; 8 MINUTES

WHITE CHEESE TART WITH RAISINS AND HONEY

SERVES 8

An Old World cheese tart from Austria with a couple of New World touches. The filling is very lightly sweetened with honey.

A good trick when sliding a delicate tart off the base of the pan is to reverse the fluted rim over it. This will support the tart as you push it, and the crust won't break.

½ cup golden raisins

2 tablespoons bourbon

1 *Pastry Shell with Lemon Peel (page 242), unbaked*

10 ounces cream cheese (preferably fresh)

3 large eggs

2 tablespoons honey

½ cup heavy cream

Dash vanilla extract

½ teaspoon Lemon Paste (page 295), or 1 teaspoon grated lemon peel

1 tablespoon cornstarch

½ cup coarsely chopped pecans

Soak raisins in bourbon for 30 minutes. Preheat convection oven to 350 degrees. Bake pastry shell for 20 minutes.

In a large bowl or a food processor, whisk together cream cheese, eggs, honey, cream, vanilla, Lemon Paste, and cornstarch. Add raisin mixture and pecans. Pour into pastry shell and bake for 20 minutes, until just set. Let cool in the pan for 2 minutes, then remove rim and slide tart off the base onto a rack. Serve at room temperature.

PREPARATION TIME: 30 MINUTES SOAKING; 10 MINUTES /
OVEN TIME: 20 MINUTES; 20 MINUTES / EASY

WHITE CHEESE
TART WITH CHERRY GLAZE   SERVES 8

An old-fashioned white cheese tart always comes as a delectable surprise. It's not too sweet, the cheese has a little tang to it, and the fruit glaze tastes of fruit, not of sugar or sticky jam. (Try to get fresh cream cheese; the commercial type contains a slick gum.)

1 *Pastry Shell with Lemon Peel (page 242), unbaked*

8 *ounces cream cheese (preferably fresh), softened*

1/3 *cup sugar*

2 *large eggs*

1/2 *teaspoon vanilla extract*

1/4 *cup sour cream*

CHERRY GLAZE

1 *16-ounce package frozen unsweetened dark cherries*

1/4 *to 1/2 cup fresh orange juice*

Pinch cinnamon

1 *tablespoon sugar*

1 *teaspoon Lemon Paste (page 295), or grated peel of 1 lemon*

1 *tablespoon cornstarch*

1 *tablespoon Kirschwasser*

Preheat convection oven to 350 degrees. Bake pastry shell for 15 minutes. Remove it from the oven. In a large bowl or a food processor, whisk together the cream cheese, sugar, eggs, vanilla, and sour cream. Pour into tart shell and bake for 20 minutes. While tart is baking, drain cherries in a colander set over a bowl.

Remove tart from the oven, let it cool in the pan for 2 minutes, then remove rim and slide tart off the base onto a rack.

Add enough orange juice to the cherry juice to make ¾ cup. Transfer juice to a saucepan and add cinnamon and sugar. Bring to a boil, and stir in cherries and Lemon Paste. Dissolve cornstarch in 1 tablespoon water, add Kirschwasser, and stir into mixture. Boil for a few seconds, until mixture thickens and clears. Let cool to lukewarm, then pour into tart shell. Chill before serving.

PREPARATION TIME: 35 MINUTES / OVEN TIME: 15 MINUTES

CAKES

ALMOND MERINGUE LAYER CAKE
WITH PRALINE BUTTERCREAM

SERVES 8

Luxury-class pâtisserie does take a little work, but if you can bake hard meringue and make buttercream, neither of which is all that difficult, you can put together a superb dessert that will compare favorably to anything offered in the best restaurants or the most expensive pastry shops. And it will cost you very little and earn you extravagant compliments, which are two of the many advantages of being a dedicated cook!

1¾ cups ground almonds

½ cup sugar

2 tablespoons all-purpose flour

4 large egg whites

½ cup sliced almonds, with skins

BUTTERCREAM

½ cup sugar

¼ cup water

4 large egg yolks

12 tablespoons unsalted butter, softened

3 tablespoons Praline Paste (page 297)

1 tablespoon Kirschwasser (optional)

Preheat convection oven to 325 degrees. Line a 17 by 12-inch baking sheet with baking parchment. Mark three 6½-inch circles on the parchment by drawing around a plate. Fit a pastry bag with a plain round ¼-inch tube.

In a small bowl, blend almonds, three fourths of the sugar, and flour together. In a large bowl, whisk egg whites until they start to hold their shape. Slowly add remaining sugar, and then beat until stiff. Fold in nut mixture with a rubber spatula, deflating the mixture as little as possible, and transfer to the pastry bag. Starting at the center, pipe out a tight spiral to fill one of the circles on the parchment. Repeat with the other two circles. Bake meringue layers for 20 minutes, and cool on rack.

Increase oven heat to 350 degrees. Place sliced almonds on a baking sheet and bake for 5 minutes, or until lightly colored. Let cool.

Make the buttercream: In a heavy saucepan, combine sugar and water and boil to soft ball stage, 230 degrees on a candy thermometer. (If necessary, skim the sugar of froth, and wash the sides of the pan down with a brush dipped in cold water, to prevent sugar crystals from forming.) In the meantime, beat egg yolks in the bowl of an electric mixer. With whisk rotating at low speed, pour sugar syrup over egg yolks in a thin stream. When incorporated, beat fast until mixture is cold, about 7 minutes. Beat in creamy butter, bit by bit, Praline Paste, and Kirschwasser.

To assemble cake, place a meringue layer flat side down on the base from the tart pan, which will make it easier to handle. Spread with buttercream. Cover with a second meringue layer and spread with buttercream. Top with the third meringue layer, flat side up, and spread with buttercream. Holding the cake at a slight angle on the palm of one hand, spread sides evenly with buttercream and sprinkle with toasted almonds. Scatter almonds on top of cake. Chill before serving, and transfer to platter.

PREPARATION TIME: 40 MINUTES / OVEN TIME: 25 MINUTES

BLUEBERRY CAKE

Somewhere between a tart and a cake, this is an excellent choice for breakfast. Blackberries or pitted cherries can be substituted for the blueberries, and you can use frozen unsweetened fruit in winter. The cake is quickly mixed in a food processor and baked in a fluted tart pan. If you find that the edges have browned but the cake is still undercooked in the middle, place the rim of a slightly larger tart pan upside-down over the cake as it finishes baking, or use a "doughnut" of aluminum foil.

6 *tablespoons unsalted butter*

½ *cup sugar*

2 *large eggs*

1 *tablespoon heavy cream (optional)*

Dash vanilla extract

1 *teaspoon grated lemon peel*

1 *cup (5 ounces) all-purpose flour*

¼ *teaspoon baking powder*

Pinch salt

12 *ounces blueberries*

Confectioners' sugar

Preheat convection oven to 350 degrees. Butter and flour a 9-inch fluted tart pan with removable base.

Combine butter and sugar in the bowl of a food processor and process until light and smooth. Add eggs one by one, then the cream, vanilla, and lemon peel. Sift flour, baking powder, and salt together onto a sheet of paper. Form paper into a cone and add to batter through the feed tube, processing just long enough to mix. Transfer mixture to the prepared tart pan, using a rubber spatula to form an even shell in the pan. Fill with blueberries. Bake for 35 minutes, or until cake is golden brown and well risen. Let it cool in the pan for 2 minutes, then remove sides and slide cake off the base onto a cake rack. Dust with confectioners' sugar before serving. Serve warm or at room temperature.

PREPARATION TIME: 10 MINUTES / OVEN TIME: 35 MINUTES / EASY

CHOCOLATE ANGEL CAKE WITH WALNUTS

Most people call this type of cake angel food cake, though it was originally called angel cake, presumably because it is so light it could fly away, not because angels eat it. (What angels eat may be as thorny a question as what language they speak, or how many of them can stand on the head of a pin!) This chocolate version is less sugary than the standard one, and is really at its best the day after it is baked. Some people insist on tearing an angel cake apart with two forks so as not to squash it, but a finely serrated knife works very well and the slices look more attractive. This cake freezes well; let it thaw at room temperature. It is wonderful with morning coffee, or served as a dessert with vanilla ice cream and Cold Chocolate Sauce (page 292).

Scant ⅔ cup (3 ounces) cake flour

¾ cup (3¾ ounces) confectioners' sugar

3 tablespoons unsweetened Dutch-process cocoa

⅓ cup chopped walnuts

9 ounces egg whites, 8 or 9, at room temperature

Pinch salt

¾ teaspoon cream of tartar

¾ teaspoon vanilla extract

¾ cup sugar

Confectioners' sugar for decoration

Preheat convection oven to 325 degrees. Have ready a clean, dry angel cake tube pan.

Combine cake flour, confectioners' sugar, and cocoa in a bowl, and sift together. Stir in walnuts. In a large bowl, beat egg whites until they start to hold their shape. Then add salt, cream of tartar, and vanilla. Beat in sugar at low speed, then increase speed to high and continue beating until mixture holds stiff peaks. Sift flour mixture over beaten egg whites, folding it in gently but thoroughly and deflating the mixture as little as possible. Transfer mixture to the tube pan. Smooth the top with a spatula, and rap pan sharply on the countertop to deflate any large air bubbles. Bake for 40 minutes.

Invert tube pan over the neck of a bottle, and leave to cool upside down. (Gravity will help to keep the cooling cake lofty.) When it has cooled, loosen sides of cake with a knife and unmold. Sift with confectioners' sugar before serving.

PREPARATION TIME: 15 MINUTES / OVEN TIME: 40 MINUTES

CHOCOLATE GINGERBREAD   SERVES 8

Reminiscent off a French pain d'epice, or spice "bread," this is very easy to make and keeps well for several days. If making by hand, add the milk and vanilla alternately with the flour mixture, a little at a time.

1¼ cups (6¼ ounces) all-purpose flour

1 teaspoon baking powder

¼ teaspoon baking soda

½ teaspoon ground ginger

¼ teaspoon salt

4 tablespoons unsalted butter, softened

¼ cup sugar

6 tablespoons honey

1 large egg

2 ounces unsweetened chocolate, melted

⅓ cup milk

½ teaspoon vanilla extract

Confectioners' sugar

Preheat convection oven to 325 degrees. Butter and flour an 8-inch square cake pan.

Sift flour, baking powder, baking soda, ginger, and salt together. In bowl of food processor, cream butter with sugar and honey. Add egg and melted chocolate. Combine milk and vanilla, and add to the chocolate mixture. Add flour mixture last, processing only long enough to mix. Pour into the prepared pan, and bake for 25 minutes.

Unmold cake and cool on a rack. When it has cooled, sift confectioners' sugar over the top.

PREPARATION TIME: 20 MINUTES / OVEN TIME: 25 MINUTES

FLOURLESS
CHOCOLATE SOUFFLÉ CAKE

This intense, rich, but not overly sweet chocolate cake can be made the day before it is to be served, but the dusting of confectioners' sugar should be added at the last minute. Crème Anglaise (see page 293) makes the perfect accompaniment, but is not absolutely essential. If you do use it, pour a pool onto each dessert plate and top with a wedge of cake.

7 *ounces best-quality semisweet chocolate, coarsely chopped*

7 *tablespoons unsalted butter, cut into pieces*

1 *tablespoon Cointreau, or 1 teaspoon Orange Paste (page 295), or grated peel of 1 orange*

1 *teaspoon vanilla extract*

2 *tablespoons finely ground almonds, with or without skins*

5 *large eggs, separated*

½ *cup plus 1 tablespoon sugar*

Confectioners' sugar

Preheat convection oven to 275 degrees. Butter and flour a 9-inch round cake pan with 2-inch sides, and line with a circle of baking parchment.

Place chocolate, butter, Cointreau, vanilla, and ground almonds in the top of a double boiler or in a metal bowl. Heat over barely simmering water, stirring occasionally. Remove from the heat as soon as chocolate is melted. Let cool to lukewarm.

In the bowl of an electric mixer, whip egg whites until foamy, then gradually add half the sugar. Continue beating until stiff peaks form. Transfer meringue to a clean, dry bowl.

Place egg yolks and remaining sugar in mixer bowl (there is no need to wash wire whisk or bowl), and whip until mixture is pale and thick and a slowly dissolving ribbon forms when it is dropped from a spoon.

Using a large rubber spatula, fold lukewarm chocolate mixture into egg yolk mixture. Next fold in the egg whites lightly but thoroughly, as if for a soufflé. Pour batter into prepared pan, and bake for 1 hour and 20 minutes.

Let cake stand for 1 minute, then loosen sides with a knife. (Be careful not to cut into sides of cake.) Unmold onto a cake rack, then quickly peel off paper and reverse onto a second rack so that cake is right side up. Cake will have a crisp, slightly cracked "sugar bloom" on the outside, and will sink slightly, which is normal. Let cool, and sprinkle with confectioners' sugar before serving.

PREPARATION TIME: 30 MINUTES / OVEN TIME: 1 HOUR AND 20 MINUTES

*F*RENCH APPLE CAKE   *S E R V E S   8*

A simple and thoroughly delicious light cake that is good for breakfast, or with tea or coffee at any time of day. It can be mixed in a food processor. Add the sifted flour last and do not overmix afterward, or the cake will be heavy. The cake will keep for several days.

Heaping 1½ cups (8 ounces) cake flour

1½ teaspoons baking powder

2 small Golden Delicious apples, 4 ounces each

8 tablespoons unsalted butter

1¼ cups (5 ounces) confectioners' sugar

3 large eggs

6 tablespoons milk

½ teaspoon vanilla extract

1 tablespoon Calvados or dark rum

¼ cup apricot jam, heated and strained

Preheat convection oven to 325 degrees. Butter and flour an 8-inch cake pan with 2-inch sides.

Sift flour and baking powder together and set aside. Peel apples and cut in half. Remove centers with a melon baller or the tip of a knife, and cut out the stalk. Place apples flat side down and cut into ¼-inch-thick slices.

In a large bowl, cream butter and confectioners' sugar together until very light and fluffy. Beat in eggs one by one. Whisk in milk, vanilla, and Calvados. Sift flour over mixture and incorporate, mixing only long enough to form a smooth batter. Spread half the batter in the prepared cake pan, and cover with a layer of apple slices, using up all the odd-sized pieces. Cover with remaining batter, and smooth top with a rubber spatula. Arrange a wreath of apple slices on top of batter. Bake for 1 hour, until a cake tester inserted near the center comes out clean. Leave cake in the pan for 2 minutes, then unmold and cool right side up on a rack. Brush with apricot glaze when cold.

PREPARATION TIME: 15 MINUTES / OVEN TIME: 1 HOUR / EASY

Hazelnut Meringue and Chocolate Cream Gâteau

An elegant dessert for very special occasions, this is basically a combination of crisp meringue layers sandwiched together with whipped cream flavored with chocolate and Cognac. The edges of the cake are covered with chopped toasted hazelnuts. It is not overly sweet but it is rich, so small slices are served.

4 ounces whole hazelnuts, unpeeled	1 tablespoon Cognac
½ cup sugar	2 tablespoons unsalted butter
4 large egg whites	¾ cup heavy cream
Pinch salt	1 cup chopped hazelnuts for decoration, lightly toasted
4 ounces semisweet or bittersweet chocolate, coarsely chopped	

Preheat convection oven to 325 degrees. Line a baking sheet with baking parchment, and mark off three 2½ by 10-inch rectangles with a pencil. Stick the baking parchment to the baking sheet with dabs of butter at the corners. Have ready a pastry bag fitted with a plain round ¼-inch tip.

Grind hazelnuts to a powder (preferably in a nut mill, which makes fine flakes without releasing the nut oil), and combine with half the sugar. Beat egg whites until they start to hold their shape, then add salt and remaining sugar. Beat until very stiff. Lightly fold nut mixture into the meringue without deflating it. Transfer to the pastry bag, and fill the three rectangles with meringue, piping the mixture in lines that touch each other. Bake for 20 minutes, or until crisp. Remove from the baking sheet onto a rack. (If meringue is difficult to remove, pour a little water under the paper to create steam on the hot baking sheet. Wait 2 minutes, then reverse paper onto the baking rack. The meringue layers will then peel off easily.)

Combine chocolate, Cognac, and butter in a bowl or the top of a double boiler set over simmering water. When chocolate has melted, remove mixture and let cool to barely lukewarm. Whip cream until it just starts to hold its shape, then add chocolate mixture and whip together. (Do not overmix or you will make butter.) Place one meringue layer flat side down on a serving plate, and cover with a layer of chocolate cream. Cover with a second layer of meringue and spread with cream. Top with the third layer of meringue, flat side up. Spread sides and top of cake with chocolate cream. Make an S-shaped pattern on the top of the cake with a decorating comb or serrated knife. Scatter toasted chopped hazelnuts on sides of the cake and place on a serving platter. Refrigerate until serving time.

PREPARATION TIME: 25 MINUTES / OVEN TIME: 20 MINUTES

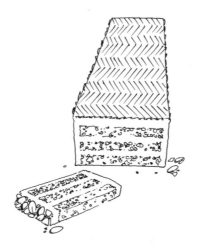

EXTRA-LIGHT
ORANGE POUND CAKE

A traditional pound cake is made with a pound of butter, a pound of sugar, a pound of flour, and a pound of eggs. The sugar and butter are creamed together, the eggs beaten in one by one, and the flour folded in last. It is very dense when baked. The same proportions of ingredients are used in this cake, but they are combined in a different manner. The result is a cake with an exceptionally light and delicate texture. It will rise best if low-gluten cake flour is used, but all-purpose flour can be substituted.

To make a marbled Chocolate-Orange Pound Cake, hold back about 1 cup of the batter in the mixing bowl and stir in 2 ounces of lukewarm melted semisweet chocolate. Add this to the batter in the cake pan and stir in very lightly with a fork.

1 *cup unsalted butter*

4 *large eggs*

1 *cup sugar*

½ *teaspoon vanilla extract*

Grated peel of 1 orange

1½ *cups plus 1 tablespoon (8 ounces) cake flour, sifted*

Small pinch salt

½ *teaspoon baking powder*

Confectioners' sugar

Preheat convection oven to 325 degrees. Butter and flour a 12-cup, 12-inch fluted bundt pan. Melt butter and cool to lukewarm.

Place the eggs, sugar, and vanilla in the bowl of an electric mixer. Whip until the mixture is pale and thick, and forms a slowly dissolving ribbon when dropped from a spoon. Remove bowl from stand and grate orange peel directly into the bowl, so that the fine spray of aromatic oil is not lost. Sift flour, salt, and baking powder together in a bowl, and then sift into batter, folding it in lightly but thoroughly with a rubber spatula. Pour the melted butter around the edges of the bowl, and fold in. Deflate the mixture as little as possible, but make sure that it is smooth. Pour batter into the prepared pan, and bake for 30 minutes, until a toothpick inserted in the center of the cake comes out clean. Let it cool in the pan for 1 minute, then shake gently to loosen and turn out onto a rack to cool completely. Dust with confectioners' sugar before serving.

PREPARATION TIME: 15 MINUTES / OVEN TIME: 30 MINUTES

PLUM CAKE

Despite the name, this cake contains no plums. It's an old English recipe that dates back to a time when they called all dried fruit, particularly raisins and currants, plums. It is very good with your morning coffee. In the old days raisins had to be cut open to have the seeds removed, which also released the flavor. Today, even though they are seedless, it is a good idea to chop raisins a little before using them in cakes.

1 *cup raisins*

3 *tablespoons dark rum*

7 *tablespoons unsalted butter, softened*

Heaping ½ cup sugar

4 *large eggs, separated*

½ *teaspoon vanilla extract*

1 *teaspoon Orange Paste (page 295), or grated peel of 1 orange*

Heaping 1 cup (5½ ounces) cake flour, sifted

½ *teaspoon baking powder*

Preheat convection oven to 350 degrees. Butter and flour an 8-inch round cake pan with 2-inch sides, and line it with a circle of baking parchment.

Combine raisins and rum in a small saucepan and bring to a boil. Simmer until the rum has evaporated, about 10 minutes. Let cool to lukewarm. (To cool off quickly, place pan briefly in the freezer.)

Cream butter and half the sugar together in a large bowl until very light and fluffy. Beat in egg yolks all at once, then add vanilla, raisins, and Orange Paste. Beat egg whites in another bowl until they start to hold their shape. Add remaining sugar and continue beating until stiff. Fold half the egg whites into the batter, then fold in half the cake flour and the baking powder. Fold in remaining egg whites and remaining flour. Transfer batter to the prepared pan, and smooth the top. Bake for 30 minutes. Unmold, peel off paper, and let cool right side up on a rack.

PREPARATION TIME: 15 MINUTES / OVEN TIME: 30 MINUTES

DESSERTS

APRICOT CLAFOUTIS

Clafoutis is an old French country dessert that usually contains sour cherries. This is a modern version, made with less flour and less sugar than the traditional recipes.

8 *ounces soft dried apricots*

½ *cup white wine*

1 *cup water*

¼ *cup sugar*

1 *strip orange peel, 3 inches*

Pinch cinnamon

CUSTARD

1 *cup milk*

¼ *cup sugar*

2 *large eggs, well beaten*

½ *cup (2½ ounces) all-purpose flour, sifted*

2 *cups milk*

½ *teaspoon vanilla extract*

Preheat convection oven to 350 degrees. In an ovenproof saucepan, combine apricots with wine, water, sugar, orange peel, and cinnamon. Bring to a boil. Cover, transfer to the oven, and bake for 20 minutes, until tender. Drain and squeeze dry, reserving liquid.

Butter a 9-inch round baking dish with 2-inch sides, and dust generously with sugar. Make custard mixture: Combine milk, sugar, eggs, flour, and vanilla in a bowl. Blend well. Place apricots in the prepared baking dish, and pour custard mixture on top. Bake for 45 minutes. Let cool, and then chill.

Place reserved apricot cooking liquid in a small saucepan and bring to a boil. Simmer until reduced to 1 cup, about 10 minutes, then chill. Serve clafoutis with apricot sauce.

PREPARATION TIME: 10 MINUTES / OVEN TIME: 20 MINUTES; 45 MINUTES / EASY

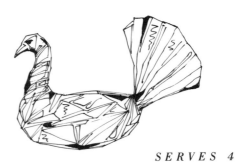

BANANAS LOHENGRIN   *SERVES 4*

Baked fruit is always an easy dessert to prepare, and in this case the presentation is charming—the foil that encloses the fruit is twisted into the shape of a swan. The trick is to work fast and not to torture the foil into too squashed a shape.

2 *tablespoons raisins*

2 *tablespoons dark rum*

2 *tablespoons apricot jam*

1 *Golden Delicious apple,*
  peeled and diced

2 *slices fresh or frozen*
  pineapple, diced

Dash cinnamon

4 *small bananas, peeled*

One hour ahead of time, place raisins in a small saucepan, add rum, and set aside to soak.

Preheat oven to 350 degrees. Heat the soaked raisins and rum but do not allow to boil. Carefully set rum alight, and stir until flames die down. Remove from the heat and blend in the jam, diced apple, pineapple, and cinnamon.

Lay four 12 by 16-inch sheets of aluminum foil on a work surface. Lay a banana across the center of each. Turn up the edges slightly so the liquid cannot run out, and top each banana with one fourth of the rum and fruit mixture. Gather up the foil over the banana, crimping it together to make a seal but leaving as much air space inside as possible. Pinch the foil together at one end of the banana, and fan out the remainder into a spread tail. Pinch the foil together at the opposite end of the banana, and curve it into a neck and head shape (see illustration). Transfer the "swans" to a baking sheet, and bake for 15 minutes. Place on dinner plates and have each diner open his or her swan at the table (slit along the top and push foil aside) to get the full aroma.

PREPARATION TIME: 1 HOUR SOAKING; 15 MINUTES / OVEN TIME: 15 MINUTES

MAKES
12 TO 14

CHESTNUT CREAM ECLAIRS

There will be about 1 cup of chestnut cream left over in this recipe, but it is difficult to make it in a smaller quantity than the one given. Pipe the extra into small ramekins and serve as a dessert with Ladyfingers (page 237), or use as a cake filling.

½ *cup water*

⅛ *teaspoon salt*

4 *tablespoons butter, cut into pieces*

  Pinch sugar

½ *cup all-purpose flour, sifted, 2½ ounces*

3 *large eggs*

1 *egg, beaten*

FILLING

½ *cup sugar*

½ *cup water*

1 *can sweetened chestnut purée, 15½ ounces*

3 *tablespoons dark rum*

1 *teaspoon vanilla extract*

1 *cup unsalted butter, softened*

Preheat convection oven to 325 degrees. Grease and flour a baking sheet.

Place water, salt, butter, and sugar in a saucepan and bring to a boil. As soon as butter has melted (water must not evaporate), add flour and stir hard until mixture forms a ball in the center of the pan.

Remove from the heat, and using a wooden spoon, beat in eggs one at a time. Beat hard after each addition. Transfer mixture to a pastry bag fitted with a plain ½-inch tube, and pipe out twelve to fourteen 4-inch-long bands onto the prepared baking sheet. Brush with egg glaze, smoothing down any peaks. Bake for 35 minutes, and let cool on a rack.

Make the filling: combine sugar and water in a heavy saucepan and boil to the soft ball stage, or 230 degrees on a candy thermometer. While sugar is cooking, beat chestnut purée, rum, and vanilla together in a bowl until creamy. Pour sugar syrup over chestnut mixture and beat until lukewarm. Beat in butter bit by bit, and continue beating until mixture is very light and fluffy. Transfer to a pastry bag fitted with a large star tube.

Slice tops off eclairs without going all the way through; in other words, leaving a hinge. Fill eclairs, using a circular motion of the pastry bag to make a series of overlapping circles of chestnut cream. Push tops down into the cream slightly, and dust with confectioners' sugar.

PREPARATION TIME: 30 MINUTES / OVEN TIME: 35 MINUTES

CHOCOLATE PÂTE À CHOUX MICE WITH ICE CREAM AND CHOCOLATE SAUCE

If you do not wish to make mice, form 2-inch round rosettes using a star tube, and top the filled desserts with a wisp of lemon peel. The baked puffs freeze well, double-wrapped, to be thawed and filled when needed.

Scant ½ cup (2 ounces) all-purpose flour	3 *large eggs*
2 *tablespoons unsweetened Dutch-process cocoa*	1 *egg, beaten*
½ *cup water*	*Vanilla ice cream*
⅛ *teaspoon salt*	1 *cup Hot Chocolate Sauce (page 293)*
4 *tablespoons unsalted butter, cut into pieces*	*Split almonds, with skins, for ears*
1 *teaspoon sugar*	*Julienned lemon peel, for tails and whiskers*

Preheat convection oven to 325 degrees. Grease and flour a baking sheet.

Sift flour and cocoa together. Place water, salt, butter, and sugar in a saucepan and bring to a boil. As soon as butter has melted (water must not evaporate), add flour mixture and stir hard until dough forms a ball in the center of the pan. Remove from the heat, and using a wooden spoon, beat in eggs one at a time. Beat hard after each addition. Transfer mixture to a pastry bag fitted with a plain ½-inch tube, and pipe out twelve to sixteen 2½-inch-long teardrop shapes onto the prepared baking sheet. Brush with egg glaze, and bake for 30 minutes. Let cool on rack.

Cut tops off puffs and fill puffs with small ovals of ice cream. Replace tops and insert two almond halves for ears (see illustration). Pour a pool of Hot Chocolate Sauce on each dessert plate, and top with one or two "mice." Insert two strands of lemon peel at the pointed end to represent whiskers, and attach a slender curl of lemon peel at the other end for a tail. (The fresh lemon tastes wonderful with the dark chocolate.)

PREPARATION TIME: 25 MINUTES / OVEN TIME: 30 MINUTES

ORANGE AND RAISIN CUSTARD WITH FRENCH TOAST TOPPING

SERVES 6

Bread and butter pudding by another—perhaps more accurate and certainly more inviting—name.

½ cup raisins

2 cups milk

1 cup half-and-half or light cream

4 large egg yolks

2 large whole eggs

½ cup sugar

½ teaspoon vanilla extract

Pinch salt

2 tablespoons finely chopped candied orange peel

6 tablespoons unsalted butter

4 slices home-style white sandwich bread, crusts removed, cut in half diagonally

Confectioners' sugar

Preheat convection oven to 300 degrees. Butter a 1½-quart shallow rectangular baking dish. Soak raisins in boiling water for 5 minutes, then drain well.

Combine milk and half-and-half in a saucepan, and bring to a boil. In a large bowl, whisk together egg yolks, whole eggs, sugar, vanilla, and salt. Pour milk over this mixture and stir. Add orange peel and raisins.

Melt butter in a large skillet and dredge the bread in it. Fit bread into the baking dish to cover the bottom completely. Pour milk and egg mixture carefully on top; the slices will rise to the surface. (Push most of the raisins and orange peel under the bread.) Bake for 40 minutes, until custard is set. Let cool and serve at room temperature, or chill. Dust with confectioners' sugar before serving.

PREPARATION TIME: 20 MINUTES / OVEN TIME: 40 MINUTES / EASY

PEACHES STUFFED WITH COCONUT AND VANILLA WAFERS, BAKED IN SHERRY

A simple, family-style dessert that is definitely good enough to offer to guests.

4 *firm ripe peaches or nectarines*

2 *tablespoons unsalted butter, softened*

¼ *cup shredded coconut*

¼ *cup crumbled Real Vanilla Wafers (page 226) or store-bought vanilla wafers, 5 or 6*

1 *tablespoon sugar*

1 *large egg yolk*

1 *tablespoon Cognac*

¼ *cup Dry Sack sherry*

½ *cup water*

Preheat convection oven to 325 degrees. Peel peaches by blanching in boiling water for a few seconds; the skins should then slip off. Cut in half and remove pits. Arrange peaches cut side up in a 9-inch shallow baking dish.

Blend butter, coconut, vanilla wafers, sugar, egg yolk, and Cognac together, and fill cavities of peaches. Pour sherry and water around fruit, and bake for 20 minutes. Serve warm, with the sauce spooned over the fruit.

PREPARATION TIME: 10 MINUTES / OVEN TIME: 20 MINUTES / EASY

PEARS IN ALMS-PURSES WITH PAPAYA SAUCE

A showy dessert that looks much more complicated than it really is: Pears are wrapped in ready-prepared phyllo, baked to a golden brown, and served with a simple papaya sauce that is made in a food processor.

Always use a neutral-tasting bottled water when making sauces; tap water can have a strong mineral flavor.

4 *ripe Bartlett pears with stems*

½ *lemon*

1 *teaspoon shredded orange zest*

4 *teaspoons raspberry jam*

4 *sheets phyllo dough, thawed if frozen*

2 *tablespoons melted butter*

SAUCE

1 *small ripe papaya*

1 *tablespoon sugar*

1 *to 2 tablespoons fresh lemon juice*

2 *tablespoons neutral-flavored sparkling water*

Preheat convection oven to 375 degrees. Peel pears, leaving the stems on, and rub with cut side of lemon to preserve the color. Remove core from underneath. Stuff the hollow with one fourth of the orange zest and a teaspoon of jam.

Lay a sheet of phyllo on a work surface. Brush one half lightly with melted butter, and fold it over. Place a pear in the center, upright, and gather phyllo together at the top, around the stem. Twist the pastry leaves gently to secure them around the stem (they will stay in place), and brush the outside of the pastry lightly with melted butter. Repeat with remaining pears, and place them on a baking sheet. Bake for 15 minutes.

While the pears are baking, make the sauce: Peel papaya, cut it in half, and discard seeds. Cut fruit in chunks and place in a food processor. Add sugar, lemon juice, and sparkling water, and purée. Serve pears hot, with room-temperature Papaya Sauce.

PREPARATION TIME: 20 MINUTES / OVEN TIME: 15 MINUTES / EASY

PUMPKIN SOUFFLÉ SALZBURG STYLE, WITH CRANBERRY SAUCE

SERVES 6 TO 8

Even traditionalists who think that Thanksgiving is synonymous with pumpkin pie will be impressed by this original and delicious version of *Salzburger Nockerl* or Emperor's Pancakes. To save time, you can substitute 1 cup of plain (unflavored and unsweetened) canned pumpkin purée for the freshly cooked article.

12-ounce piece of raw pumpkin or other yellow winter squash

1 *teaspoon Lemon Paste (page 295), or grated peel of 1 lemon*

½ *teaspoon vanilla extract*

1 *tablespoon unsalted butter*

½ *cup sugar*

3 *tablespoons all-purpose flour*

Pinch cinnamon

5 *large eggs, separated*

8 *ounces canned sweetened whole-berry cranberry sauce*

½ *cup fresh orange juice*

1 *tablespoon orange liqueur (optional)*

Preheat convection oven to 350 degrees. Wrap pumpkin in aluminum foil and bake for 1 hour, until tender.

Grease a shallow 8 by 10-inch oval or rectangular baking dish generously with butter, and dust with sugar. (Use one that is attractive enough to bring to the table.) Scrape pumpkin pulp off the skin and purée in a food processor—there should be 1 cup. Place purée in a saucepan with Lemon Paste, vanilla, butter, half the sugar, flour, and cinnamon. Cook for 1 minute, stirring with a whisk. Remove from the heat and beat in egg yolks. Beat egg whites until they start to hold their shape, then add remaining sugar and continue beating until stiff. Fold into yolk mixture. Using a rubber spatula or a large serving spoon, make four mounds or "pillows" of the mixture in the prepared dish. Bake at 350 degrees for 22 minutes.

While soufflé is baking, combine cranberry sauce, orange juice, and liqueur in a saucepan, and heat gently. Remove the soufflé from the oven and serve immediately, making sure that each diner gets some of the caramelized crust. Serve sauce alongside.

PREPARATION TIME: 15 MINUTES   /   OVEN TIME: 1 HOUR; 22 MINUTES

VANILLA SOUFFLÉ
WITH FRESH RASPBERRY SAUCE

Soufflés of all kinds bake and rise extremely well in a convection oven because of the even heat. Be sure to include a little of the crispy sugar coating with each serving.

1½ tablespoons butter, softened

¼ cup sugar

¼ cup cornstarch

1 cup milk

1 teaspoon vanilla extract

5 large egg yolks

6 large egg whites

SAUCE

1 cup fresh raspberries

1 tablespoon sugar

1 tablespoon raspberry jam

1 tablespoon Cognac

Preheat convection oven to 350 degrees. Grease a 1-quart soufflé dish with 1 tablespoon of the butter, and dust with 1 tablespoon of the sugar.

Combine 1 tablespoon of remaining sugar and cornstarch in a saucepan. Add milk, and stir until smooth. Heat to boiling, whisking constantly. Stir in the remaining ½ tablespoon butter, vanilla, and egg yolks. Beat egg whites until they form soft peaks. Add remaining 2 tablespoons of sugar and beat until firm, moist peaks form. (Do not beat until dry or it will be difficult to incorporate.) Gently fold whites into the warm mixture, and pour into the prepared soufflé mold. Bake for 22 minutes.

While the soufflé is baking, make the Raspberry Sauce: Combine the raspberries, sugar, jam (which adds a little thickness), and Cognac in a blender or food processor. Blend until smooth, then push through a sieve to get rid of the seeds. Remove the soufflé from the oven and serve immediately, with the room-temperature Raspberry Sauce.

PREPARATION TIME: 15 MINUTES / OVEN TIME: 22 MINUTES

YELLOW SUMMER SQUASH PUDDING WITH RASPBERRY SAUCE

SERVES 6 TO 8

Very few guests will be able to identify the surprising main ingredient in this fresh-tasting pudding!

1 *pound yellow summer (crookneck) squash*

4 *tablespoons unsalted butter*

1 *cup heavy cream*

Scant ½ cup sugar

1 *teaspoon vanilla extract*

½ *teaspoon Lemon Paste (page 295), or grated peel of 1 lemon*

4 *large eggs*

Heaping ½ cup (3 ounces) all-purpose flour

1¼ *cups Raspberry Sauce (page 294)*

Preheat convection oven to 350 degrees. Butter a 9-inch baking dish with 2-inch sides, and line it with a circle of baking parchment. Butter the parchment, then dust the dish with sugar.

Trim summer squash and slice. Heat butter in a saucepan, and add squash, cream, sugar, vanilla, and Lemon Paste. Bring to a boil and simmer for 2 minutes. Transfer to a food processor and purée. Beat eggs in a large bowl, and incorporate flour. Whisk in purée. Pour mixture into the prepared baking dish, and bake for 20 minutes, until a knife blade inserted near the middle comes out clean. Let cool.

When pudding is lukewarm, turn it out onto a platter and peel off baking parchment. Chill, and serve with Raspberry Sauce.

PREPARATION TIME: 15 MINUTES / OVEN TIME: 20 MINUTES / EASY

WINE CREAMS

These delicate creams are flavored with Chinese five-spice powder, which is a mixture of star anise, Sichuan peppercorns, fennel or aniseed, cloves, and cinnamon. If you cannot get it, substitute a very tiny pinch each of powdered aniseed, clove, and cinnamon, but do not be too generous or you will overpower the little custards.

1 *cup gewürztraminer (sweet white wine)*
Pinch *Chinese 5-spice powder*

1 *strip lemon peel*
1 *cup heavy cream*
2 *tablespoons honey*
4 *large eggs*

Preheat convection oven to 300 degrees. Combine wine, 5-spice powder, and lemon peel in a saucepan, bring to a boil, and set aside to infuse for 5 minutes.

Pour wine into a bowl, discarding lemon peel, and whisk in cream, honey, and eggs. Put a paper towel in the bottom of a shallow baking pan (to shield the custards from direct heat), and arrange six ½-cup ovenproof porcelain ramekins or small custard cups on top. Fill ramekins with cream mixture, and remove foam by drawing a paper towel across the surface. Pour enough hot water into the baking pan to reach halfway up the sides of the ramekins. Cover pan with foil, and punch a few holes in it to let the steam out. Bake for 25 minutes. Serve the creams chilled.

PREPARATION TIME: 10 MINUTES / OVEN TIME: 25 MINUTES / EASY

DESSERT SAUCES; USEFUL ODDS AND ENDS

COLD CHOCOLATE SAUCE

Always use good-quality chocolate in cooking; poor grades or chocolate chips usually turn grainy.

4 *ounces semisweet or bittersweet chocolate, cut into small pieces*

2 *tablespoons unsalted butter, softened*

1 *tablespoon Cognac or dark rum*

½ *cup strong hot coffee*

Place chocolate, butter, and Cognac in the bowl of a food processor. With the motor running, add hot coffee through the feed tube. Process for a few seconds, until smooth. Transfer to a bowl and refrigerate until cool (sauce will thicken), about 15 minutes.

PREPARATION TIME: 5 MINUTES / OVEN TIME: NONE / EASY

HOT CHOCOLATE SAUCE

Serve with ice cream, or over cold poached pears.

4 *ounces semisweet or*
bittersweet chocolate,
cut into small pieces

2 *tablespoons unsalted*
butter

1 *tablespoon Cognac or*
dark rum

¼ *cup strong coffee*

Combine all ingredients in the top of a double boiler, and heat over simmering water until smooth, 10 minutes.

PREPARATION TIME: 15 MINUTES / OVEN TIME: NONE / EASY

CRÈME ANGLAISE (CUSTARD SAUCE)

When you are combining egg yolks and sugar, always start whisking immediately. Do not leave the sugar lying on the yolks, as it can "burn" them and make your sauce grainy.

4 *large egg yolks*

¼ *cup sugar*

½ *teaspoon cornstarch*

2 *cups milk, chilled*

1 *vanilla bean, or ½*
teaspoon vanilla extract

Whisk egg yolks and sugar together in a heatproof bowl until thick and pale in color. Dissolve cornstarch in a little of the cold milk. Place remaining milk in a heavy nonaluminum saucepan (tin-lined copper is the best), add cornstarch mixture and vanilla bean (but not vanilla extract), and heat until little bubbles start to form around the edges. Pour half the hot milk over the beaten eggs, whisking constantly. Pour combined mixture back into the saucepan, and stir with a wooden spoon over low to medium heat until custard thickens slightly, about

1 minute. It should register 165 degrees on a candy thermometer, or lightly coat the back of a wooden spoon. Strain into a bowl (and stir in vanilla extract), and let cool. Stir occasionally to prevent a skin forming as it cools.

Rinse and dry vanilla bean, and store it buried in sugar. It will flavor the sugar, and can be reused several times.

PREPARATION TIME: 15 MINUTES / OVEN TIME: NONE

RASPBERRY SAUCE

MAKES
1¼ CUPS

The red currant jelly adds a little body and sweetness to the sauce; the bottled water (as opposed to tap water) has a pure taste.

1 *package lightly sweetened frozen raspberries, 10 ounces, thawed*

1 *tablespoon red currant jelly*

¼ *cup neutral-flavored bottled water*

Combine raspberries with their juice, red currant jelly, and water in the bowl of a food processor. Make a purée, then force it through a sieve to get rid of the seeds. If sauce is very thick, add an additional tablespoon or two of bottled water until you have a pouring consistency. Chill until needed.

PREPARATION TIME: 5 MINUTES / OVEN TIME: NONE / EASY

LEMON OR ORANGE PASTE

This is a very convenient flavoring to have on hand, and it can be made whenever lemons are plentiful and cheap since it stores so well. To make Orange Paste, substitute 5 or 6 oranges and orange juice for the lemons and lemon juice, and be sure that you do not include any white pith.

Always use bottled water when making sauces; tap water can have a mineral taste.

10 *lemons, 3 to 4 ounces each*
3 *tablespoons sugar*

¾ *cup fresh lemon juice*
¾ *cup neutral-flavored bottled water*

Peel lemons with a vegetable peeler, taking only the colored part of the skin. Combine peel in a heavy saucepan with sugar, lemon juice, and water. Bring to a boil and simmer for about 20 minutes, until the liquid has almost evaporated. Transfer to a blender (preferable to a food processor, though the latter will do), and blend until smooth, adding a little cold bottled water if necessary and scraping down the sides of the container as needed. The consistency should be somewhere between that of tomato paste and tomato purée. Store in the refrigerator in a screw-top glass jar. It will keep for months.

PREPARATION TIME: 35 MINUTES / OVEN TIME: NONE / EASY

MINCEMEAT

Homemade mincemeat tastes incomparably better than anything you can buy, and makes a good item for gift-giving at Christmastime. Use it in Mince Pies (page 246), Lattice Mincemeat Tart (page 259), and English Mincemeat Cookies (page 225).

8 *ounces dark raisins*
8 *ounces golden raisins*
1 *pound currants*
8 *ounces beef suet, finely chopped*
1 *pound tart green apples, peeled and chopped*
8 *ounces candied orange peel, chopped*
8 *ounces candied lemon peel, chopped*
8 *ounces dark brown sugar, firmly packed*
Shredded peel and juice of 1 orange

Shredded peel and juice of 1 lemon
1 *teaspoon ground nutmeg*
1 *teaspoon ground cloves*
1 *teaspoon ground ginger*
½ *teaspoon salt*
½ *cup Cognac*
½ *cup dark rum*

Chop raisins coarsely to release their flavor. (A food processor is useful here, for both raisins and suet.) Mix all the ingredients together, pack in glass jars, and seal airtight. Store in refrigerator for 2 weeks, so flavors can mellow. This mincemeat will keep for at least 3 months in the refrigerator.

PREPARATION TIME: 20 MINUTES; 2 WEEKS MARINATING / OVEN TIME: NONE / EASY

PRALINE PASTE

To make Praline-Stuffed Prunes, a delicious sweetmeat to offer with after-dinner coffee, stuff small soft pitted prunes with Praline Paste, letting a little of the paste show in the slit. Make crisscross cuts in the revealed paste with the back of a knife, then glaze the prunes with strained heated apricot jam. Place in paper cases to serve.

⅔ cup hazelnuts

⅔ cup whole almonds, with skins

2 cups confectioners' sugar

Preheat convection oven to 350 degrees. Spread nuts on a baking sheet and bake for 10 minutes, until skins start to split on the hazelnuts and nuts are lightly toasted. (There is no need to remove skins from almonds or hazelnuts.) Transfer hot nuts to the bowl of a food processor and process until very finely ground and mixture starts to turn oily. Add confectioners' sugar and continue processing until a paste forms, about 5 minutes or longer. Scrape down sides of bowl occasionally with a spatula. Store in a screw-top jar in the refrigerator; it will keep almost indefinitely.

PREPARATION TIME: 15 MINUTES / OVEN TIME: 10 MINUTES / EASY

QUICK NUT-PASTE FILLING

This creamy mixture of ground nuts and eggs is lightly sweetened (less so than the standard recipes) and used as a tart filling. It bakes into a form of rich nut sponge.

⅔ cup pecans, walnuts, or almonds

8 tablespoons unsalted butter

⅓ cup sugar

2 large eggs

2 tablespoons dark rum

1 tablespoon all-purpose flour

Grind nuts in a food processor and set aside. Process butter and sugar until very creamy. With the motor running, add eggs one at a time through the feed tube. Add ground nuts, rum, and flour. Process until smooth. Store covered in the refrigerator; it will keep for 5 days.

PREPARATION TIME: 5 MINUTES / OVEN TIME: NONE / EASY

Basic French Crêpes

It is important not to work the flour too much when you are making crêpes, or the gluten will be activated and the batter will have to rest before it can be used. When the batter is combined quickly in a food processor, it can be used immediately, and crêpes made this way are especially tender. They can be refrigerated for 4 or 5 days, or can be frozen.

3 *large eggs*
Pinch salt
Pinch sugar
1½ *tablespoons sugar (for dessert crêpes only)*
½ *teaspoon vanilla extract (for dessert crêpes only)*

1 *teaspoon Lemon or Orange Paste (page 295, for dessert crêpes only, optional). Add with milk.*
1½ *cups milk*
1 *cup (5 ounces) all-purpose flour*
2 *tablespoons unsalted butter*

In the bowl of a food processor, combine eggs, salt, and pinch of sugar. (Add larger amount of sugar and vanilla if making dessert crêpes.) Process for 5 seconds. With the motor running, add milk through the feed tube. Sift flour into a sheet of paper, and add through the feed tube, processing only long enough to mix. Melt butter in a 7½-inch iron crêpe pan and allow it to brown. Add butter to batter and pulse machine on and off to blend. Pour batter into a bowl and stir occasionally while making crêpes.

Reheat crêpe pan (grease it with a little more butter from time to time), and pour in about 2 tablespoons of batter. Tilt pan to cover the bottom, and pour any excess back into the bowl. Cook over medium-high heat for 1 minute, until lightly browned. Turn crêpe with your fingers and cook the other side for 30 seconds. Repeat with remaining batter, overlapping cooked crêpes on a baking sheet with the browned side down.

PREPARATION TIME: 30 MINUTES / OVEN TIME: NONE / EASY

MAKES 1 POUND
SHELLED MEATS

ROAST CHESTNUTS

Freshly roasted chestnuts are excellent in poultry stuffings, or tossed in butter with cooked Brussels sprouts and served with chicken or turkey.

2 pounds chestnuts in the
shell

Preheat convection oven to 400 degrees. Cut a ½-inch X on the flat side of each chestnut, through the shell. Spread chestnuts on a baking sheet, and bake for 30 minutes, until shells open. When chestnuts are cool enough to handle but still warm, peel off both outer husk and inner covering.

PREPARATION TIME: 15 MINUTES / OVEN TIME: 30 MINUTES / EASY

STOCKS, SAUCES, ET CETERA

CHICKEN STOCK

Do not add salt to chicken stock. Salt can be added to taste later, when the stock is used in sauces or soup.

4 *pounds chicken necks and backs, or carcasses, cut up*

1 *brown-skinned onion, unpeeled (skin adds color), cut in half*

1 *leek, trimmed and well rinsed*

1 *carrot, coarsely chopped*

2 *cloves garlic, unpeeled*

1 *bay leaf*

3 *sprigs parsley*

3 *sprigs thyme, or ½ teaspoon dried*

6 *peppercorns*

3 *quarts water*

Combine all the ingredients in large stockpot and bring to a boil. After 5 minutes, skim off the cloudy scum on the surface. Continue boiling rapidly for another 15 minutes, skimming regularly. Then reduce the heat, cover the pot, and simmer slowly for 2 hours.

Line a colander with several thicknesses of dampened cheesecloth and strain the stock through it into a bowl, pressing down on the solids to extract all the flavor. Let cool in the refrigerator. When stock is cold, remove the layer of fat that will have formed on the surface.

Stock will keep in the refrigerator for 3 days, or can be frozen for several months. (Freeze in 1-cup portions, or in ice cube trays, and be sure to label and date. Frozen stock is impossible to identify!)

PREPARATION TIME: 2½ HOURS / OVEN TIME: NONE / EASY

WHITE VEAL STOCK

Do not add salt to veal stock. Salt can be added later, when the stock is used in cooking.

Concentrated White Veal Jelly, which makes a wonderful addition to sauces, both enriching the flavor and adding a good consistency, can be made from veal stock: Simply reduce the clear stock until it cooks down to a thick amber syrup. This will solidify to a very firm jelly when chilled, and can be cut into 1-ounce squares, wrapped individually, and frozen.

4 *pounds veal neck bones*
1 *veal shank, cut into 2-inch pieces*
1 *calf's foot, split (optional)*

1 *onion, cut in half*
1 *bay leaf*
3 *sprigs parsley*
6 *peppercorns*
3 *quarts water*

Combine all the ingredients in a large stockpot and bring to a boil. Boil briskly for 5 minutes, skimming off the cloudy scum on the surface. Reduce heat and partially cover pot. Simmer slowly for 4 hours, adding more water if necessary to maintain the original level.

Line a colander with several thicknesses of dampened cheesecloth, and strain the stock through it into a large bowl. Let it cool in the refrigerator. When stock is cold, remove the solid layer of fat that will have formed on the surface. Stock will keep for 3 days in the refrigerator, or can be frozen for several months. (Freeze in small portions, and be sure to label and date.)

PREPARATION TIME: 4¼ HOURS / OVEN TIME: NONE / EASY

BROWN VEAL STOCK

Do not add salt to veal stock. Salt can be added later, when the stock is used in cooking.

To make Concentrated Brown Veal Jelly, which is wonderful for adding depth of flavor and a "coating" quality to sauces, use the same directions as for making Concentrated White Veal Jelly on page 301.

2 tablespoons olive oil

4 pounds veal neck bones

1 veal shank, cut into 2-inch pieces

1 calf's foot, split (optional)

1 onion, coarsely chopped

1 carrot, coarsely chopped

1 stalk celery, coarsely chopped

1 bay leaf

3 sprigs parsley

6 peppercorns

3 quarts water

½ cup tomato purée

Preheat convection oven to 375 degrees. Add olive oil to a shallow roasting pan and heat in the oven for 5 minutes. Add veal bones, shank, and calf's foot, and brown for 30 minutes, turning the pieces over after 15 minutes. Transfer to a large stockpot, adding a little water to the roasting pan and scraping up any coagulated bits. Add all the other ingredients and bring to a boil. Boil briskly for 5 minutes, skimming off the cloudy scum on the surface. Reduce heat and partially cover pot. Simmer slowly for 4 hours, adding more water if necessary to maintain the original level.

Line a colander with several thicknesses of dampened cheesecloth, and strain the stock through it into a large bowl. Let it cool in the refrigerator. When stock is cold, remove the solid layer of fat that will have formed on the surface. Stock will keep for 3 days in the refrigerator, or can be frozen for several months. (Freeze in small portions, and be sure to label and date.)

PREPARATION TIME: 4¼ HOURS / OVEN TIME: 35 MINUTES / EASY

HOLLANDAISE SAUCE, FOOD PROCESSOR METHOD

Stir a small quantity of fresh chopped herbs such as tarragon, thyme, parsley, or chives into any leftover Hollandaise and chill until firm enough to form into a roll. Wrap in foil and freeze. Cut off pats of herbed butter and use as a garnish for broiled steaks and fish.

1 *cup unsalted butter*
2 *large egg yolks*
   Pinch white pepper
2 *tablespoons very hot*
   water

1 *tablespoon fresh lemon*
   juice
   Pinch salt

Melt butter in a small saucepan, and skim off the froth. Place egg yolks and white pepper in the bowl of a food processor. With the motor running, slowly add hot water and then the butter, in a thin stream. (Do not add the milky solids at the bottom of the pan.) The sauce should thicken and become opaque. Add lemon juice and salt, and mix briefly. Taste for seasoning and adjust if necessary. Transfer sauce to a warmed container and place in a warm spot on top of the stove until required.

PREPARATION TIME: 5 MINUTES / OVEN TIME: NONE / EASY

GENOESE PESTO SAUCE

Use this garlic and basil paste in the Sirloin of Lamb with Pesto-Mushroom Stuffing on page 153, or stir it into cooked hot pasta with butter and additional Parmesan cheese.

2 *tablespoons pine nuts*

5 *cloves garlic, crushed*

2 *cups lightly packed fresh basil leaves*

½ *cup fresh Italian flat-leaf parsley leaves*

1 *teaspoon salt*

¾ *cup olive oil*

½ *cup grated Parmesan or Pecorino cheese*

Cook pine nuts in a dry nonstick skillet for 2 minutes, shaking the pan often, until lightly toasted. Combine the garlic, basil, parsley, pine nuts, salt, and ¼ cup of the oil in the bowl of a food processor. Process to a purée, then gradually add remaining oil. Add cheese last. Store in a screw-top glass jar in the refrigerator; it will keep for several weeks.

PREPARATION TIME: 7 MINUTES / OVEN TIME: NONE / EASY

CABERNET SAUCE

Serve this sauce with the Whole Calf's Liver Baked in Puff Pastry (page 189). It also complements beef and venison and, perhaps surprisingly, grilled swordfish.

1½ *cups Brown Veal Stock (page 302)*

3 *tablespoons unsalted butter*

3 *tablespoons minced shallots*

¾ *cup Cabernet Sauvignon wine*

Salt and pepper

Bring stock to a boil in a small saucepan, and boil rapidly until reduced to ¾ cup, about 8 minutes.

Heat 2 tablespoons of the butter in a small heavy saucepan and simmer shallots until tender but not brown, about 5 minutes. Add wine, bring to a boil, and cook over high heat until reduced by one half, about 5 minutes. Stir in reduced veal stock and simmer for 2 minutes. Add salt and pepper to taste. Just before serving, whisk in remaining 1 tablespoon butter.

PREPARATION TIME: 15 MINUTES / OVEN TIME: NONE

FRESH TOMATO, OLIVE OIL, AND CORIANDER SAUCE

MAKES 1 CUP;
SERVES 4

This sauce is outstanding with simply cooked fish of all kinds.

½ cup extra-virgin olive oil

1 ripe tomato, peeled, seeded, and diced

½ teaspoon chopped fresh parsley

½ teaspoon chopped fresh chervil

Pinch chopped fresh tarragon

½ teaspoon crushed coriander seeds

Juice of ½ lemon

Salt and pepper

½ clove garlic, unpeeled

One hour ahead, combine olive oil, tomato, herbs, coriander seeds, lemon juice, and salt and pepper to taste in the bowl of food processor or blender. Mix briefly until an opaque, salmon-pink liaison is formed. Taste for seasoning. Rub a warmed bowl with the garlic. Pour the sauce into the bowl, and set the bowl in a pan of hot water. Set to one side; the flavors will develop on standing.

Sauce should be served lukewarm, not hot. (If heated, it will separate.)

PREPARATION TIME: 10 MINUTES; 1 HOUR MARINATING / OVEN TIME: NONE / EASY

LEMON BUTTER SAUCE

MAKES 2 CUPS;
SERVES 8

If you heat any leftover Lemon Butter Sauce until the water has evaporated, you will have clarified butter to use in cooking.

Always use bottled water, carbonated or plain, when making sauces as ordinary tap water can have a strong taste of chlorine or other minerals.

2 tablespoons fresh lemon
  juice
½ cup neutral-tasting
  bottled water

1 cup unsalted butter, at
  room temperature but
  still firm
Salt
White pepper

In a heavy saucepan, bring lemon juice and water to a boil. Whisk in all but 2 tablespoons of the butter, 1 tablespoon at a time. Remove the pan from the heat, and whisk in the last 2 tablespoons (so the butter does not overheat and "break," or become liquid). The sauce should be opaque and the consistency of light cream. Serve with the Halibut with Avocado Mousse in Puff Pastry on page 162, or with other fish or vegetable dishes.

PREPARATION TIME: 5 MINUTES / OVEN TIME: NONE

RICH TOMATO SAUCE

Use with the Warm Smoked Salmon Mousse on page 36, or with the Gnocchi Piedmont Style, page 58.

1 *tablespoon olive oil*

1 *onion, chopped*

1 *carrot, chopped*

2 *cloves garlic, minced*

1 *ounce bacon rind, 4 by 3 inches, taken from slab bacon*

2 *tablespoons all-purpose flour*

Pinch *thyme*

Pinch *oregano*

1 *bay leaf*

2 *teaspoons black peppercorns*

1 *cup tomato juice*

½ *cup tomato paste*

Pinch *sugar*

1 *cup Chicken Stock (page 300) or canned chicken broth*

Salt

Preheat convection oven to 350 degrees. Heat olive oil in a saucepan and sauté onion for 5 minutes, until softened. Add carrot, garlic, and bacon rind, and cook for 2 or 3 minutes. Stir in flour and add thyme, oregano, bay leaf, peppercorns, tomato juice, tomato paste, sugar (to cut acidity), and chicken stock. Add salt cautiously—the bacon rind will be salty. Bring to a boil, cover, and transfer to the oven. Bake for 40 minutes. Strain, and taste for seasoning.

PREPARATION TIME: 15 MINUTES / OVEN TIME: 40 MINUTES / EASY

VINAIGRETTE

You will find that you require far less salt than usual in your salad dressings if you dissolve it in the vinegar first. Proportions of oil to vinegar are a matter of personal taste and depend upon the sharpness of the vinegar. For example, when using aged sherry wine vinegar, you will find that less oil is needed than the normal 3 to 1 ratio.

¼ teaspoon salt

2 tablespoons white or red wine vinegar, or fresh lemon juice

6 tablespoons virgin olive oil

Black pepper

VARIATIONS

½ teaspoon Dijon mustard

1 tablespoon crumbled Roquefort cheese

1 anchovy filet (omit salt in basic vinaigrette), minced

1 teaspoon finely chopped fresh thyme, tarragon, chives, basil, or parsley

In a small bowl, dissolve salt in vinegar. Beat in olive oil with a whisk. Add black pepper, and if desired, one of the variations. Taste for seasoning and adjust as necessary.

PREPARATION TIME: 2 MINUTES / OVEN TIME: NONE / EASY

BLACK OLIVE PASTE

This typically Mediterranean mixture, which is very easy to make in a food processor, is sensational spread on triangles of toast and served as an hors d'oeuvre. You can also use it in cooking, for instance with the Salmon Filets on page 69 or on pizza (see page 52). Cover the paste with a thin film of olive oil and it will keep for months—but we are rarely able to keep it around for more than a couple of weeks! Be sure to use the small, flavorful oil-cured olives imported from one of the Mediterranean countries, and buy them from a delicatessen that has a brisk turnover, so that they are not rancid. (Taste one to make sure before buying.)

1 *pound imported black oil-cured olives, dry type*	2 *tablespoons pickled capers, drained*
¼ *cup olive oil*	½ *teaspoon thyme*
4 *cloves garlic, mashed and minced*	½ *teaspoon oregano*
	Black pepper

Pit the olives and place them in the bowl of a food processor. Add remaining ingredients, and pulse the machine on and off until mixture is evenly ground. Pack in small jars and store in the refrigerator.

PREPARATION TIME: 10 MINUTES / OVEN TIME: NONE / EASY

SERVES 4   # CARAMELIZED ONION CONFIT

Serve this savory mixture with roast lamb or roast beef.

To make Caramelized Garlic Confit, separate enough heads of garlic to make 1 cup of cloves. Blanch in two or three changes of simmering water, 3 minutes altogether, trim base off garlic cloves, and remove skins. Sauté as directed for Onion Confit. Can be served with sautéed steak, chicken, or veal.

1 *cup thinly sliced onions*	¼ *cup red wine*
1 *tablespoon butter*	¼ *red wine vinegar*
Salt and pepper	1 *tablespoon Cognac*
½ *teaspoon sugar*	

Sauté onions in butter until transparent, about 5 minutes. Season with salt, pepper, and sugar, and simmer until the mixture caramelizes and turns golden brown, about 2 minutes. Add wine, wine vinegar, and brandy, and cook until the liquid has been absorbed, about 4 minutes. Confit will keep, covered, in refrigerator for up to 1 week. Reheat over very low heat, or in a double boiler.

PREPARATION TIME: 30 MINUTES / OVEN TIME: NONE / EASY

RAS EL HANOUT
(MOROCCAN SPICE BLEND)

Ras el Hanout is a Moroccan spice blend of great antiquity. It can contain as few as ten and as many as one hundred spices, some of which have alleged aphrodisiac properties. Needless to say, the more exotic components such as cantharides (Spanish fly) and cubeb peppers are difficult to find in the United States—assuming one wanted to do so—but the spice mixture listed here will give an authentic flavor to the Cornish Game Hen with Almonds and Cinnamon in Phyllo on page 100 or to the Moroccan-style Spiced Roast Chicken with Saffron Rice on page 90. For convenience, ready-ground spices are listed, but the more whole seeds, berries, bark, and so on are used, the better the flavor will be. Proportions are approximate and up to the individual cook.

4 *white or green cardamom pods*
⅛ *teaspoon mace*
¼ *teaspoon nutmeg*
¼ *teaspoon cinnamon*
½ *teaspoon white peppercorns*
4 *whole cloves*
¼ *teaspoon turmeric*

¼ *teaspoon ginger*
⅛ *teaspoon lavender seeds*
2 *dried rosebuds (optional; available in some health food stores)*
¼ *teaspoon aniseeds*
6 *allspice berries*
Pinch cayenne pepper

Remove cardamom seeds and discard pods. Combine all ingredients in a mortar and grind to a powder with the pestle, or grind in a mini-chopper or blender, and then shake through a sieve. Store airtight, away from the light.

PREPARATION TIME: 10 MINUTES / OVEN TIME: NONE / EASY

MENUS

AN EFFORTLESS MONDAY-NIGHT DINNER FOR SIX

*Cold Smoked Salmon Mousse
with Fresh Tomato, Olive Oil, and Coriander Sauce
Boned Turkey Wings Stuffed with Pork and Spinach
Wild Rice Pilaf
Chocolate Angel Cake with Vanilla Ice Cream and Chocolate Sauce*

The secret here is to cook on Sunday; then reheat the turkey wings and pilaf on Monday. The salmon mousse can be part of Sunday's menu; it's a double recipe that is designed to be eaten hot one day and cold the next, with a different sauce.

The chocolate angel cake will serve 12, so it too can be made and served on Saturday or Sunday; Monday's guests will be none the wiser. The chocolate sauce can be hot or cold, as you please.

A VERY SPECIAL BIRTHDAY DINNER

*Goat Cheese and Pear Canapés
Crab Cakes with Green Pea Sauce
Cornish Game Hen "Pears" with Braised Cabbage
Apricot Tart with Crème Brûlée*

Make the apricot tart first; it has to be well chilled before the thin layer of brown sugar on top is caramelized. The game hens and cabbage and the crab cakes can also be prepared ahead of time, but the canapés should be made at the last minute or the pear will discolor.

A CONTEMPORARY THANKSGIVING FEAST

Salmon Quenelles with Lobster Sauce
Breast of Turkey Stuffed with Pork Filet
Gratin of Corn with Spinach
Pecan Cornbread
Pumpkin Soufflé Salzburg Style, with Cranberry Sauce

Guests expect turkey, pumpkin, corn, and cranberries at Thanksgiving; it's nice to offer these traditional foods in an unexpected way. Make the salmon quenelles and prepare the turkey early in the day and refrigerate them, but let them come to room temperature before cooking. The gratin of corn and the cornbread are simple to prepare, and the soufflé is easy to assemble at the last minute.

A PREPARE-AHEAD FORMAL DINNER FOR FOUR

Red Snapper Wrapped in Zucchini
Sirloin of Lamb with Prosciutto and Mint
Bulgur Pilaf
Flourless Chocolate Soufflé Cake with Crème Anglaise

Prepare the fish and the lamb and refrigerate them, but let them come back to room temperature before cooking. The pilaf can be made ahead and reheated, and the cake and custard sauce can be made 24 hours in advance if this is more convenient.

A DINNER TO IMPRESS YOUR BANK MANAGER OR A RICH BUT FRUGAL UNCLE

Asparagus Soufflé
Pot-au-Feu, California Style
Pears in Alms-Purses with Papaya Sauce

This dinner is not only inexpensive, it is also delicious! If asparagus is not in season and at its cheapest, make a cheese soufflé instead. The pot-au-feu with turkey drumsticks and aromatic vegetables is exceptionally tasty, and the contrast with the garnish of pickled gherkins, horseradish cream, and coarse salt is sensational. The meat is taken off the bones in the kitchen, so there's no problem with carving. The pears in alms-purses, or beggar's bundles, are a delicate joke. The golden phyllo dough bundles look very inviting and taste wonderful.

A WEEKEND BRUNCH

The Original Eggs Benedict
Alsatian Pizza with Cream Cheese and Bacon
Blueberry Cake / French Apple Cake
Orange Juice / Champagne / Coffee

Very few of your guests will have experienced the delicious original French version of Eggs Benedict, as reputedly invented by the Benedictine monks—poached eggs on a bed of creamy mashed potatoes mixed with tender poached salt cod. The pizza, actually a rustic country tart from Alsace, is exceptionally tasty. Both the blueberry cake and the apple cake can be served slightly warm if you prefer; neither is too sweet.

A *DINNER TO CELEBRATE CHRISTMAS*

Warm Smoked Salmon Mousse with Rich Tomato Sauce
Roast Turkey with Pecan Cornbread and Chestnut Stuffing
Gratin of Potatoes with Cream / Stuffed Pattypan Squash
Hazelnut Meringue and Chocolate Cream Gâteau

This is a traditional feast, but with some memorable original touches. The mousse is mixed in a food processor and then poached in the oven—nothing too difficult about that. The tomato sauce can be made well ahead of time. Turkey is always amazingly successful when roasted in a convection oven: crisp on the outside and juicy within, and it takes far less time than in a conventional oven. The potatoes for the gratin must be sliced and then baked immediately, or they will discolor, but it is an easy dish. The fluted squash can be cooked ahead and kept warm without courting disaster. The very festive gâteau takes a modest amount of effort and should be tackled early so that it can be chilled, but the results are well worth it. You can decorate the top with a couple of real holly leaves, if available. If you are serving between 8 and 12 people, make a double recipe of the salmon mousse, which is baked in individual molds. Double the amount of potato gratin, using two baking dishes, and allow two pattypan squash per person. Prepare a double-size gâteau, making it twice as long (not wider) for easy slicing.

An Elegant Afternoon Tea for Boxing Day (December 26)

*Tiny Tea Sandwiches made with French Sandwich Bread
or Brioche, spread with sweet butter and lightly
salted watercress leaves*
Lattice Mincemeat Tart
Pecan Cloud Cookies
Hazelnut Sponge Fingers with Chocolate
Extra-Light Orange Pound Cake
Chestnut Cream Eclairs
Earl Grey Tea / Dry Sherry / Darjeeling Tea

The day after Christmas is known as Boxing Day in Britain because that was the day on which Christmas boxes, or gratuities, were handed out to the servants in true "Upstairs, Downstairs" style. The boxes and the servants have long gone, but afternoon tea is still with us. Most people are charmed with an invitation to tea during the holidays—it makes a change of pace. It is also an easy way to entertain a relatively large number of guests.

A Dinner to Celebrate the First Day of Your Diet

Spaghetti Squash with Garlic and Red Bell Pepper
Breast of Turkey, Oven Steamed over Herbs
Gratin of Potatoes with Chicken Stock
Vanilla Soufflé with Fresh Raspberry Sauce

Seriously, this is a surprisingly low-calorie meal. Bake the squash ahead of time, and prepare the turkey breast for cooking. The potatoes should be sliced and baked right away or they will discolor, but it is not a complicated dish. The vanilla soufflé is simple to prepare at the last minute, and of course the raspberry sauce can be made ahead of time.

A DINNER TO IMPRESS THE SENIOR PARTNER
AND HIS WIFE

Crab Cakes with Green Pea Sauce
Quail with Cracked Coriander and Wilted Spinach Salad
Rack of Lamb with Herbed Yogurt Sauce
Chocolate Pâte à Choux Mice with Ice Cream and
Hot Chocolate Sauce
Glazed Praline-Stuffed Prunes

Unless you are very confident, practice this menu on friends first so that you can time the progression of the courses without getting flustered. The crab cakes can wait in the refrigerator until they go in the oven. The quail require boning first, but roast in just a few minutes. The rack of lamb must be properly prepared by the butcher, but then is exceptionally easy to cook and carve. The chocolate pâte à choux mice can be baked early in the day and require only filling with ice cream and a little decoration before they are served. The praline-stuffed prunes are not at all difficult to make, but are very difficult to resist.

A PRE-THEATER SUPPER

Scallops with Scallions
Cornish Game Hens with Kumquats
Wild Rice Pilaf
Goat Cheese and Pear Tart

This is a very light and delicate menu with lots of texture and color contrasts. It won't make your guests want to nod off during the play, and it's an easy menu for the cook to orchestrate. Make the tart first. The scallops can be prepared and refrigerated until ready to go in the oven; the pilaf can be made ahead, and the game hens prepared ready for roasting.

AN EASTER DINNER

Asparagus and Prosciutto in Puff Pastry Cases
Lean Duckling with Green Olives
Beet Mousse / Crisp Buttered Potato Cake
Apricot Clafoutis

The clafoutis has to chill after it has been baked, so make this first. Beets are dense and take a surprisingly long time to bake, so cook those next—the beet purée is mixed in a food processor and then kept warm over hot water. The puff pastry cases are made ahead, filled, and reheated for 5 minutes just before serving. The potato cake can bake while the duck is roasting; only the duck sauce has to be combined at the last moment.

AN INFORMAL PATIO PARTY

Cold Shrimp and Sole Pâté with Dill and Yogurt and Herb Sauce
Crustless Artichoke Tart with Bell Peppers
Onion Pizza with Black Olive Paste
Breast of Veal Stuffed with Spinach
Paella with Rabbit
Slow-Rising Country Loaves with Aniseeds
Wine Creams / Fresh Strawberry Tart

The important thing about choosing a menu for this kind of gathering is to select foods that look colorful and inviting, are easy to eat, and don't spoil if left standing. The pâté and the artichoke tart are served cold; the pizza is actually better lukewarm than hot; and the breast of veal is delicious served cold in very thin slices. The paella should be kept warm on a hotplate, with serving plates alongside. The wonderfully rustic bread is made in a food processor (no kneading!), and both the wine creams and the strawberry tart can be made ahead of time.

A COMFORTING SUPPER FOR A WET AND CHEERLESS NIGHT

Fettucine Baked with Blue Cheese
Medallions of Pork with Prunes and Red Currant Jelly
Gratin of Green Beans with Almonds
Upside-Down Quince Tart

There are times when nothing but comfort food will do, and what could be more satisfying than creamy pasta, pork chops that are actually juicy and tender, green beans, and a nicely caramelized upside-down tart? If quince are not in season, substitute Golden Delicious apples.

A CASUAL SUNDAY NIGHT SUPPER FOR FRIENDS

Gnocchi Roman Style, with Tomato Sauce
Veal Shanks with Ginger and Green Peas
Spaghetti Squash with Garlic and Red Bell Pepper
Apple-Pecan Tart with Meringue Topping

Nothing too complicated here. The gnocchi can be made the day before if that suits your schedule. The veal shanks require very little attention and are sure to be tender. The spaghetti squash is baked and then tossed with a simple sauce at the last minute. The tart is also made ahead.

AN EASY INFORMAL DINNER FOR FOUR

Marinated Shrimp with Herbs
Chicken Legs with Mushrooms, Artichokes, and Scallions
Baguettes
Bananas Lohengrin

If you are making your own baguettes, which are essential for mopping up the buttery juices from the shrimp and the good sauce that comes with the chicken, bake them while the shrimp are marinating. Bone the chicken legs and prepare the vegetable garnish ready for cooking, and assemble the dessert beforehand. If your guests enjoy opera, be sure to play some appropriate Wagnerian music when you serve the swan-shaped dessert—they'll appreciate the joke.

INDEX

Honey(ed)
    apple pie, 249
    bran muffins, 223
    chicken wings with sesame oil and,
        19
    -mustard glaze, butterflied chicken
        with, 76
    and soy sauce, leg of lamb
        marinated in, 146
    white cheese tart with raisins and,
        263

Ice cream, chocolate pâte à choux mice
    with chocolate sauce and, 283

Jalousie, apple and almond, 248
Japanese eggplant with lamb, feta, and
    mint stuffing, 44
Jelly
    cookies, 226
    mint, lamb shanks with potatoes
        and, 145
    red currant, medallions of pork with
        prunes and, 127
Juniper berries, marinated leg of lamb
    with, 147

Kalamata olives, sole with, 73
Kumquats, Cornish game hens with,
    174

Ladyfingers, 237
Lamb
    casserole of macaroni, feta, and, 62
    chops
        double rib, with herb stuffing in
            phyllo, 187
        with leeks and potatoes, 152
        shoulder, with eggplant and
            lemon, 151
    Japanese eggplant with stuffing of
        feta, mint, and, 44
    leg of
        marinated in honey and soy sauce,
            146
        marinated with juniper berries,
            147
    rack of
        with herbed yogurt sauce, 150
        with rosemary and bread crumbs,
            149
    "sausages" with eggplant purée, 143
    shanks
        with lentils, 144
        with potatoes and mint jelly, 145

Lamb *(cont.)*
    sirloin of
        with pesto-mushroom stuffing, 153
        with prosciutto and mint, 154
Leeks
    filet of pork with, in puff pastry, 184
    gratin of turnip, potato, and, 204
    shoulder lamb chops with potatoes
        and, 152
Lemon
    -apricot glaze, almond tart with, 252
    -blueberry muffins, 222
    butterflied chicken with sherry and,
        78
    and goat cheese tart, 257
    paste, 295
    pastry shell with peel of, 242
    pot roast, 136
    sauce
        butter, 306
        creamy, 167
    shoulder lamb chops with eggplant
        and, 151
    soufflé tart, 260
    veal shanks with tomato and, 133
Lentils, lamb shanks with, 144
Lime, rabbit with sauce of mustard,
    cream, and, 158
Liver
    calf's, whole, baked in puff pastry,
        189
    chicken
        mousse with tomato sauce, 18
        and prune and coppa appetizers, 17
Lobster sauce, salmon quenelles with,
    33

Macaroni, casserole of lamb, feta, and,
    62
Macaroons, coconut, 231
Madeleines, 238
Meat. *See also* Beef; Lamb; Pork; Veal
    cabbage rolls, bacon-wrapped, 121
    loaf, spiced turkey and pork, 116
Menus, 311–319
    casual Sunday night supper for
        friends, 318
    comforting supper for a wet and
        cheerless night, 318
    dinner
        to celebrate Christmas, 314
        to celebrate the first day of your
            diet, 315
        Easter, 317
        easy informal, for four, 319

Plum cake, 277
Pork. *See also* Ham
    boned turkey wings stuffed with
        spinach and, 109
    breast of turkey stuffed with filet of,
        113
    filet of
        with caper and cornichon sauce,
            123
        with leeks in puff pastry, 182
    loin of, with mustard and sage, 124
    medallions of
        with ginger and Chinese five-spice
            powder, 126
        with prunes and red currant jelly,
            127
    stuffing, roast saddle of rabbit with,
        181
    and turkey meat loaf, spiced, 116
    and veal tourte, 40
Potato(es)
    baked, creamy salt cod in, 31
    cake, crisp buttered, 200
    galette, orange roughy with, 164
    gnocchi Piedmont style, with Fontina
        and, 58
    gratin of
        with cream, 195
        with turnips and leeks, 204
    lamb shanks with mint jelly and,
        145
    mousse of carrot, rutabaga, and, 192
    oven-fried, with garlic and parsley,
        198
    patties with goat cheese and parsley,
        199
    red, roast chicken with baby
        artichokes and, 97
    shoulder lamb chops with leeks and,
        152
    stuffed baked, with chives, 202
    and zucchini tart, 201
Pot-au-feu California style, 115
Pot roast, lemon, 136
Poultry. *See* Chicken; Cornish game
        hens; Duck(ling); Squab;
        Turkey
Pound cake, orange, extra-light, 276
Praline
    buttercream, almond meringue layer
        cake with, 266
    paste, 297
Prosciutto
    and asparagus in puff pastry cases,
        22

Prosciutto *(cont.)*
    chicken breasts with, en papillote,
        82
    sirloin of lamb with mint and, 154
Prune(s)
    and chicken liver and coppa
        appetizers, 17
    medallions of pork with red currant
        jelly and, 127
    rabbit confit with, 182
Pudding
    yellow summer squash, with
        raspberry sauce, 290
    Yorkshire, prime rib of beef with, 140
Puff pastry
    asparagus and prosciutto in, 22
    baked apples in, with yogurt sauce,
        245
    filet of pork with leeks in, 182
    halibut with avocado mousse in, 162
    quick, 244
    whole calf's liver baked in, 189
Pumpkin
    pancake with scallions, 203
    soufflé Salzburg style, with cranberry
        sauce, 287

Quail, with cracked coriander and
        wilted spinach salad, 171
Quenelles, salmon, with lobster sauce,
        33
Quiche
    mussel, 38
    with sorrel and spinach, 37
Quince tart, upside-down, 251

Rabbit
    to cut, 157
    with lime, mustard, and cream
        sauce, 158
    paella with, 156
    two-way, 180–182
        rabbit confit with prunes, 182
        roast saddle of rabbit with pork
            stuffing, 181
Raisin(s)
    bread, 215
    and orange custard with French toast
        topping, 284
    rum, and chocolate cookies, 228
    white cheese tart with honey and,
        263
Ras el hanout (Moroccan spice blend),
        310
Raspberry sauce, 294